THE
TENEMENT
LANDLORD

THE
TENEMENT
LANDLORD

GEORGE STERNLIEB

Rutgers University Press

New Brunswick, New Jersey

The Urban Renewal Demonstration Project and the publication of the first
edition of this volume were made possible through an Urban Renewal
Demonstration Grant awarded by the Urban Renewal Administration,
Department of Housing and Urban Development, under the provisions of
Section 314 of the Housing Act of 1954, as amended, to Rutgers, The State
University. The first edition was published by the Urban Studies Center
of Rutgers University, of which the author was a staff member.

TABLE OF CONTENTS

LIST OF EXHIBITS

ACKNOWLEDGEMENTS

This study would have been impossible without the wholehearted coopera-tion of my associates. Mrs. Mildred Barry was in charge of the field work and acted as a most creative second in command. Mr. Howard Nacht took charge of the title search and statistical procedures, with the assistance of Mr. Robert Gibson and Mr. Alan Yuttal. I would like to thank all of the field interviewers and single out particularly Mr. Lawrence Besserer for his imagination and drive in digging out and securing interviews with some of the "hard core" landlords.

My colleagues, Professors David W. Blakeslee, Stephen S. Castle, Wil-liam A. Dymsza, Salomon J. Flink, Louis T. German, and Donald Grune-wald, were continual sources of encouragement and suggestion. In addition, Dean Martin Myerson of the University of California at Berkeley, Profes-sor Bernard Frieden of M.I.T., and Professor William Nash of Harvard read the manuscript and made many suggestions toward its improvement.

Mr. Howard Cayton and Mr. Don Patch of the Urban Renewal Admin-istration and Dr. Jerome Pickard of the Urban Land Institute were, as any-one who has worked with them can testify, invaluable sources of help. My wife, Dr. Phyllis Fox, took on much of the burden of proofreading and computer programming. Miss Carol Wozniak and Mrs. Mary Picarella went through the laborious typing chores of the several drafts and the pressures of deadlines in a thoroughly effective fashion. Mr. William Riddle and Mr. Peter Piro drew the charts.

Financial support for the project was received from the Urban Land Institute, the Lincoln Foundation, and the Urban Renewal Administration.

Mr. J. Carl Cook of the Rutgers Bureau of Economic Research and his assistant, Miss Patricia Felton, served as editors and arbiters of the finished product. Whatever claims to artistic merit the finished production may have are largely due to their efforts.

INTRODUCTION

The American city faces a crisis of function; questions of race and class are secondary to this basic fact. The city's major historic role in the United States has been as a recipient of successive waves of migrants. Painful and even miserable living conditions have been mitigated by a national social structure loose enough to permit rapid mobility. Meanwhile the city has provided some entrepreneurs with a source of cheap labor, and for the migrant to it the city has offered employment at levels of skill which he could meet.

The concentration of businesses and jobs, the availability of neighborhood shopping districts and other service areas once made the central city a reasonably attractive and satisfactory place for living and working, particularly for low-income families or persons. These city advantages are less and less persuasive today. Innovations in transportation and communication are making centralness less and less essential. The telephone and the airplane have made wider and wider areas almost as accessible as the inner core of the great city. Jobs are relocated outward from the hard core of the city. As these changes become plainer and more visible to all eyes it becomes clear that we, as a society, are much better at building from scratch than we are at rebuilding.[1]

In an age where capital investment per worker plays a significant role, cheap labor in itself is less crucial than it used to be. The most affluent of the world's poor, the low-skilled slum dweller of the United States is now in competition with Formosa, with Hong Kong, with the Philippines; he is not in a competitive position. When low labor costs are a significant element, importing an end product is frequently much less expensive than utilizing local labor to create it.

When this study was first planned, it was fashionable to discuss the question of how to retain the white middle class in the central city. At present the problem is more and more that of maintaining any middle class—be it black, white or any other hue.[2] The city as an institution cannot survive in any desirable form merely by serving as a reservation for those who cannot make it to the suburbs.

One of the basic elements of the city's earlier growth, the continual flow of fresh immigrants, has now for the first time been reduced. Puerto Rican migration is relatively stable, with nearly as many Puerto Ricans going back to the island as coming to the mainland. Black migration across the Mason-Dixon line has slowed very substantially as job opportunities open in the South and as the dominant political forces in the region realize that its labor pool must be sustained even at the cost of integration.

There is no group to replace the current immigrants into the city as they move upward and outward.

In spite of very tight housing markets, American cities are generating zones of abandonment—areas of housing so poor as to be without takers.[3] This fact has enormous implications for the city's housing. Much of the folklore of code enforcement, of health regulation, and of other governmental or near governmental efforts to maintain the city's housing for the poor has presumed a basic high level of profit in low-end housing. The rallying cry has been that the landlords are growing fat and that if we could only get them to disgorge an appropriate part of the money they are securing from their rentals, good maintenance could be secured while still preserving enough profit to insure fresh private investment. This contention is based, however, on the supposition that there is a profitable and vigorous low-end housing market. The landlord will improve and the wherewithal to improve will be available only if a high degree of profit is shown by the city's low-income housing, not only in the present but as an investment for the future. If the latter is not evident, the landlord's response all too frequently will be to milk the building and, when faced with too many violations and too many problems, just simply "throw it in." The rising rate of the return required for adequate maintenance and the problems of producing that return are a frequent source of ethnic clashes between owner and tenant.

This study is an effort to delineate the economic realities of the private low-end housing market in one city. Newark, the scene of the research, is in many ways representative of other American cities. Its problems are not unique but are the common lot, to greater or lesser degree, of a majority of the United States' older municipalities. It is easy to get lost in the noise attendant on the urban scene and to lose sight of the evolution of basic parameters. These are all too often obscured by questions of personalities: of rat-raising landlord, or anecdotes about untutored tenantry, what City Hall is or isn't doing, and all the other sharp-cornered immediacies of every day urban life. This is a self-indulgence that demands a very high price.

A year after this study concluded, a major riot shook the city of Newark. Despite the tragedy involved in the loss of life, I would suggest that this was essentially a noise element rather than a basic parameter. The trends that were evident before the riot have continued since. The migration of jobs out of the city, now described as a result of the riot, substantially preceded it. The housing degeneration discussed in this study has continued. It is the basic factor with which any public policy must deal.

What is new and promising is the increasing feeling on the part of the Black community that the city as such is to be nurtured because the Black community will fall heir to it. But the heritage is a very worn and battered one.

What is the potential of the private housing market for enhancing the lives of the people of the city? The city and its housing must be seen as way stations on the road toward upward economic and social mobility. Housing is an input rather than an end in itself. Tenement ownership by minority group members can provide an essential source of capital accumulation, and a key input toward "making it." When combined with resident ownership it also offers substantial promise of improving the quality of the housing—and the morale of the tenants.

But where are the resources to maintain and enhance the level of urban necessities—health services, sanitation requirements, and the schools of the central city? Housing does not exist in a vacuum. The physical and social setting inherited by the newest and perhaps the last of a long series of immigrant groups does not provide the incentives which gave encouragement to earlier immigrants. Much will be required in the public sphere to make that legacy truly useful, not least some positive and imaginative governmental shaping of private housing programs.

George Sternlieb

Newark, N. J.
1969

REFERENCES

1 On jobs see for example, Sternlieb et al, *Newark, New Jersey Population and Labor Force* (Rutgers, 1967) and H. Bienstock, *Work and Workers in the New Urban Environment* (N. Y. Bureau of Labor Statistics, nd.) On the costs of rehabilitation see the series of working papers issued by Dr. Frank Kristof, Housing Development Administration, New York City, particularly #14.
2 On this point see New York State Commission for Human Rights, *Non-whites in Suburbia* (N. Y., 1969).
3 See Sternlieb, "Bulldozer Renewal," *Journal of Housing,* April, 1968.

SUMMARY OF FINDINGS

This is a study of the impact of slum ownership and the realities of the market on the maintenance and rehabilitation of slum tenement houses. Government policies on financing, on rehabilitation, on code enforcement, and on taxes are viewed in terms of their effect upon the market and ultimately upon the landlords' response.

The basic goal was to define the optimum bundle of carrots and sticks with which to secure upgrading of slum housing.

Summary

There is no single one-shot panacea, be it code enforcement, financing, or tax relief, which will substantially improve the maintenance of slum tenements or induce owners to rehabilitate their parcels. Without question, the effect of all of these in a concerted effort would be considerable; they face, however, the reality of a weak market and a lack of entrepreneurial interest on the part of major landowners.

Maintenance of parcel as a function of ownership was analyzed in detail. It was found that the prime generator of good maintenance is owner-residence. It is only this factor that produces the degree of close supervision required for good maintenance of slum properties. In addition, owner-residence provides a substantial bridge in the tenant-landlord discontinuity. In the author's opinion, this type of ownership pattern should be encouraged by financing aid which is not available under present legislation. It must, however, be coupled consistently with increased levels of municipal service in slum areas, rigorous code enforcement and, most important of all, appropriate advisory services for the relatively unsophisticated new owner.

There is consistent evidence that the weakening of the slum realty market is causing present maintenance procedures to degenerate. The necessity, therefore, for an action program with which to secure proper maintenance and rehabilitation of slums is increasing.

Ownership Patterns

—The number of resident, white owners is decreasing very rapidly. The bulk of those who are left are quite elderly.

—One third of the parcels in the sample are owned by Negroes, the bulk of whom are resident owners.

—The new Negro owners are avoiding the hard-core slums.

—In essence, the worst housing areas have the highest concentration of major owners. Analyses of date of acquisition, by area, as a function of race, indicates that the latter is increasingly dominated by white large-scale slum landlords.

—Multiple-slum parcel owners are specialists in slum properties, typically owning no other kind.

The Impact of the Acquisition Process on the Maintenance of Slum Properties

—The bulk of recent transactions in slum tenements are financed by purchase money mortgages.

—Conventional lending sources, such as banks and savings and loan institutions, play a relatively minor role in the acquisition process. Their absence is in direct proportion to the degree of housing decay. The number of acquisitions financed by them is decreasing over time.

—The new Negro buyer pays inflated purchase prices to cover financing costs. Not uncommonly these excess charges are 50 to 100 percent of the normal purchase price.

—The cash squeeze on the new owner is made even more onerous by the short-term nature of typical, purchase money mortgage agreements; the latter are typically no more than eight years in duration.

—The new resident owners are frequently victimized by high pressure, home-improvement salesmen of a variety of kinds. They are in great need of counseling.

The Impact of the Weakening Market Structure

—Vacancy rates in the hard-core slums are increasing sharply, with larger scale landlords being hardest hit.

—The typical, large-scale landlord reaction has been to reduce maintenance expenditures rather than to reduce rents, with a minority making improvements to secure tenantry.

—The multiplier used to capitalize gross rents for retail tenements is falling. Presently it is three and one-half to four times.

—The weak resale and finance markets definitely inhibit rehabilitation efforts.

The Tenantry and Rehabilitation

—The proportion of parcels occupied by nonwhites is directly proportional to the scale of the landlords' holdings.

—Nonwhites pay significantly higher rents than whites located in the same area.

—A basic problem of slum maintenance and rehabilitation is the attitude of tenantry, largely a function of their basic alienation from the absentee landlord. Any effort toward rehabilitation which does not face up to this reality is pure romanticism.

The Financing Question

—It is only the larger holders who presently have easy access to financing.

—Financing help in itself will not generate rehabilitation.

—Fear of legal action and of a weak market makes very high rates of return mandatory before large-scale owners can be induced to take any action. Their present attitude is that the market is too weak to support substantial rehabilitation effort by them, regardless of financial aid. Owner residents would be more amenable to improvement if appropriate financing could be secured.

—Aged owners are numerous, and regardless of the availability of financing, they are, with few exceptions, uninterested in rehabilitation investment.

Code Enforcement

—The level of municipal service must be raised to insure improvement of slum areas. There is substantial evidence that when a neighborhood "changes" the quality of municipal service suffers.

—Code enforcement, though essential, does not in itself insure proper maintenance. Present municipal efforts, while most useful, cannot fight the realities of the market.

Urban Renewal and Rehabilitation

—The great majority of slum owners feel that urban renewal land-taking is equitable.

—The greatest fear of urban renewal is among small owners who are grossly uninformed on urban renewal procedures.

—Unless there is some municipally endorsed and substantially financed program for land clearance, vacant tenements, no matter how decayed, will be permitted to stand. The alternative values of the vacant land are so low as to make this normative landlord behavior.

—Given the availability of housing for people displaced because of urban renewal, the program is much more practicable now than was the case several years ago.

Impact of Taxes

—Taxes are the largest single operating expense of the slum tenement.

—Big owners fear taxes least; small owners are most fearful.

—In the weak tenement market the pressure of increased taxes cannot be passed on.

—High taxes inhibit the improvement of slum properties by reducing their profitability.

—The uncertainties of local tax administration and rate increases are as harmful as the actual tax impact.

—Many landlords avoid making improvements because of fear of reassessment. There is an incredible range of ignorance on what constitutes a reassessable improvement.

—Slum tenements are equitably assessed in terms of market and drastically underassessed in terms of municipal expenditures.

—Land values in slums are commonly on a par with equivalent suburban acreage zoned for multiple residency. Tax relief in itself would be helpful, but is no guarantee of rehabilitation.

Methodology

Newark, the scene of the study, was chosen as representative of many of America's older cities, possessing in an advanced degree the bulk of their problems.

A structured random sample of five hundred sixty-six parcels in three different categories of census tracts was chosen. Tax, transfer, and financing data were accumulated as well as descriptions of landlord maintenance of the individual structures. Successful depth interviews were later secured with three hundred ninety-two of the parcels' owners. Ownership of the balance of the parcels was substantially identified in terms of occupational characteristics, ethnic origins, and so on.

Analysis, both of parcel characteristics and also of landlord statements, was partitioned by three sets of housing characteristics and cross partitioned in terms of dominant ethnic strain present in the tracts in question. Landlord responses to the questionnaire were analyzed by five categories of size of holdings from single parcels to twelve or more parcels held.

Chapter 1

THE NATURE OF THE PROBLEM

DURING 1948 the *Chicago Law Review* published an article on "The Needs and Problems of Urban Renewal," followed closely by one on the "Problems of Atomic Energy Control." Nearly twenty years afterward it is interesting to note that the latter area, thought to represent one of the most technically involved subjects of human endeavor, has largely been resolved. Commercial atomic energy is with us and the juridical harnessing of the atom has continued apace.

These advances provide a most useful contrast with the former subject, that of urban renewal. The very term itself has been subject to so much variation in meaning, both statutory and philosophical, as to defy simple comparisons. Its meaning has moved from a description of the effort thought to be required to return our cities to their former greatness, both real and apocryphal, to providing a better environment for the socially disenfranchised; from a concentration on the physical surroundings to a realization that it is people who are its appropriate concern.

The early romanticism surrounding renewal of the city—the feeling that all its ills could be cured by any one of a collection of cures: more parking, expressways, potted trees downtown, physical destruction of the slums, public housing, and any of a host of other panaceas—has given way to the serious confrontation with the problems of age, education, and poverty. The basic problems of slum housing are still with us. They are, however, seen more and more as part of the overall context of a broader problem.

This study is dedicated to defining certain aspects of the housing problem. Though the bulldozer approach to the rejuvenation of our older cities

1

may be required in certain cases, the sheer enormity of the urban-blight problem has brought forth many efforts to work in the direction of urban renewal and rehabilitation through existing real estate market mechanisms. The supply of older residences is at least forty times the size of annual additions to the housing stock. As such, it warrants far more research and understanding than it has been given. The basic question is: *Can the housing market be reshaped so as to provide a decent environment for depressed urbanites?*

The housing market is essentially a free market within governmentally-set parameters. The point must be stressed that there is not now, nor has there been for a very long time, a free market in housing *per se*. Rather, there is a circumscribed ball field within which the players must observe basic ground rules.

In the suburbs these rules are most obvious in their effects. From the financing, which makes the housing possible, to the zoning and lot restrictions, which define its placement and not infrequently its caliber and cost, the effects of government policy on the "free" market are clear. In housing for low-income families, with the exception of public housing, the factor of government power and action is not so obvious, but it is present nevertheless. Housing code enforcement, mortgage guarantees or their effective absence, and tax policy are the principal weapons of the government over the existing stock of rental housing. These parameters have not acted effectively to dissipate slum conditions. Can they be changed in order to attain societally desired ends in our cities?

This study attempts to define the optimum combination of carrots and sticks to aid in attaining that goal. The carrots represent some compound of improved financing and/or improved tax policy, and the sticks represent code enforcement and implementation, etc., with which to reshape the market.

Despite the existence of considerable general information plus a few detailed case studies, there is a substantial lack of systematic studies of the interaction of local municipal policies and the real estate market, especially as these policies bear on the maintenance of real property in a satisfactory physical condition, or the rehabilitation of substandard properties. In order to guide tax policy and other related government policies in the direction of dealing more effectively with urban blight, intensive study of the owners and managers of urban realty is required.

Future legislation will be more effective and government action more fruitful if generated from a sound basis of market fact. The role of the market and the financial, social, and regulatory factors, which shape the decision making of individual property owners and managers, must be studied in detail in order to design more effective and more satisfactory modes of attack on blight.

What are the effects of municipal and other governmental taxes and tax policies on the urban property owner? How does he react to building and housing codes? Do current assessment policies inhibit potential rehabilitation? What is the effect of urban renewal programs?

Complementing the answers to these questions must be a parallel study of the potential capacity of reshaped public policies to activate property owners and managers toward rehabilitating urban realty holdings. Also, the potential of the "big three" of government action in this field—tax policy, financing, and code enforcement—must be defined in order to secure the cooperation of the entrepreneur in rehabilitating the residential slum areas of major cities.

In order to provide useful insight, it is essential not to ignore subjective elements in the analysis. Property owners and managers must be understood not merely as profit makers, but as human beings capable of all sorts of complex motivations beyond the simple acquisition of gain. Effective public policy makers need to comprehend the nature of the real estate market and the character of the participants in its processes. Without better market understanding, there is danger that public actions will be frequently blunted in their intended effects, that some of the results may be the reverse of those intended, or that "side effects" will create new and difficult problems requiring further public attention. The goal is to provide new guidelines for the policy makers within a market context.

Before turning to a description of the research methodology and its arena, it is worthwhile to examine briefly some of the major parameters of the slum housing scene. The topic to be reviewed initially is the size of the blight problem, followed by a discussion of the major attack upon the problems of poor housing, urban renewal, public housing, rehabilitation, and the problems of financing and taxes which have bedevilled it.

The Size of the Blight Problem

There are few areas of urban analysis that are not controversial. The very size of the blight problem is no exception to this statement. In one of the basic efforts to define this question, Dyckman and Isaacs, *Capital Require-*

ments for Urban Development and Renewal,[1] a modular "case" city was postulated. Based upon the authors' analysis, this city would require expenditures for the purpose of adequately housing its citizens in excess of the sum total of the capital value of all existing housing facilities. A total figure of $780- to $800-billion appears to represent fairly the national cost of renewal as postulated by the authors.

In a survey of Northeastern New Jersey, the basic age level of the housing stock was equated with the necessity for renewal. The analysis indicated that:

> About a half million of the region's housing units are now over forty years old. Of these, four hundred thousand are in core municipalities. The dwellings built during the construction boom of the 1920's are expected to add about half again as many units to this category in the 1960's. Allowing for demolition and other expected withdrawal activities, the number of dwelling units that will be forty years old or older in 1970 will be about seven hundred thousand.[2]

Even the question of whether the slums are increasing in size or decreasing is far from settled. For example, according to the New York State Temporary State Housing Rent Commission:

> Our slums grow faster than they can be razed. New construction in the postwar period—fourteen million nonfarm units up to 1958—has done little more than provide for the growing number of households.[3]

More recent students of the problem have been much more sanguine.

> Aside from an easing of housing shortages and overcrowding, the quality of old housing also improved in the last decade. In cities of over one hundred thousand population, 2.6 million units, 20 percent of the housing stock, was substandard in 1950. By 1960 a combination of renovation and demolition had reduced this number to 2.0 million, or 11 percent of the total. Here too, the extent of the improvement was striking. In the dozen largest metropolitan areas more than half of the substandard units of 1950 that were surveyed in 1959 had been put into sound condition through repairs or plumbing additions. Powerful forces have been at work in the private housing market for improved conditions in the cities. Public policy could make a major contribution toward raising environmental standards by nurturing and promoting this type of rehabilitation in the old areas.[4]

In a sense this is representative of the confusion which surrounds the definition of *slum*. In terms of the base lines of physical characteristics, there can be no doubt that there has been a substantial upgrading of American housing conditions. When based, however, upon the improved standard of living which is the American "norm," this improvement is largely illusory. *The gap between this norm and the typical living conditions of poor urbanites is perhaps wider today than it was twenty years ago.*[5]

American attitudes toward urban renewal have undergone many permutations. The early period, which saw framing of the first Urban Renewal Act in the late 1940's, may be characterized as one in which the idea was essentially a total attack on the slums as breeding places of ignorance and misery. The basic approach was that if these areas could be removed, with them would go their concomitants: poverty, disease, and high crime rates. This may be characterized essentially as the plumbing approach toward housing the poor—the thought that good plumbing would produce "good citizenry" (by "good citizenry" was meant citizenry whose habits would conform to middle-class mores).

In recent years an attack has been leveled on this attitude from a variety of sources, spearheaded by sociologists such as Herbert Gans, and more recently by talented journalists such as Jane Jacobs. The attitude has been to stress the positive aspects of what is conventionally referred to as *slums.* The warmth, the feeling of belongingness, and the wealth of diversity—both visual and functional in the city's overcrowded "poor" housing areas—have been seen in a more positive light.[6]

As one researcher put it:

> Housing sometimes appears obsolete only so long as it is inhabited by members of a lower social class, as amply demonstrated in the Georgetown and Capitol Hill sections of Washington, on Baltimore's Tyson Street, and sections of Greenwich Village and Chelsea in New York City.[7]

It should be noted, however, that most of the advocates of "warmth" and "togetherness" are typically members of middle-class intellectual groups. There is no question that among certain ethnic enclaves the housing which is the despair of the municipal planner may be uniquely desirable; these are, however, comparatively rare exceptions. For example, in a substantial study done of attitudes of Negro residents of Newark, the focus of concern among the respondents was on housing. In response to a question asking "What are the major problems facing Negroes in Newark today?" fully two-thirds of the total responses referred to that category; even jobs were mentioned less frequently, and no other problem area was discussed with any comparable frequency.[8]

The Communications Factor

The effect of slum housing on the "psyche" of its inhabitants has changed markedly over the years. One of the more common criticisms of Negro protest movements in America currently is that essentially similar housing conditions prevailed for a number of depressed immigrant groups in the past. Certainly anyone reading the description of the New York slum ghettos at the turn of the century could not help but agree. It is indeed doubtful whether similar urban housing conditions still exist in this country. The important differentiation, however, is the factor of mass communications. Through the media of communications, the standard of "appropriate" life of appropriate conditions of tenure in housing has risen very markedly. At the turn of the century there was no common denominator of appropriate expectation for all people. *Today the degree of popular knowledge of the discrepancy between the irresistibly promulgated standard of what the good life is for middle-class Americans, and that which is actually endured among depressed urban groups is the chief differentiator between the present period and that of the past.* Past approaches toward the problems of slum housing, such as public housing and physical rehabilitation, have foundered on this rock of public unawareness. Is there a practicable solution? This question will be considered in the final chapters of this study.

Improvements in Housing Conditions

Exhibit 1–1 derived from Frieden's, *The Future of Old Neighborhoods,* indicates the substantial improvement which has been made in the degree of overcrowding in our major metropolitan areas. Frieden makes a strong case for permitting the free market to continue, what he indicates as a function in this Exhibit, its improvement of general housing conditions. Though the point has much validity, the significance of the table can be seriously questioned. A substantial part of the improvements indicated is merely the dilution of center-core, overcrowded units by suburban additions of one-family housing. While there has been a substantial improvement in the overcrowding picture, at least as defined by the 1.01 or more occupants per room criterion, the general standards of what is appropriate housing have

EXHIBIT 1-1

OVERCROWDED HOUSING* IN SELECTED METROPOLITAN AREAS, 1950 AND 1960

METROPOLITAN AREA 1950: Standard Metropolitan Area 1960: Standard Metropolitan Statistical Area or Standard Consolidated Area	UNITS OCCUPIED BY:							
	WHITES†				NONWHITES			
	1950		1960		1950		1960	
	Overcrowded Dwelling Units Number	Percent	Overcrowded Housing Units Number	Percent	Overcrowded Dwelling Units Number	Percent	Overcrowded Housing Units Number	Percent
New York (SMA-SCA)	436,000	12.4	361,000	8.6	62,000	24.4	105,000	22.3
Chicago (SMA-SCA)	170,000	11.7	151,000	8.5	55,000	35.9	74,000	27.3
Philadelphia (SMA-SMSA)	64,000	7.1	53,000	4.9	27,000	21.9	30,000	16.3
Los Angeles (SMA-SMSA)	133,000	9.7	163,000	8.0	16,000	22.7	30,000	17.4
Detroit (SMA-SMSA)	72,000	9.6	80,000	8.6	19,000	25.3	26,000	17.5
St. Louis (SMA-SMSA)	73,000	16.6	64,000	11.8	20,000	35.2	23,000	28.0
Washington, D. C. (SMA-SMSA)	31,000	9.3	29,000	6.2	21,000	28.7	29,000	22.6
San Francisco-Oakland (SMA-SMSA)	51,000	7.8	49,000	6.0	16,000	29.8	19,000	19.7

* Overcrowded units defined as those with 1.01 or more occupants per room.
† Including whites with Spanish names.
Source: Frieden, *The Future of Old Neighborhoods*, p. 26.

also moved up. To this degree one can seriously question whether the *relative* disadvantage, concerning housing of the underprivileged, particularly those who are nonwhite, has been altered substantially. Given the enormous amount of new suburban housing both extant and projected, will this suffice to improve urban housing standards?

The Filtering Concept

The filtering concept revolves around the idea that as people at the top of the economic scale move into better housing, they leave behind residences which are filled by their less fortunate brethren. The analogy is frequently used of the new car, used car market. The purchaser of the new car typically makes available a used car for someone who can afford the latter which in turn commonly releases an older used car to someone and, in sum, a whole series of upward shifts to better cars is predicated. The basic concept is that the people at the top of the economic scale can only be satisfied with new housing and greater luxury and/or new cars. In turn, by vacating their previous homes or cars, they depress the value of the housing market and the gradient of housing in turn is improved. Thus, at the bottom is found a small vacuum of houses no longer desirable, and all the people on the housing ladder, or car ladder, move up the scale into new and/or better units.

This analogy has been attacked on a number of grounds. Perhaps the most basic is that of racial segregation which does not permit equal access to used housing. Other criticisms center around the deterioration of the housing stock in the process of filtering down. Perhaps the most succinct statement of the latter point is that of Ira S. Lowry. His reasons for disagreement are summed up as follows:

> The price decline necessary to bring a dwelling unit within reach of an income group lower than that of the original tenant also results in a policy of under-maintenance. Rapid deterioration of the housing stock is the cost to the community of rapid depreciation in the price of existing housing.[9]

In essence, Lowry raises the question of whether, in the process of creating the vacuum, the standards of maintenance of the dwelling units are not so structured as to create new slums, little better, if any, than those which in turn are vacated by the new occupants.

Certainly the emigré moving from the hard-core blight of the usual ghetto into newly vacated areas may find the previously middle-class housing somewhat the worse for wear and tear. It is, however, usually substantially better than the area that he has vacated.

Rent Levels

Is the process of filtering down accompanied by a change of rents? One researcher, Leo Grebler in his *Housing Market Behavior*,[10] raises the question of whether filtering down should be thought of in terms of the same physical houses at lower rents over the period of years as they degenerate, or the same group of houses costing less in stabilized dollars as a proportion of total living costs, or whether the rentals on the same group of houses should represent a smaller part of the typical occupants' income. The choice, which he finally selects as being perhaps the most valid, is the relationship of rents on the groups of houses in question to rents of the overall area at some past time vs. the equivalent ratio at the present time.

In any case, the actual rentals per unit of slum housing have not decreased as a result of the hegira of the middle class, judging from the Newark research which will be discussed later. Whether in the absence of this hegira they would have increased is an open question.

One of the more obvious problems that confronts the renter looking for new and better apartment living at relatively inexpensive rates is the fact that there has been such a dearth of new rental housing. The period of the Thirties, beset with foreclosures of mortgages and high vacancy rates, obviously generated very little. The war and postwar years saw the growth of Federal-enabling legislation which permitted the development of private one-family housing at prices very competitive to those of rental housing, thus inhibiting the development of the latter. This has meant that in the lower-priced housing the alternatives in many cases have been limited to either the public housing projects or the slum on a "take it or leave it" basis. As Winnick comments:

> . . . Government efforts to bring new housing within the reach of lower income groups seem to have proved more successful with ownership than with rental housing. While the Government has by no means reached the limits of liberal mortgage terms for either type, it has exercised more restraint in rental housing. It is easier for officials to justify the benefits of easy credit directly to the home owner, who is regarded as a consumer rather than as an investor. Renters can be benefited only by acting through investors, and easy credit for investors can lead to undue personal enrichment.[11]

Obviously, the process of filtering down is obstructed by the structured condition of the market. When vacancies occur in a white neighborhood, and the only potential renters are Negroes, this does not necessarily mean that the Negroes are free to enter the neighborhood even if they are economically equipped to pay the rents. Ultimately, as shall be noted in more detail in the next chapter, these barriers, at least in Newark, have tended to break down. To that degree one can envision the new housing opportunities opened for middle-class whites in the suburbs, whether they be rental units in garden apartment houses or one-family tract developments, as ultimately benefiting the housing condition of the urbanite.

Rehabilitation as an Inhibitor of Filtering

Conversely, at least some commentators on the scene see any efforts at keeping the middle class in the city as, in essence, cutting back the opportunities for upgraded housing among socially and economically depressed groups.

Grigsby, for example, stresses the necessity of encouraging mobility out of areas that are medium good to permit families from the very poor areas to move up the line. Any investment opportunities in rehabilitation which detract from new building would be contrary to this end, and in Grigsby's opinion, hinder the speed at which housing is upgraded.

> It appears clear that in most localities, a rejection of the older, inlying housing stock by those families who can afford something better in the suburbs, has been the primary, immediate cause of improved housing for the population generally.
>
> . . . The erection of new dwelling units creates a potential flow of housing too, and reduced prices for lower-income groups. Rehabilitation has precisely the opposite effect. To the extent that it draws demand away from a new construction market, it retards the rate in which the dwelling units are released to families of modest means.[12]

The author continues to point out that this still leaves the basic hard core of the very low-income families. These "can only be cut by more rapidly rising incomes or some form of public assistance."

Certainly, the filtering concept of housing is becoming increasingly valid as the proportion of the city available to nonwhite entry is increased, and as the hegira of the middle class from these areas continues. One of the limitations of the filtering concept is the fact that, as pointed out by Grebler in the study cited earlier of the lower East Side and as corroborated by research in Newark for this report, the very bottom of the barrel, the broken-down housing which is beneath any reasonable standard of appropriateness, continues to stay on the market. The alternative uses for lots in the hard-core slum areas are so limited as to make it more profitable for the landlord to maintain a parcel as long as there is any possibility of securing some rental from the parcel.

The question of whether rehabilitation and efforts at improving the urban scene, so as to keep the middle class from moving out, actually hinder the improvement of housing conditions for low-income groups is a most academic one. Certainly as important as the physical conditions of housing is the essential racial mix which is required for healthy growth, both for the city and its inhabitants. An all-Negro ghetto is as socially undesirable as a mixed bad-housing area; neither fits the goal of housing with mixed occupancy.

In the process of urban renewal, the question of whether the potential source of housing for the depressed is restricted, rather than enlarged, is also an open one. Certainly, if in the course of urban renewal better housing is removed than that which the hard-core slumites presently occupy, the potential for upgrading housing for the latter is being removed. This is one of the major accusations which has been leveled against the urban renewal program.

Urban Renewal

The Urban Renewal Program, an effort to upgrade land use and provide for demolition of slums through Federally-aided land acquisition, has received considerable criticism during the last several years. The time required between starting early urban renewal projects and actual land-taking and completion disenchanted many observers. The degree of displacement of the poor and socially declassed, those least able to afford alternative accommodations, has similarly been criticized.

There are also questions raised as to urban renewal's capacity to penetrate to the core of blighted areas. Do the market realities permit the urban renewal process to really stamp out the hard core of blight? Though the program was originally advocated by municipal authorities faced with the problems of securing additional ratables for revenue purposes, there has been some disillusionment on this score also. The lag between the demolition of existing taxpaying properties and the creation of new ones has been most costly.

Those cities such as Newark, which have extensive urban renewal programs, have found that the great bulk of their capital expenditures must be confined to the urban renewal program in order to meet the matching funds requirement of the Federal Government. This, in turn, has created "a backlog of unfulfilled needs which have grown to a very large proportion."[13] In Newark's case, projected expenditures for the period 1964–1969 for the functions of urban renewal will come very close to hitting the limit on the city's borrowing capacity. These problems are rapidly being meliorated as more experience is gained in the program and appropriate modifications are instituted. There still remains the question of the ultimate results of frequently unskilled and relatively unplanned efforts of improving the city. These were vividly voiced by Mr. William Slayton, then Urban Renewal Commissioner, when he said:

> What are the bottlenecks of urban renewal? Are they functions of time or are they functions of limited objectives? . . . These bottlenecks of time are recognized and frequently condemned. Frequently, also they are broken. Are these the real bottlenecks of urban renewal? . . . The real bottlenecks of urban renewal are not functions of time or process, but the difficulty of refashioning our cities in a rational esthetic and comprehensive pattern.[14]

The question raised by Mr. Slayton is a very deep and profound one and is worth restating. *What is the optimum reality of the city in terms not of recapturing some past glamour, but rather in terms of bettering the outlook and morale of its inhabitants?* The most effective arguments against urban renewal have been those raised most recently by the newly aroused verbal center-core residents who find themselves being displaced by the activity.

Displacement Size and Relocation Problem

The basic problem was voiced clearly ten years ago by Fisher when he pointed out that standards can only be boosted in housing if vacancies are available.[15] While this is an obvious necessity, some critics of the program claim that it has been lost under the exigencies of getting programs going.

Clearly housing conditions are not improved by demolishing *occupied* substandard housing if, in the process, the total supply of accommodations which the displaced family can afford is reduced. To as great an extent as possible, demolition should be the consequence of abandonment, not the cause of it. The complement of this rather elementary point was stressed in the early public housing legislation which provided that each new low-cost housing project must be accompanied by an equivalent amount of slum clearance. Both concepts seem to have been lost in most current residential renewal efforts. When, as is typically the case, housing and slum in blighted areas is replaced by new homes for higher-income groups, there is no assurance that the displaced families will be better or even equally well housed. Their fate hinges on vagaries of the filtering process, which cannot function effectively when the excesses of supply over demand are being diminished rather than increased.[16]

The problem has, of course, been accentuated by the racial difference which frequently exists between the nonwhite, center-core city dwellers, and the dominant white majority in the outer areas. The supply of housing available to the former has been narrowed by urban renewal clearance, while not infrequently the supply was not added to by the results of the improvements made upon the cleared sites. The continual nibbling at the problem through amended legislation is apt witness to this. The 1965 Housing Act, however, is a product of the experience gained from nearly two decades of urban renewal activity. As such it shows signs of greatly improving the program.

At the same time that the shape of early urban renewal efforts has been drawing criticism, the public housing effort in many major cities has been slowing down.

Public Housing

The failure of private enterprise to provide adequate housing facilities for the socially disadvantaged in center-core cities has been made up in part by the development of public housing. From 1950 to 1956, for example, fifty-seven out of every one hundred housing units started in Newark were in public housing. The latter were one and one-half times as numerous as starts of units in private two-or-more-family structures.[17] The relative paucity of new multiple-family housing generated by the private market in Newark since that time is indicated by the annual compendiums of the New

Jersey Department of Labor and Industry, the State of New Jersey—*Residential Construction Authorized By Building Permits.* At this writing nearly 10 percent of the City of Newark's total housing units are in public housing projects.

Could public housing possibly provide a complete solution to the problem of housing the poor in the central city? Even the advocates of public housing would be forced to accept a negative response to this question. Certainly from the viewpoint of those who would be potentially the occupants of public housing, there is a very real question as to whether the program would be a substantial success if enlarged to that degree. Millspaugh reports that though slightly more than 50 percent of the families displaced by urban renewal would be eligible for low-rent public housing, less than 20 percent have actually moved into public housing.

> In a survey of families to be relocated from New York's West Side renewal project, it was found that 68 percent were apparently eligible, but only 16 percent said they wanted to live in public housing.[18]

The distaste of substantial groups of the poor for public housing is indicated by Back's study of slum and public housing dwellers in Puerto Rico. Despite the very poor housing conditions of a statistically controlled sample, about 30 percent were quite unyielding and said:

> Under no condition would they move into a housing project. Half as many more would move only if they had to do so. The other responses, which we get infrequently, all had to do with the payment of rent, if they had low rent or no rent at all, etc.[19]

The reasons for the distaste of public housing by the poor are grouped by Millspaugh as follows:

1. The desire to stay close to the old neighborhood, whether public housing is available there or not.

2. The feeling that a stigma is attached to residents of public housing.

3. An unwillingness to accept the rules and regulations that go with publicly administered housing; among other things, slum families often wish to spend a smaller proportion of family income on housing than is required in public housing.

4. Dislike of the physical character of public housing projects. (Relocatees mention distaste for elevator living, for concrete floors, and so on.)[20]

In addition to these problems, resident and income restrictions are such that many of the poor cannot qualify for public housing. For example, a study of urban renewal in Northeastern New Jersey indicates that the areas most likely to be subject to urban renewal have the greatest proportion of normally ineligible newcomers to the area.[21] The degree of segregation which is the normal concomitant of the politically derived placement of public housing and the effects on the morale of the inhabitants of the institutionalization of typical projects[22] are merely some of the arguments against public housing. This is not to detract from the great value that public housing in appropriate proportions may have to the city's mix of accommodations. Certainly it has been a pace-setter in improving the physical housing of the poor.

A much more sophisticated approach toward public housing is currently in evidence. The use of extant housing and of smaller scattered units is a welcome departure from the monolithic concentrations of the past and may provide new vigor for the program.

During its last session, Congress heard proposals for augmenting the rent-paying capacity of the poor and thus providing a greater degree of housing choice, rather than subsidizing the housing needs of the poor through direct construction of public housing units by the government. This approach is considered in Chapter 12.

Given the revised urban renewal program and the new approaches in public housing, the sheer size of the existing housing stock has greatly strengthened efforts at organized rehabilitation.

Rehabilitation

In a study done in 1944 by the Chicago Housing Authority of the possibilities of rehabilitation, the following questions were asked:[23]

1. Is rehabilitation of a slum area physically possible?

2. Is rehabilitation under private ownership economically sound?

3. Will rehabilitation of a slum area by The Housing Authority provide housing for low-income families more economically than new construction?

The questions are more than twenty years old but their answers are far from clear-cut. Newspapers and magazines are filled with sanguine stories of successful rehabilitation efforts. However, as an overall program, the success of rehabilitation efforts is certainly open to question. As Julian Levi has pointed out, based upon his Chicago experience:

> Rehabilitation of properties in blighted areas remains an experimental program—success has yet to be demonstrated. Moreover, the program will either succeed or fail on area-wide terms. The successful rehabilitation of a single structure is most meaningful if further rehabilitation within the area is thereby generated. Limited success and prestige rehabilitation programs . . . do not permit broad generalizations. The challenge of the program requires reversal of economic and social forces achievable only through a massive effort, involving the elements of adequate public facilities, required clearance, code enforcement, economies in material and labor, and financing assistance not yet generally mounted.[24]

The problem of securing appropriate financing is a recurrent theme in all of the reports on rehabilitation efforts. Government efforts to provide adequate financing have, according to some critics, been stymied by the bureaucracy of lending agencies.[25] The need for "take-out" financing, i.e. the ability to mortgage out improvements, if professional rehabilitators are to be brought on to the scene is clearly indicated by Nash.[26]

The problem of securing financing on any terms in so-called black-listed areas of the slums has often been presented as a major inhibitor of rehabilitation efforts.[27] How realistic is this problem?

Obviously, the problem for the individual investor or property owner in a decision to improve a specific parcel is complicated by the question of whether his neighbors will similarly respond. A common platitude in the real estate field, which will be discussed in later chapters, is that it's the height of foolishness to improve a parcel over and above its neighborhood.

The Tax Question

Local government, throughout the United States, is largely financed by property taxes. Although this varies considerably from community to community depending upon state aid and the prevalence of other types of taxation, the national figure is roughly 50 percent.[28] In New Jersey, as shall be seen later, the figure is considerably higher. Any plan which diminishes the municipal tax base is dreaded. Its concomitant frequently is an increase in the tax rate and a dynamic degenerative cycle of exodus of ratables leading to tax rate increases and further exodus.

In addition, there is the question of the effect of high tax rates on maintenance. Are rehabilitation efforts inhibited by the fear of upward boosts in taxation? What is the capacity of tax abatements or tax limitations towards securing improved housing? To a number of commentators upon the scene, the property tax is one of the leading factors leading to poor maintenance.

> Property tax, as it is based upon valuation, increases as properties improve. Any number of observers, in some studies, testify that such a basis for a tax leads to neglect of property.[29]

> . . . the fiscal deterrent assumes not just a supplemental but the primary role in blocking urban renewal. It may defer private renewal, not just for decades, but indefinitely, because of reverberating neighborhood effects, from deterioration of old buildings, which progressively rob sites of their renewability. . . . There are large areas in our central cities which would be renewed forthwith in the absence of the fiscal deterrent.[30]

> . . . (A) tax that imposes substantial penalties upon improvement, rewards decay, and encourages land speculation may have high social costs. It would appear to be a major contributor to the economic and fiscal ills of urban areas.[31]

In the opinion of Arthur Weimer, Dean of the Graduate School of Business of Indiana University:

> Our real estate tax system works in reverse. Instead of giving the owner an incentive to improve his property, there is an incentive to let it run down. Every time he improves it, he courts higher taxes, and he capitalizes the tax, and this is a tremendous investment. Since these taxes are capitalized, the decision may have a tremendous impact on the future.[32]

The Newark Central Planning Board stated the case from the viewpoint of municipal authorities as one in which:

> Our present tax system of *ad valorem* taxation compels us to tax new construction the most, and dilapidated, older structures the least. The result is a tax bonus for slum ownership and a tax penalty for the creation of modern standard houses. Yet, a similar dilemma is posed by the rehabilitation of structures. Property owners have complained that their concern, lest improving their property, will result in their assessments being increased.[33]

How realistic are these appraisals? What is their impact on the landlord? And, if their weight is accepted, how reversible are the effects of taxation?

Summary

In this chapter attempts have been made to define some of the basic conditions and background affecting the slum tenement and to define govern-
mentally inspired efforts to amend these difficulties. In sum, the government
has made substantial efforts at reviving the central core of our cities. None of
these efforts, whether it be public housing or the urban renewal effort or
present efforts at rehabilitation, though useful, have proven completely effective in and of themselves. The private market through generating great
quantities of new housing, largely in the suburbs and one-family though it
may be, has also affected the center-city housing market through the par-
tial vacuum which it has created in former middle-class areas. Despite this,
the process of filtering down, enormously substantial as has been its contribution, is still far from satisfying the demands of society for better housing
in the central city. In the meantime, the gap between the aspiration level of
our society and the realities of center-city slums continues to expand.

This study is an effort to examine the dynamics of the private sector of
the market, particularly where it intersects with governmental policy. It
also attempts to define those areas in which the market may be reshaped to
provide more adequate housing within appropriate price ranges for the
central cityites.

In Chapter 2 is presented a detailed look at the scene of the major part
of the field work for this study—Newark. The physical aspects of Newark
and its population shifts will be examined. After a brief description of the research methodology, the focus will turn in Chapter 3 to the tenantry. Who
lives in the slum areas as they have been defined? What are the landlord-
tenant relationships? What are the white-Negro relationships, which are so
significant in the housing market of most major cities? The concern here is
particularly with the tenants, rent discrimination against tenants and their
capacity to pay, as well as the effects of all of these on the maintenance of
parcels.

Chapter 4 undertakes an analysis of slum operations and profitability.
How profitable are slums? What kinds of operating ratios are extant within
them? What kinds of return on investment are there? What are the risks
and rewards of slum ownership? What does housing code enforcement actually mean to the landlords of slum tenements in the city?

From the operational point of view, Chapter 5 turns to the acquisition
procedure—tenement trading and the buying and selling of parcels. The

major topics of concern will be turnover rates, slum-rent multipliers, the capital gains potential of slums, and the problems of financing and mortgaging. All of these must be viewed within the context of the basic question—the landlord's capacity and will to improve.

Chapters 6, 7, 8, and 9 take up the question of who owns the slums. Why did they buy slum properties? What are the different types of landlords? Are there variations in attitude, response, capacity, and will to improve among the several types of landlords? What is the effect of area upon the response of the landlord? What elements make for "good" or "bad" landlords?

Chapter 10 is concerned with the question of financing. What is the potential of mortgage aid in generating rehabilitation efforts?

In Chapter 11 the tax factor is examined in detail. Are slum properties overassessed? What is the effect of present reassessment practice on improvement procedure of landlords? How substantial are real estate taxes as a percentage of income? And most significantly of all, what is the capacity of tax abatement to generate additional investment in rehabilitation on the part of the landlord?

The final chapter revolves around the potential role for government and the policies required to secure rehabilitation. *Is there some optimum mix of strategy to energize the market in improving the housing conditions and the aspiration levels of the center cityite?*

REFERENCES

1 John W. Dyckman and R. R. Isaacs, *Capital Requirements for Urban Development and Renewal* (New York: McGraw-Hill, 1961), p. 16.

2 Northeastern New Jersey Regional Urban Renewal Survey, *A Guide to Urban Renewal* (Trenton, New Jersey, 1963), p. 25.

3 New York State Temporary State Housing Commission, *Prospects for Rehabilitation* (Albany, N. Y., 1960), p. 1.

4 Bernard J. Frieden, *The Future of Old Neighborhoods* (Cambridge, Mass.: M.I.T. Press, 1964), p. 23. See also the similar comments of William C. Grigsby in *Housing Markets and Public Policy* (Philadelphia, Pa.: University of Pennsylvania Press, 1963), p. 254ff.

5 On this point see Robert M. Fisher, *Twenty Years of Public Housing* (New York: Harper & Brothers, 1959).

6 A full description of the literature in this area is in Alvin L. Schorr, *Slums and Social Insecurity* (U. S. Department of Health, Education and Welfare, Social Security Administration, Division of Research and Statistics, 1963).

7 Martin Millspaugh, "Problems and Opportunities of Relocation," *Law and Contemporary Problems* (School of Law, Duke University, Winter, 1961), p. 32.

8 Market Planning Corporation, *Newark—A City in Transition,* Volume I (N.P. 1959). Hereinafter cited as MPC I and MPC II for Volume II of the report.

9 Ira S. Lowry, "Filtering and Housing Standards—A Conceptual Analysis," *Land Economics,* (August, 1960), p. 370.

10 Leo Grebler, *Housing Market Behavior In a Declining Area* (New York: Columbia University Press, 1952), pp. 55–63.

11 Louis Winnick, *Rental Housing: Opportunities for Private Investment* (New York: McGraw-Hill, 1958), p. 77.

12 Grigsby, *Housing Markets and Public Policy,* pp. 267, 275, and 286. For a study of the cost/rent impact of rehabilitation, see N. Y. State Temporary State Housing Rent Commission, *Prospects for Rehabilitation* (Albany, 1960). See also Millspaugh, *The Human Side of Urban Renewal* (New York: Washburn, 1960).

13 Newark, New Jersey, Project Conference Committee, *Capital Program 1964 to 1969* (Newark, N. J., Dec., 1963), p. 7.

14 William L. Slayton, "Bottlenecks of Urban Renewal," *Federal Bar Journal* (Summer, 1961), p. 281.

15 Fisher, *Twenty Years of Public Housing,* pp. 51–52.

16 Grigsby, *Housing Markets and Public Policy,* p. 286. See also Martin Anderson, *The Federal Bulldozer* (Cambridge, Mass.: M.I.T. Press, 1964), p. 67. As a rebuttal, however, a check by the Bureau of the Census during the period from November 1964 to January 1965 of 2300 households moved during the summer of 1964 indicates that 94 percent of them found accommodations in standard housing, though at higher rentals. See HHFA. *The Housing of Relocated Families,* March, 1965.

17 Fisher, *Twenty Years of Public Housing,* p. 17.

18 Millspaugh, "Problems and Opportunities of Relocation," pp. 11, 12.

19 Kirk W. Back, *Slums, Projects and People* (Durham, N. C.: Duke University Press, 1962), p. 59.

20 Millspaugh, "Problems and Opportunities of Relocation," p. 12. Note that while the specific reasons may be rationalizations, the fact of some distaste is clear.

21 Northeastern New Jersey Regional Urban Renewal Survey, *A Guide to Urban Renewal,* pp. 39–40.

22 See Martin Meyerson and Edward C. Banfield, *Politics, Planning and the Public Interest* (Glencoe, Ill.: Free Press, 1955), on the former point and Metropolitan Housing and Planning Council of Chicago, *Interim Report on Housing the Economically and Socially Disadvantaged Groups in the Population* (Chicago, 1960), p. 14, on the latter point.

23 Chicago Housing Authority, *The Slum . . . Is Rehabilitation Possible?* (Chicago, 1960), p. 1.

24 Julian H. Levi, "Problems in the Rehabilitation of Blighted Areas," *Federal Bar Journal* (Summer, 1961), p. 317.

25 See David B. Carlson, "Rehabilitation: Stepchild of Urban Renewal," *Architectural Forum* (1962).

26 William W. Nash, *Residential Rehabilitation . . .* (New York: McGraw-Hill, 1959).

27 See, for example, Jane Jacobs, "How Money Can Make or Break Our Cities," *The Reporter* (October 12, 1961), p. 38.

28 For more precise analysis see *The National Tax Journal,* (1962), pp. 435–436.

29 Schorr, *Slums and Social Insecurity,* p. 91.

30 Mason Gaffney, *Property Taxes and the Frequency of Urban Renewal* (Paper presented at National Tax Association, Pittsburgh, September 17, 1964, mimeo).

31 Harvey Brazer, *Some Fiscal Implications of Metropolitanism* (Washington, D. C.: Brookings Institution, 1962), p. 82.

32 United States Savings and Loan League, *Proceedings—Conference on Savings and Residential Financing* (Chicago, Illinois, May 10–11, 1962).

33 Newark Central Planning Board, *New Newark* (Newark, N. J., 1961), p. 54. For discussion of the regressive effects of real estate taxation, see Walter A. Morton, *Housing Taxation* (Madison, Wisconsin: University of Wisconsin Press, 1955).

Chapter 2

THE CITY AND ITS ANALYSIS

In using Newark, New Jersey, as the focal point of the study, our attention is centered on a city which is an advanced prototype of most older eastern municipalities. The detailed changes in population, both in number and racial characteristics, and the changing function of the city as a whole, which is the subject matter of this chapter, may be specific to Newark. As general phenomena, however, they're all too familiar to most of our older eastern cities and several of the newer western ones as well. The specific efforts described here of both aroused citizenry and municipal authorities to turn back the tide through urban renewal and rehabilitation programs in terms of the specific details are uniquely those of Newark. Once again, however, as general phenomena there are many similarities to efforts in other cities.

The decay of the residential real estate market, as well as all of the demographic shifts, are perhaps sharper in Newark than in any other major northern city. Is Newark merely a forerunner of the situation to come in other cities? What lessons can municipal authorities in other cities gain from the Newark experience? Most important of all, what will be the raison d'être of the older city in the future?

Newark, as indicated by the map shown in Exhibit 2–1 on page 23, is the center of a broad industrial belt at one end of the nation's great pipe-line between New York and Norfolk. Its broad industrial base is a tribute to its location and to the variety of nationalities which have dominated its population at one time or another. The breweries of the "1848'ers" still exist side by side with the leather works stimulated by Yankee Seth Boyden. In-

EXHIBIT 2–1

MAP OF NEWARK AND SURROUNDING CITIES

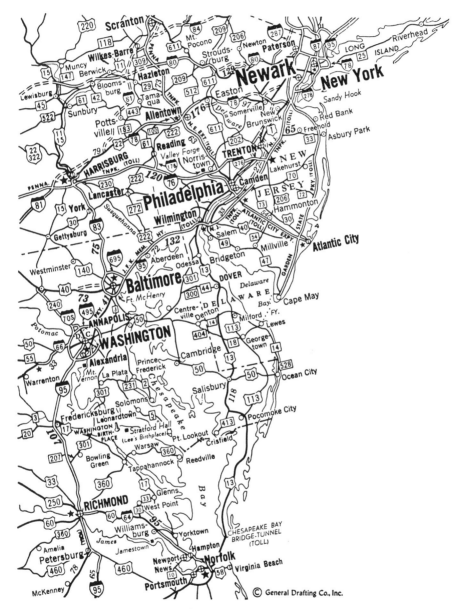

© General Drafting Co., Inc.

creasingly important, however, are a variety of warehousing and near-warehousing-type activities calculated to serve the New York market. As a major financial center in its own right and home of several of America's largest insurance companies, the white collar base of the city's economy is equally substantial. Newark's original industrial growth was greatly stimulated by its superb transportation facilities. No less than six railroads serve the city.

The growth and development of alternative transportation means and particularly the improvement of New Jersey's highways have resulted in a variety of alternative industrial locations being made available. While Northern New Jersey has acted as a magnet for industry from the New York side of the Hudson, the bulk of new development has bypassed the older New Jersey industrial centers for highway-oriented facilities. The requirement of parking facilities, the fashion of horizontal rather than vertical industrial plant development, the increased tax rates of the older cities, and certainly not least, the changing racial composition of the city have played major roles in slowing the development of the economic base of the city.[1]

Population Shifts in Newark

As Exhibit 2–2 on page 25 indicates, Newark's population rose very rapidly from 1880 to 1920. The percentage increase from census to census averaged nearly 30 percent. The numerical increases continued, although at a diminishing rate, through 1930. It was in the decade of the 1930's that the city lost population for the first time. Though there was a small population increase in the 1940's, the trend was reversed in the following decade with a population loss of 7.6 percent.

These overall data, however, mask internal shifts which were even more consequential. In a 1914 issue of Dau's *Blue Book,* a social register of New Jerseyites, nearly 18 percent of the nine thousand five hundred families listed had Newark addresses. Indeed, many of the slum areas that are to be considered later are listed as locations for the socially elite. By 1957 a researcher doing a study on group relations in Newark could say, "So frequently do their leaders move to the suburbs, (referring to the exodus of social leaders from the city) that continuity of effort is sometimes impaired. There is no phenomenon in Newark akin to New York City's luxury apartments. There is no middle-income housing project. As status and incomes rise, whites enter the new promised land of our era, the suburb."[2]

EXHIBIT 2–2

NEWARK TOTAL POPULATION BY DECADE

Year	Number	Percent Change
1880	136,508	+29.9
1890	181,830	+33.2
1900	246,070	+35.3
1910	347,469	+41.2
1920	414,524	+19.3
1930	442,337	+6.7
1940	429,760	−2.8
1950	438,776	+2.1
1960	405,220	−7.6

Source: U. S. Census.

This phenomenon is far from unique to Newark, and it should not be coupled necessarily with the changing racial composition of the city's population.[3] Undoubtedly, however, the process was accentuated by the fact that the vacuum, created by the white population of the city upgrading its residences into the newly-vacated better areas, was filled by the socially declassed—the Negro.

Exhibit 2–3 on page 26 shows the change in the number of white inhabitants from 1940 to 1960. In Area 1* the white population loss was 23.7 percent in the decade of the Forties. This was accelerated in the next ten years to a 61.1 percent white population loss. The seven census tracts in this group lost over 70 per cent of their white inhabitants in twenty years.

The other groups are somewhat similar. As is natural, based upon the preselection of A and B groups, the rates of change of white population are quite different. In both cases, however, for both 2B and 3B the rate of white population loss has been accelerating. For the sample areas as a whole, the

---

* While a fuller description of the research methodology will be reserved for the latter part of this chapter and Appendix 1, it should be noted here that for the purposes of analysis, five groups of census tracts have been segregated from the balance of the city. The first group, Area 1, is the set of seven census tracts with less than one-fifth of the units "sound," based upon the 1960 Housing Census. Groups 2A and 2B have the same housing characteristics; between one-fourth and one-half of the units are sound. Group 2A, however, consists of those tracts which are largely Negro-occupied; 2B are those which are still largely white-occupied. Groups 3A and 3B consist of the twenty-one tracts in the city whose housing is more than 50 percent, but less than 67 percent sound. As in the case of the Number 2 groups, 3A is largely Negro, and 3B is largely white-occupied. See the map in Exhibit 2–4 on page 27 for the locations of these tracts and Exhibit 2–5 on page 28 for their housing condition. Thus, the area of prime focus consists roughly of 40 percent of the city's one hundred tracts.

EXHIBIT 2–3

CHANGE IN THE NUMBER OF WHITE INHABITANTS, 1940–1950–1960 BY SAMPLE AREAS, BALANCE OF CITY, AND CITY AS A WHOLE

	1940	1950		1960		Total
	Population	Population	Percent Change 1940–50	Population	Percent Change 1950–60	Percent Change 1940–60
Area 1	20,916	15,960	−23.7	6,205	−61.1	−70.3
Area 2A	31,038	24,911	−19.7	9,060	−63.3	−70.8
Area 2B	12,533	12,391	−1.1	8,076	−34.8	−35.6
Area 2 combined	43,571	37,302	−14.4	17,136	−54.1	−60.7
Area 3A	36,181	29,440	−18.6	12,167	−58.7	−66.4
Area 3B	44,651	44,403	−.6	33,983	−23.5	−23.9
Area 3 combined	80,832	73,843	−8.6	46,150	−37.5	−42.9
Total sample areas	145,319	127,105	−12.5	69,491	−45.3	−52.2
Balance of Newark	238,215	236,044	−.9	196,398	−16.8	−17.6
Newark City total	383,534	363,149	−5.3	265,889	−26.8	−30.7

Percentage changes were determined using the formula: $\dfrac{1950-1940}{1940}$ = Percent Change 1940–1950.

$\dfrac{1960-1950}{1950}$ = Percent Change 1950–1960.

$\dfrac{1960-1940}{1940}$ = Percent Change 1940–1960

Source: *U. S. Census*: 1940, 1950, 1960.

EXHIBIT 2–4

NEWARK SAMPLE AREA DETAIL

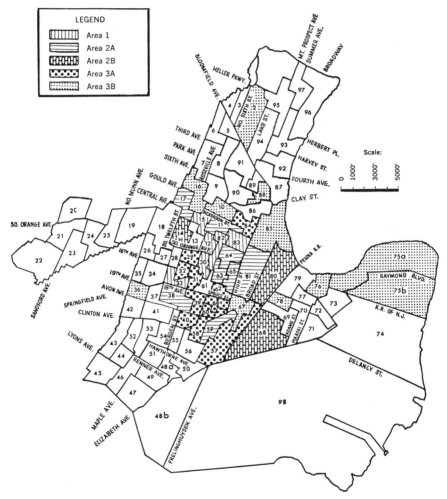

Census Tracts, Newark, New Jersey, Central Planning Board, November 1960.

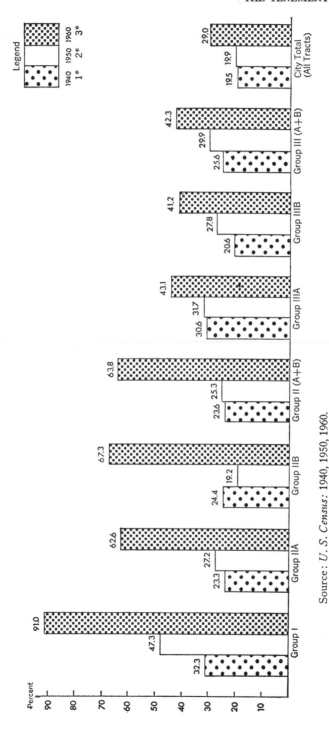

EXHIBIT 2–5

STATE OF REPAIR OF UNITS

Source: *U. S. Census:* 1940, 1950, 1960.

* Note that the terms used to define housing condition have varied between censuses

DEFINITIONS: 1—1940 "Needing major repair" 2—1950 "No private bath or dilapidated"
3—1960 "Deteriorating or dilapidated"

white population decline between 1940–1950 was 12.5 percent while the balance of Newark lost only 0.9 percent. In the decade of the Fifties, the sample areas as a whole lost 45.3 percent of their white population, while the balance of Newark was losing 16.8 percent. In sum, in the twenty years covered by Exhibit 2–3, the sample areas lost more than half of their white population, while the balance of Newark lost less than a fifth.

Exhibit 2–6 on page 30 shows the equivalent changes in the total number of nonwhite inhabitants. As can be seen, the decline in the number of white inhabitants was largely offset by Negro immigration. It is evident from this Exhibit that the pattern of segregation of Negro housing facilities within the city has altered considerably over the 1940–1960 period. In 1940, for example, the sample areas had nearly thirty-nine thousand of the city's forty-six thousand nonwhites. By 1960, though the bulk of the nonwhite population of Newark lived within the sample areas, more than forty thousand were living in the balance of Newark.

The significance of this broader housing market will be touched on in more detail in later chapters. It should be noted here, however, that unlike many other cities (or perhaps as a forerunner of other cities?) the total areas of Newark available for nonwhite housing have increased very, very substantially in recent years. This should not minimize, however, the fact that the core of the city's blighted tracts are largely Negro-occupied. There are less than half as many whites living in the sample area as of 1960 as were living there in 1940. In 1960 nearly 60 percent of the population within the sample areas was nonwhite. In 1940 it was little more than 20 percent.

The pattern of change can be most extreme. For example, in Census Tract 33, there were only forty-six nonwhites out of a total population of four thousand two hundred seventy-five in 1940, and in 1950 there were only two hundred fifty-four of the total population of four thousand one hundred eighty-six. By 1960 the number of nonwhites had increased to two thousand three hundred eighty-nine out of a total population of four thousand two hundred twenty-seven. Though the tract described here is an extreme case, it is closely paralleled by a number of others.

Exhibit 2–7 on page 31 shows total changes in the number of inhabitants from 1940 to 1960, and Exhibit 2–8 on page 32 shows the changes in housing unit occupancy. The pattern of shift is clear. The sample areas, in the decade of the Forties, increased in population somewhat more quickly than the city as a whole. This changed quite radically in the following ten-year period. While the sample areas lost 12.3 percent of their total population,

EXHIBIT 2-6

CHANGE IN THE NUMBER OF NONWHITE INHABITANTS, 1940–1950–1960 BY SAMPLE AREAS, BALANCE OF CITY, AND CITY AS A WHOLE

	1940	1950		1960		Total
	Population	Population	Percent Change 1940-1950	Population	Percent Change 1950-1960	Percent Change 1940-1960
Area 1	8,827	14,530	+64.6	19,078	+31.3	+116.1
Area 2A	8,606	15,783	+83.4	26,683	+69.1	+210.1
Area 2B	1,970	2,926	+48.5	4,420	+51.1	+124.4
Area 2 combined	10,576	18,709	+76.9	31,103	+66.2	+194.1
Area 3A	16,637	24,311	+46.1	36,117	+48.6	+117.1
Area 3B	2,943	5,054	+71.1	10,606	+109.9	+260.4
Area 3 combined	19,580	29,365	+50.0	46,723	+59.1	+138.6
Total sample areas	38,983	62,604	+60.6	96,904	+54.8	+148.6
Balance of Newark	7,243	13,023	+79.8	42,427	+225.9	+485.9
Newark City total	46,226	75,627	+63.6	139,331	+84.2	+201.4

Percentage changes were determined using formulas: $\dfrac{1950-1940}{1940}$ = Percent Change 1940–50.

$\dfrac{1960-1950}{1950}$ = Percent Change 1950–60.

$\dfrac{1960-1940}{1940}$ = Percent Change 1940–60

Source: U. S. Census: 1940, 1950, 1960.

EXHIBIT 2-7

CHANGE IN TOTAL NUMBER OF INHABITANTS, 1940–1950–1960
by SAMPLE AREA, BALANCE OF CITY, AND CITY AS A WHOLE

	1940		1950		1960		Total	
	Population	—	Population	Percent Change 1940–1950	Population	Percent Change 1950–1960	—	Percent Change 1940–1960
Area 1	29,743	—	30,490	+2.5	25,283	−17.1	—	−15.0
Area 2A	39,644	—	40,694	+2.6	35,743	−12.2	—	−9.8
Area 2B	14,503	—	15,317	+5.6	12,496	−18.4	—	−13.8
Area 2 combined	54,147	—	56,011	+3.4	48,239	−13.9	—	−10.9
Area 3A	52,818	—	53,751	+1.8	48,284	−10.2	—	−8.6
Area 3B	47,594	—	49,457	+3.9	44,589	−9.8	—	−6.3
Area 3 combined	100,412	—	103,208	+2.8	92,873	−10.0	—	−7.5
Total sample areas	184,302	—	189,709	+2.9	166,395	−12.3	—	−9.7
Balance of Newark	245,458	—	249,067	+1.5	238,825	−4.1	—	−2.7
Newark City total	429,760	—	438,776	+2.1	405,220	−7.6	—	−5.7

Percentage changes were determined using the formulas: $\dfrac{1950-1940}{1940}$ = Percent change 1940–1950.

$\dfrac{1960-1940}{1940}$ = Percent Change 1940–1960. $\dfrac{1960-1950}{1950}$ = Percent change 1950–1960.

Source: *U. S. Census:* 1940, 1950, 1960.

EXHIBIT 2–8

PROPORTION OF HOUSING UNITS OCCUPIED BY NONWHITE BY GROUP AND
SUBGROUP AS A PERCENTAGE OF TOTAL OCCUPIED UNITS

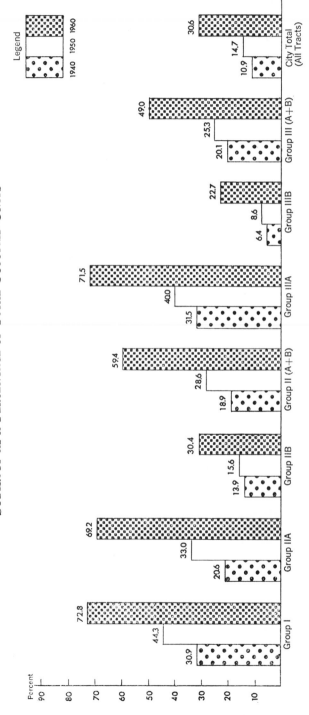

Source: *U. S. Census:* 1940, 1950, 1960.

the balance of Newark was losing only 4.1 percent. In this loss of population, Area 1 and Area 2 lead the way. As will be shown in more detail later, Area 1, the receiving depot for the initial wave of Negro migrants, is now rapidly emptying out as other more desirable areas are available.[4] The transition in 2B, which also will be examined in more detail in later chapters, is a function of whites moving out and defacto segregation inhibiting their replacement with an equivalent number of Negroes.

It is this context of population shift, both in number and in socio-economic condition, which sets the basic parameters of the housing market in Newark. Not one of the Group 1 tracts increased in white population after 1940. Only one of the Group 2B tracts, Number 80, increased in white population from 1940 to 1950. In the following ten years the number of whites was halved in this tract. In Group 3A there is one tract which increased in white population from 1940 to 1950, and this too lost more than half of its white population by 1960. In Group 3B there were two tracts out of the ten, which increased in white population from 1940 to 1950. Only one of these maintained its increase through the following decade. (For a complete tract racial change listing, see Appendix II on page 237.)

Longevity of Slum Property in Newark

The existence of slums in Newark is not a novelty. The clippings file maintained faithfully by the Newark Public Library is filled with material dating back to the turn of the century, indicating that the old Third Ward (roughly identical with Group 1 tracts) was the focus of the city's indignation even at that time. Crime, fire, disease—all of these seemed to be centered there. But this was essentially a localized phenomenon. In 1946 a publication of the Housing Authority of the City of Newark, entitled *The Cost of Slums in Newark,* pointed to essentially the same areas which had drawn the fire of city critics for decades before. From the viewpoint of the researcher, one of the provocative questions is whether the "growth of blight in the city," usually identified with population shifts, is actually a discrete phenomenon, or whether it is merely the growth of *realization* of the city's blighted condition as a function of up-graded public standards. A glance at Exhibit 2–5 on page 28 gives some insight into the physical attributes of the Newark poor-housing areas. The data shown is for 1940, 1950, and 1960, divided into five groups, plus the city total. (Notice that there is no direct comparability between the several censuses. The data must be used, therefore, within the same time spans.) The Group 1 tracts have obviously been the poorest area of the city since 1940. By 1960 there was very little in them which, by the definitions of the census used at that time and within the time-altered judgments of the field surveyors, was judged as sound. Groups 2A and 2B are essentially similar in housing characteristics as of 1940. By 1950, however, the soon-to-be dominantly Negro 2A area had degenerated much more than the 2B area. The measure of stability was restored by 1960 with both areas being roughly two-thirds unsound. A somewhat similar division is apparent when Groups 3A and 3B are examined. Group 3A in 1940 was nearly as poor as Group 1 in contrast with 3B. Although 3B has remained essentially white, in terms of state of repair of units, by 1960 both 3A and 3B were remarkably similar.

Three basic generalizations arise from this Exhibit:

1. Substantial blight areas existed throughout the major groupings as early as 1940.
2. Those areas which are more blighted than their neighbors are the first to be given over to Negro occupancy.
3. There is little to choose from in changes of housing quality between areas initially of similar housing quality which are later split between white and nonwhite residents. Blight's continuance is largely indifferent to color.

It should be noted that the vast bulk of the housing in our sample areas is rental. In Group 1, for example, the proportion is 83.5 percent of all occupied housing. For the city as a whole, it is 73.4 percent.

Vacancy Rates and Overcrowding

As will be indicated in greater detail later, there is data which shows a growing vacancy rate in the Newark slums. While from the landlord's point of view the decrease in population which has characterized the areas under study has softened the rental market, it has considerably helped the overcrowding problem.

In Exhibit 2–9, Central City Housing Utilization, 1950 and 1960, on page 35, the number of dwelling units with 1.01 or more occupants per room has changed substantially in the older residential cores of the area. In Newark, for example, this decreased from 15.1 percent to 13 percent. In the sample areas substantial improvement was experienced in absolute

EXHIBIT 2–9

CENTRAL-CITY HOUSING UTILIZATION, 1950 AND 1960

	Number and Percent of (Nonseasonal) Units with 1.01 or More Occupants per Room			
	1950		1960	
	Number	Percent	Number	Percent
Manhattan	99,846	16.5	92,386	13.3
Bronx	90,811	21.6	70,926	15.3
Brooklyn	138,369	17.6	110,053	12.9
Newark	18,216	15.1	16,600	13.0
Jersey City	12,418	14.8	10,077	11.4

Source: Frieden, *The Future of Old Neighborhoods*, p. 161.

terms; however, this still means that, according to the 1960 census, more than 18 percent of the dwelling units in the hard-core slums are substantially overcrowded. (I think it can safely be stated, in addition, that though the relative gain is clear cut, the absolute level of overcrowding is probably understated by the census gathers' respondents.) In any case the area remains one of aged, relatively decrepit housing, with little open space or playground facilities, and with very little in the way of new, privately constructed housing. (The prevalence of bars, of junkyards, and other sources of blight is codified in Exhibit 12 of Appendix I on page 53. The Appendix also contains data on construction, commercial occupancy, etc.)

Importance of Housing

How important is housing to the residents of the slum areas? Exhibit 2–10 on page 36 portrays the results of a survey of two thousand five hundred ninety-five Negro Newarkites on the major problems facing Negroes in Newark. The most frequent reference is to housing. Getting better housing, for example, got 39 percent of the response; high rents, 17 percent; and housing discrimination, *per se*, 10 percent. Even references to employment were far fewer. Complaints about neighborhood conditions and rent levels predominated in the results of the survey. (The question of rent levels will be taken up in the next chapter.)

Certainly one of the most harmful elements in the slums of Newark is the prevalence of vacant and/or abandoned parcels. In the course of the field

EXHIBIT 2-10

OPINIONS OF NEGRO RESPONDENTS AS TO THE MAJOR PROBLEMS
FACING NEGROES IN NEWARK, BY NEIGHBORHOOD

Major Problems Facing Negroes	Total Percent
References to Housing	
Getting better, decent housing	39
High rents	17
Housing discrimination	10
References to Employment	
Jobs are scarce	22
Job discrimination, unequal job opportunities	19
Negroes' lack of training, preparation for jobs	2
Responses in Terms of Shortcomings of Negroes Themselves	
Negroes' own conduct	5
Negroes don't stick together	4
General Responses	
Discrimination, segregation	4
References to inadequate city services	2
References to schools	1
All responses indicating that Negroes have no problems peculiar to own group. (Problems are same as those of all others.)	4
All other responses	2
Don't know, no answer	15
	100*
	(2,595)

* Totals add to more than 100 percent due to multiple responses.
Source: *MPC-II*

study, and later interviewing, no less than sixteen out of a total of five hundred
sixty-six parcels in the random sample fitted this category. They were either
burnt out, boarded up, or in some cases basically vacant and open to the
wind and the derelicts of the neighborhood. Each of these parcels was re-
visited six months after having been observed. No less than twelve were
still in the same condition as had been observed initially. Each of these
parcels serves as a source of contamination for the entire neighborhood.
While the city in theory has a policy of requiring that vacant parcels be
cleared off the land, this is obviously far from the usual practice. In a number of cases, parcels were observed that had been vacant, according to
neighbors, for upwards of three years. Their effect on real estate values will
be discussed more fully later. Their effect on the human environment is
most deleterious.

The Tax Problem

The changes in population have been particularly significant in increasing municipal expenditures in Newark. Data from the State of New Jersey, Department of Institutions and Agencies, Division of Public Welfare, indicates that for nearly every category of welfare assistance, Essex County's expenditures were more than double those of its nearest New Jersey rival—Hudson County. With Newark the major reservoir of the unfortunate in Essex County the relationship as shown in Exhibit 2–11 is all too clear.

EXHIBIT 2–11

NEWARK'S CONTRIBUTION FOR WELFARE BY YEAR, 1941–1963

Year	Health Service	Welfare— Public Assist. Poor and Relief	Hospitals (Aid to Maintenance)	Other	Total
1941	$ 778,591.58	$2,486,825.71	$1,154,432.00	—	$ 4,419,849.29
1943	817,985.00	751,351.20	1,226,002.00	$198,325.00	2,993,663.20
1945	967,237.10	473,313.61	1,303,061.00	—	2,743,611.71
1947	1,705,617.50	662,839.50	2,113,284.04	—	4,481,741.04
1949	1,836,072.60	1,884,977.78	2,549,110.60	—	6,270,160.98
1951	1,762,426.74	1,648,034.93	2,873,554.00	292,359.90	6,576,375.57
1953	2,014,997.57	1,113,188.88	3,508,048.42	319,550.00	6,955,784.87
1955	2,155,868.89	1,963,638.73	3,844,689.72	—	7,964,197.34
1957	2,416,637.37	1,460,862.25	4,428,240.63	—	8,305,740.25
1959	2,131,553.04	1,385,450.42	5,738,599.48	—	9,255,602.94
1962	2,576,024.31	1,205,545.66	7,145,204.30	—	10,926,774.27
1963	2,529,014.58	2,536,542.77	7,439,520.72	—	12,505,078.07

Source: *Annual Report of the Division of Local Government, State of New Jersey, Statements of Financial Condition of Counties and Municipalities,* New Jersey Department of the Treasury, Division of Local Government, 1941–1963, Trenton, N. J.

Paralleling this problem is the increase in tax rates. The current tax rate is $6.60 on nominally 100 percent of value. (See Exhibit 2–12 on page 38, Newark Tax Rate per $100 Evaluation.) The dynamics of expenditures in older cities need little amplification here. The symptoms of a relatively static tax base and increased need are a platitude in every major American city.[5] As shall be shown in detail in Chapter 11, Newark's situation is intensified by New Jersey's dependence on land-based taxes; to a greater or lesser degree, however, it is close to being universal.

EXHIBIT 2-12
NEWARK TAX RATE PER $100 OF VALUATION

1927—$1.895	1947—$2.985
1928— 1.915	1948— 3.25
1929— 1.90	1949— 3.38
1930— 1.97	1950— 3.42
1931— 1.99	1951— 3.46
1932— 1.90	1952— 3.78
1933— 1.64	1953— 3.89
1934— 1.825	1954— 4.275
1935— 1.68	1955— 4.235
1936— 1.905	1956— 4.215
1937—$1.845	1957— 4.47
1938— 2.305	1958— 4.805
1939— 2.275	1959— 5.105
1940— 2.425	1960— 5.125
1941— 2.575	1961— 5.055
1942— 2.645	1962— 5.37
1943— 2.655	1963— 5.79
1944— 2.65	1964— 6.60
1945— 2.73	
1946— 2.78	

Based on 100 percent of true value.
See text for actual experience ratio.

Conclusion of Newark Background

It is within this context of rapid population shift, of an aged city whose core is composed largely of inadequate housing, of a city that partakes of the fiscal and human problems which are nearly universal among American municipalities, that Newark's efforts at renewal and rehabilitation have taken place. The scale of these efforts has been considerable. Frequently, however, they have been too little and too late in terms of the dynamism of change within the city. Newark remains a city of much hope in the face of great problems.[6]

Methodology

The material which follows is based upon intensive analysis of five hundred sixty-six slum tenements, i.e. parcels having three or more apartment units within the slum areas of Newark. The parcels chosen on a random basis are essentially representative of the housing types within this category in the city. As noted earlier, for the purposes of analysis, the city was divided into five different housing/racial categories. (For a full analysis of the methodology see Appendix I on page 40.)

Sales, mortgage, and tax data were secured for all the sample parcels, and lengthy depth interviews were obtained from the owners of three hundred ninety-two of the five hundred sixty-six parcels. The nonrespondents, as more fully explained in Appendix I, are roughly similar to the respondents. The major exception is the relative paucity of owners of abandoned parcels who could be found. The field survey and choice of parcels were completely independent of the research on ownership. Surveyors, therefore, were not aware of who owned individual parcels in appraising the quality of maintenance and upkeep. The appendices give full descriptions of the parcel-choice and interview techniques which were employed.

REFERENCES

1 For an analysis of the changing economic base of the older city, see George Sternlieb, *The Future of the Downtown Department Store* (Cambridge: Harvard University Press, 1962).

2 Chester Rapkin *et al., Group Relations in Newark, 1957, A Report to the Mayor's Commission On Group Relations* (N. Y.: Urban Research, 1957), p. 70. While a number of new middle income developments have been planned or built since Rapkin's study, the basic premise still holds.

3 On this point see Walter Firey, *Land Use in Central Boston* (Cambridge: Harvard University Press, 1943).

4 The extent of population thinning at the older city core is examined in detail by Hans Blumenfeld, "The Tidal Wave of Metropolitan Expansion," *Journal of the American Institute of Planners* (Winter, 1954).

5 For the specifics of the New Jersey situation, see Morris Beck, *Property Taxation and Urban Land Use in Northeastern New Jersey* (Washington: Urban Land Institute, 1963). For an overall view, see Ruth L. Mace, *Municipal Cost-Revenue Research in the United States* (Chapel Hill, N. C.: University of North Carolina, 1964).

6 Harold Kaplan, *Urban Renewal Politics* (N. Y.: Columbia University Press, 1963) gives an excellent, though controversial, view of the course of renewal and rehabilitation efforts in Newark.

SAMPLING METHODOLOGY

Housing Conditions and Demographic Partitions

The basic sample target was a representative sample of Newark slum tenements (parcels with three or more rental units) divided into several categories of blighted areas.

There were three basic way stations on the road toward the ultimate parcel choice. The first of these was the question of what criterion should be used to measure the degree of blight; the second was the question of what geographical subsets were to be used in describing areas; and the third was the question of what degree of blight to use as sample partitions.

For these purposes the *United States Census of Housing: 1960* for Newark, New Jersey, was utilized. The census presents data on housing units by three categories—sound, deteriorating, and dilapidated. (For a full description of these terms, please see Appendix III on page 243.) Obviously the subjective judgments of the field survey groups used by the census play a major role in determining the categories in which the housing units are placed. There are a number of discrepancies between the census data and studies done both by the Newark City Planning Board and the Newark Housing Authority. Nevertheless, for purposes of a rough sort of the city's areas the data proved reasonably reliable. When the proportion of sound housing for each of the city's census tracts* was listed in an array from

---

* *Definition of Census Tract*—"Census tracts are small areas into which large cities and adjacent areas have been divided for statistical purposes. Tract boundaries were established cooperatively by local committees and the Bureau of the Census, and generally designed to be relatively uniform with respect to population characteristics, eco-

those tracts with the least sound housing to those with the most, there were two obvious clusters. As the table in Exhibit A–1 on page 42 indicates, there were seven census tracts with less than 20 percent of their housing units sound.

Yet another cluster was present for the eleven tracts with less than 50 percent of sound housing. In order to see whether there would be significant differences in landlord opinion and reaction in areas which had considerable pockets of blight, but which overall were still basically sound, a third set of tracts was chosen from the next twenty-one. The very best of these tracts had 66.7 percent of its housing classified as sound. (For a full list of all of Newark's tracts see Appendix II.)

A map was then drawn showing the three sets of tracts. This map was taken by the project leader to several tenement managers and Newark real estate speculators who, after a brief discussion of the importance of neighborhood in determining investment, were shown the map and asked whether this map was a reasonable representation of the variations in Newark "low end" neighborhoods. In all cases they confirmed the overall validity of the sets chosen. This is not to indicate that there are not blocks in Area 2 as bad as anything in Area 1, or, for that matter, that in Area 3 there are not pockets of blight which would be out of place at all in Area 1. It does mean, however, that in terms of an overall neighborhood context, usually of approximately twenty blocks, the sets chosen made some sense to seasoned real estate investors. Area 1, the hard-core area, had as its worst tract one in which only 2.3 percent of the housing units were classified as sound. Its best tract had 17.7 percent classified that way. In Area 2 the range was 26.7 percent to 46.6 percent. Group 3 started at 50.2 percent and went up through 66.8 percent sound. Notice, by the way, the discontinuity between the groups. There is no abrupt step between the top of Group 3 and the balance of the city. Our upward boundary was set at an offhand estimate of two-thirds sound.

For the purposes of later analysis, another partition was found worthy of note. This is the proportion of housing occupied by nonwhites. For Group 1, this ran from a low of little less than half, 48.7 percent, to a high of 92.9

---

nomic statuses, and living conditions. The average tract has about four thousand residents. Tract boundaries are established with the intention of being maintained over a long time so that comparisons can be made from census to census." Source: U. S. Bureau of the Census, *U. S. Censuses of Population and Housing: 1960 Census Tracts,* Final Report PHC (1)—105.

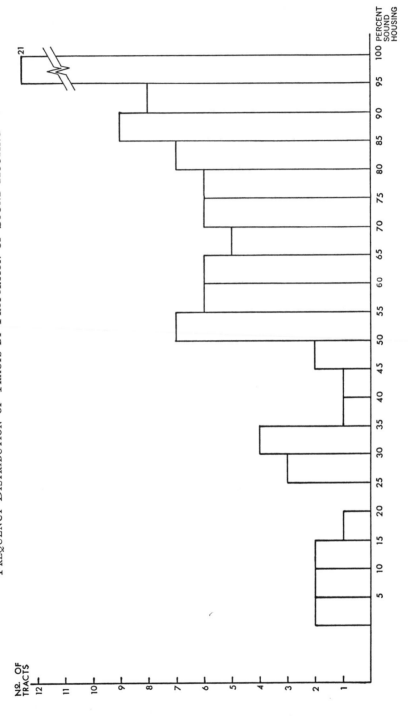

EXHIBIT A-1

FREQUENCY DISTRIBUTION OF TRACTS BY PROPORTION OF SOUND HOUSING

percent. Current opinion indicates a comparative homogenization of the Group 1 tracts. Both for Groups 2 and 3, however, there were decided dichotomies.

In Group 2A, for example, the proportion of nonwhites in 1960 ran from a low of 56.2 percent to a high of 84.4 percent with a relatively even distribution through the eight tracts concerned. Group 2B goes from a low of 22.1 percent to a high of 42.4 percent. Similarly, when Tract Group 3 was prepared in a rank ordering, there was an obvious division into two different subgroups with eleven census tracts running from 41.2 percent to 95.1 percent nonwhite occupancy and ten tracts running from a low of 6.8 percent to a high of 34.2 percent. The exhibits in the main body of the work are based, therefore, at least in part, on five subsets based on a combination of housing characteristics and also nonwhite occupancy. Exhibit A–2 summarizes the tract group categories. In order to economize on survey costs, the number of tracts in Group 3 was reduced by means of a random number table from twenty-one to thirteen (seven in subset 3A and six in subset 3B).

EXHIBIT A–2

TRACT GROUP CATEGORIES

Group	Number of Tracts	Housing Characteristics Percent Sound	Proportion of Occupied Housing Units Occupied by Nonwhites
1	7	2.3–17.7	48.7–92.9
2 {A	8	29.1–46.8	56.2–84.4
{B	3	26.7–38.0	22.1–42.4
3 {A	11	50.2–66.7	41.2–92.6
{B	10	51.2–66.8	7.9–31.1

Block and Parcel Choice

The Newark Census Tracts within each of the three Housing Sets were then detailed in terms of the number of those census blocks they contained which had twenty or more renter-occupied dwelling units. For each tract enough blocks were chosen using a random number table to secure approximately forty to fifty blocks per set one, two, and three, respectively. The number of blocks per tract, however, regardless of the paucity or abundance of blocks with twenty or more renter-occupied dwelling units within the tract, was limited to five by means of a random number table. The parcel surveyors were then sent out to the chosen blocks. (The instructions for the parcel surveyors and the parcel check list are incorporated in Appendix IV on page 251.) Starting at a designated corner of the specified block, the field surveyor counted all parcels on the block which had three or more rental units. He then used a random number table to determine which of those parcels were to be incorporated into the sample. For no block were more than five parcels chosen. In theory this should have yielded two hundred to two hundred fifty parcels in each area. Because of blocks which contained fewer than five appropriate parcels, this was not the case. In addition, three parcels were discovered to be in tax-exempt hands and were, therefore, dropped from the sample. For Area 1, there are one hundred eighty-six parcels, while there are one hundred eighty-two in Area 2, and one hundred ninety-eight in Area 3, for a total of five hundred sixty-six parcels. Exhibit A–3 summarizes the numbers involved.

EXHIBIT A–3

SUMMARY OF BLOCK AND PARCEL CHOICE

	Number of Tracts	Number of Blocks Chosen	Total Parcels Counted	Parcels in Sample
Area 1	7	39	609	186
Area 2	11	42	622	182
Area 3	13	52	829	198
				566

As stated earlier, a parcel for the purpose of this study was defined as an individual tenement with three or more rental units. This latter stipulation introduced a number of problems. There have been a number of both legal and nonlegal conversions of one- and two-family houses into multiples which would meet the category standards. Distinguishing these parcels from their unaltered equivalents, however, was frequently difficult. Unlike the situation in middle-class rental units, postal boxes are not an adequate indication of the number of rental units. Wherever there was doubt, tenants on the parcel were questioned. When there was no one at home and entrance into the parcel was prevented by a locked front door, neighboring tenants and store owners were questioned. Undoubtedly, the sample does contain some two-unit buildings despite this precaution. In Exhibits A–5 and A–6 on pages 45–46 of this appendix a breakdown of the parcels by number of dwelling units is presented.

EXHIBIT A-4
PROPORTION OF DWELLINGS OCCUPIED, PARTIALLY OCCUPIED, AND VACANT

	AREA 1		AREA 2A		AREA 2B		AREA 3A		AREA 3B		TOTAL	
	Number	Percent	Number	Percent	Number	Percent	Number	Percent	Number	Percent	Number	Percent
Occupied*	166	89.2	117	91.4	49	90.7	105	91.3	75	90.4	512	90.5
Partially Occupied	14	7.5	11	8.6	3	5.5	9	7.8	5	6.0	42	7.4
Vacant	6	3.2	—	—	2	3.7	1	0.9	3	3.6	12	2.1
Total	186	100.0**	128	100.0	54	100.0	115	100.0	83	100.0	566	100.0

* Note: Four were vacant by time of interview.
** Totals are not precise because of rounding.

EXHIBIT A-5
SIZE OF PARCEL
NUMBER OF APARTMENTS OBSERVED

	AREA 1		AREA 2A		AREA 2B		AREA 3A		AREA 3B		TOTAL	
	Number	Percent	Number	Percent	Number	Percent	Number	Percent	Number	Percent	Number	Percent
3–6 Units	159	85.5	111	86.7	52	96.3	105	91.3	75	91.5	502	88.8
7–12 Units	23	12.4	10	7.8	1	1.9	7	6.1	6	7.3	47	8.3
13–24 Units	4	2.2	7	5.5	1	1.9	2	1.7	1	1.2	15	2.7
25 or More	—	—	—	—	—	—	1	0.9	—	—	1	0.2
Total	186	100.0	128	100.0	54	100.0	115	100.0	82	100.0	565	100.0
Unobserved	—	—	—	—	—	—	—	—	1	—	1	—

EXHIBIT A-6

OUR SHEET INDICATES THAT ＿＿ HAS ＿＿ TO ＿＿ APARTMENTS, IS THAT CORRECT?*

	AREA 1		AREA 2A		AREA 2B		AREA 3A		AREA 3B		TOTAL	
	Number	Percent	Number	Percent	Number	Percent	Number	Percent	Number	Percent	Number	Percent
3–6 Units	94	73.4	60	67.4	33	89.2	64	81.0	44	83.0	295	76.4
7–12 Units	22	17.2	8	9.0	—	—	3	3.8	3	5.7	36	9.3
13–24 Units	1	0.8	5	5.6	1	2.7	2	2.5	2	3.8	11	2.8
25 or More	—	—	—	—	—	—	—	—	1	1.9	1	0.3
Sleeping Rooms	1	0.8	4	4.5	—	—	4	5.0	—	—	9	2.3
Other	—	—	—	—	—	—	2	2.5	—	—	2	0.5
Less than 3 Units	10	7.8	12	13.4	3	8.1	4	5.0	3	5.7	32	8.3
Total	128	100.0	89	100.0	37	100.0	79	100.0	53	100.0	386	100.0
NA			1				1				2	
DK			1				3				4	

*Based on interviews with landlords.

The Field Survey Parcel Check List

The basic goal of the field survey was first, as indicated above, to secure a random sample of tenements in the areas of Newark which had been defined. In addition, a basic description of the parcel, its condition and maintenance was desired. In the Exhibits which follow are detailed the results of this survey.

As Exhibit A-4 indicates, there are three categories of occupancy: those dwellings which were described as occupied, those which were partially occupied, and those which were vacant. If the categories are taken in reverse order, the vacant parcels were those parcels which were completely vacant. The reasons for this, as was later discovered, were various: a number of the parcels were burned out; some were in the process of being restored, and several were boarded up, with no signs of tenancy. The partially-occupied category required much more judgment on the part of the field surveyors. These were parcels which showed signs of substantial vacancy. In a number of cases a part of the parcel had been either demolished or obviously vandalized. In a number of cases they were parcels which had been substantially rebuilt and were just in the process of being rented. The occupied parcels, on the other hand, although they had the normal quota of "For Rent" signs, exhibited none of the characteristics of the other two sets.

There is little variation in the proportion of these categories by area. *As a whole, however. 9.5 percent of the parcels investigated were either vacant or substantially unoccupied.*

Exhibit A–5 shows the size of parcel and the number of apartments as noted by the field surveyors. As is indicated, the bulk of Newark tenements are relatively small with six or fewer units. A very few ran in the thirteen and over categories. This obviously is a factor of considerable significance in terms of the costs of maintaining and supervising rental units in Newark. Larger units obviously can more easily afford the services of a full-time resident janitor or superintendent. Smaller units, on the other hand, can have only part-time supervision at best. Area 1, the hard-core slum area, has the largest number of parcels with more than six units. The number of apartments observed required a considerable degree of judgment on the part of the field surveyors, and obviously there was much room for error.

The size of parcel was checked out in the personal interviews. By adding back in the "less than three units" which were claimed by landlords as a category to the three- to six-unit figure, it can be seen that the field survey universe and interviews have roughly the same size of unit proportions. Notice, as shown in Exhibit A–6, sleeping rooms, *per se*, played a relatively minor role in the sample. When this subject was checked in depth with a number of landlords, it was discovered that the familiar pattern is for apartments to be rented to individuals who then, in turn, sublease individual rooms as sleeping rooms. The giving over of an entire parcel to sleeping rooms, however, is comparatively infrequent, representing only 2.3 percent of the interviewed group.

The bulk of the construction in the sample set is frame. The proportion of masonry runs from 22.9 percent in Area 3B to 31.2 percent in Area 1. More than half of the frame structures have been covered with asphalt siding of one form or another, and, as Exhibit A–7 on type of construction indicates, a substantial proportion of them are in bad condition.

Condition of Parcel

The next category in the field survey directions was aimed at defining the quality of the parcel being surveyed. This is obviously a difficult task involving a variety of subjective elements. There were three questions which were directed to this end. The first of them appraised the quality of external appearance. The field surveyors were asked to compare the parcel to its immediate neighbors. Was it poorer than its neighbors, the same as its neighbors, or better than its neighbors? The results appear in Exhibit A–8.

The field surveyor was then asked to define the absolute quality of the landlords' maintenance of such elements as garbage facilities, halls, stairs, fire escapes, porches and steps. This too was categorized by reasonably-kept, poorly-kept, and well-kept. A substantial difference from area to area is evident in Exhibit A–9. Nearly one-quarter of all parcels were rated as poorly-kept by the surveyors in Area 1. This ratio drops substantially for the other areas to a low of 7.4 percent in 2B (based on a relatively small sample in this latter area).

Of the well-kept parcels, Area 1 has the smallest proportion, roughly one out of seven. Although Area 2 as a whole is poorer than Area 3, Area 2A is far worse than Area 2B. A similar relationship exists between Areas 3A to 3B. In the last, which is the "best housing area," largely white-occupied, nearly one-third of all parcels are well-kept. For the sample area as a whole, 61.6 percent are reasonably-kept, 19.3 percent are poorly-kept with a similar proportion well-kept.

EXHIBIT A-7
TYPE OF CONSTRUCTION

	AREA 1		AREA 2A		AREA 2B		AREA 3A		AREA 3B		TOTAL	
	Num-ber	Per-cent	Num-ber	Per-cent	Num-ber	Per-cent	Num-ber	Per-cent	Num-ber	Per-cent	Num-ber	Per-cent
Frame	46	24.7	33	25.8	17	31.5	39	34.2	22	26.5	157	27.8
Frame with reasonable to good siding	65	34.9	48	37.5	22	40.7	38	33.3	38	45.8	211	37.3
Frame with bad siding	17	9.1	8	6.3	1	1.9	9	7.9	4	4.8	39	6.9
Masonry	58	31.2	39	30.5	14	25.9	28	24.6	19	22.9	158	27.9
Total	186	100.0	128	100.0	54	100.0	114	100.0	83	100.0	565	100.0
Not Recorded							1				1	

EXHIBIT A-8

QUALITY OF EXTERNAL APPEARANCE
(COMPARED TO NEIGHBORING PARCELS)

	AREA 1		AREA 2A		AREA 2B		AREA 3A		AREA 3B		TOTAL	
	Number	Per cent	Number	Per cent	Number	Per cent	Number	Per cent	Number	Per cent	Number	Per cent
Poorer than neighbors	25	13.4	17	13.3	3	5.6	9	7.8	13	15.7	67	11.8
Same as neighbors	130	69.9	90	70.3	43	79.6	90	78.3	62	74.7	415	73.3
Better than neighbors	31	16.7	21	16.4	8	14.8	16	13.9	8	9.6	84	14.8
Total	186	100.0	128	100.0	54	100.0	115	100.0	83	100.0	566	100.0

EXHIBIT A-9

ABSOLUTE QUALITY OF LANDLORD MAINTENANCE BY AREA

	AREA 1		AREA 2A		AREA 2B		AREA 3A		AREA 3B		TOTAL	
	Number	Per cent	Number	Per cent	Number	Per cent	Number	Per cent	Number	Per cent	Number	Per cent
Reasonably Kept	113	60.8	78	60.9	36	66.7	79	68.7	43	51.8	349	61.6
Poorly Kept	46	24.7	27	21.1	4	7.4	19	16.5	13	15.7	109	19.3
Well Kept	27	14.5	23	18.0	14	25.9	17	14.8	27	32.5	108	19.1
Total	186	100.0	128	100.0	54	100.0	115	100.0	83	100.0	566	100.0

The surveyors were then asked to compare the street upon which the parcel being rated was situated with the general area. A word of definition is in order here. By the street was meant the block frontage on which the parcel was located. By the general area was meant the frontage across the street which it faced and the several blocks in the immediate area, with greatest weight being placed upon the facing frontage. (See Exhibit A–10 on the following page.)

Nonresidential Use

One of the most striking characteristics of the slums is the number of parcels which have commercial occupancy to some degree. This can be the small grocery store, the automobile repair shop, the plumbing and roofing contractors' headquarters, and so on. Two measures of commercial occupancy were defined. The first was a minor degree—occupancy which would generate in the surveyor's opinion less than 30 percent of the total parcel rent roll. The second was rated as a "significant category," i.e. over 30 percent of parcel rent. Obviously, these are rough judgments on the part of the surveyors. They were checked, however, in nine cases by this writer and only one substantial discrepancy was noted. Area 1 has by far the greatest degree of commercial occupancy. Nearly one-quarter of all parcels in the sample had commercial occupancy of some nature. Area 2A was next with a total of 15.6 percent. Interestingly enough, both B categories had less commercial occupancy than A categories. For the slum areas as a whole, the figure was 16.4 percent (Exhibit A–11).

These commercial facilities, convenient as they often are for local residents, provide a substantial cornerstone of blight. The older areas of the city are obviously over-stored. Many boarded-up stores in otherwise occupied parcels were found. A good proportion of the commercial occupancy was provided by bars.

Exhibit A–12, *Proximity of Nuisances,* is indicative of the problem. More than half of the parcels in Area 1 were on the same block front as a "nuisance"—defined as a bar, loitering area, a neighborhood hang-out (in one case), junk yards, factories, heavy traffic areas, and so on. Twenty-three out of the one hundred eighty-six parcels in that area had more than one problem of this kind. The proportion of bars in Area 1 is overwhelming. Nearly one out of every five parcels was reasonably close (i.e. within a half block) to a bar.

EXHIBIT A–10
QUALITY OF STREET BLOCK VS. AREA

	AREA 1		AREA 2A		AREA 2B		AREA 3A		AREA 3B		TOTAL	
	Number	Per-cent	Number	Per-cent	Number	Per-cent	Number	Per-cent	Number	Per-cent	Number	Per-cent
Same As	120	64.5	82	64.1	37	68.5	88	76.5	57	68.7	384	67.8
Better Than	38	20.4	25	19.5	10	18.5	12	10.4	12	14.5	97	17.3
Poorer Than	28	15.1	21	16.4	7	13.0	15	13.0	14	16.9	85	15.0
Total	186	100.0	128	100.0	54	100.0	115	100.0	83	100.0	566	100.0

EXHIBIT A–11
DEGREE OF COMMERCIAL OCCUPANCY

	AREA 1		AREA 2A		AREA 2B		AREA 3A		AREA 3B		TOTAL	
	Number	Per-cent	Number	Per-cent	Number	Per-cent	Number	Per-cent	Number	Per-cent	Number	Per-cent
Minor—Less than 30% of total parcel rent	38	20.4	17	13.3	3	5.6	16	13.9	10	12.0	84	14.8
Significant—Over 30% of total parcel rent	6	3.2	3	2.3	—	—	—	—	—	—	9	1.6
None	142	76.3	108	84.4	51	94.4	99	86.1	73	88.0	473	83.6
Total	186	100.0	128	100.0	54	100.0	115	100.0	83	100.0	566	100.0

EXHIBIT A-12

PROXIMITY OF NUISANCES
(NEWARK)

TYPE OF NUISANCE	AREA 1		AREA 2		AREA 3		TOTALS	
	Disa-bilities	Percent of Total Parcels	Disa-bilities	Percent of Total Parcels	Disa-bilities	Percent of Total Parcels	Disa-bilities	Percent of Total Parcels
Bars	40	21.6	23	12.7	44	22.4	107	19.0
Loitering	6	3.2	3	1.7	4	2.0	13	2.3
Junkyards	24	13.0	28	15.5	23	11.7	75	13.3
Factories	34	18.4	34	18.8	26	13.3	94	16.7
Heavy Traffic	25	13.5	71	39.2	100	51.0	196	34.9
Other	—		—		—		—	
None	83	44.9	73	40.3	65	33.2	221	39.3
Single nuisances	79		66		83		228	
Two or more nuisances	23		42		48		113	
Total parcels in sample	186		182		197		565	
Total live parcels in sample	185[1]		181[1]		196[2]		562[3]	
	185 = 100%		181 = 100%		196 = 100%		562 = 100%	

NOTE: The disabilities add up to a total which is higher than the total number of parcels because of multiple-disability parcels.

[1] One parcel not observed.
[2] Two parcels not observed.
[3] Four parcels not observed.

It is obvious that the city's liquor licensing in the hard core has been more than generous. While it may be far from realistic to assume that in the absence of the bars the housing conditions in the hard core would improve, certainly the environment would be enhanced as far as the residents are concerned.

The mixed land-use factor so characteristic of Newark is also evident here. Notice that the prevalence of factories is highest both in Area 1 and Area 3B. Area 3B is something of a phenomenon. It is an old industrial area that has become residential, largely populated by the immigrant stock derived from the turn of the century immigration. It is essentially a Polish and Italian area, euphemistically referred to as the Ironbound. Obviously, if one contrasts the housing conditions in Area 1 with those of Area 3B, the simple, mechanical approach of equating mixed land-use and blighted housing conditions is far from complete. Area 1, though quite heavy in this category, is far lighter than Area 3B. The latter, on the other hand, though its housing conditions are far from completely satisfactory, still is an infinitely better environment than that of Area 1.

Essentially this completed the field choice and survey of the parcels. From this point attention was turned to defining ownership and acquisition of the parcels.

Ownership

Defining the ownership of slum tenements is a far from easy task. In the case of Newark the researchers were fortunate in having the *Essex County Real Estate Directory* available. This is a service which compiles frequently updated ownership lists which include transaction data. Unfortunately, the prevalence of nominal transfers, i.e. transfers usually without consideration as between members of the same family or between holding corporations, must be researched in order to find last bonafide sales. With the help of title experts, Miss Dorothea Kaas and Howard Nacht, this difficulty was overcome. Exhibit A–13 on page 55 gives the proportion of nominal transfers between the last bonafide sale and the present. As can be noted there, over one-quarter of the last bonafide sales had had at least one nominal transfer between "true" sale being generated and the present.

Titles were researched back to 1939. In all cases that were not clear, actual title deeds were researched. Although initially data were obtained on nominal ownership by deed, this is far from indicative of the true owners of the parcels in question (Exhibit A–13 on page 55). It was found, for

EXHIBIT A-13
PROPORTION OF NOMINAL TRANSFERS
BETWEEN TIME EXISTING LANDLORD SECURED PARCEL AND PRESENT
BY AREA

	AREA 1		AREA 2A		AREA 2B		AREA 3A		AREA 3B		TOTAL	
	Number	Percent	Number	Percent	Number	Percent	Number	Percent	Number	Percent	Number	Percent
No Nominal Transfer	146	83.7	91	72.2	42	77.8	75	65.2	65	78.3	419	74.1
Nominal Transfer	40	16.3	37	27.8	12	22.3	40	34.8	18	21.7	147	25.9
Total	186	100.0	128	100.0	54	100.0	115	100.0	83	100.0	566	100.0

example, that many major holders held parcels individually, and conversely that the existence of a corporation did not necessarily mean a multiple holder. Similarly, the addresses of owners, as obtained from the title search and by the cooperation of the Newark tax authorities, was far from adequate. Many owners use addresses of convenience, which are far from indicative of their real residences. These addresses, however, did provide a first lead for the next stage of the research, contacting the individual landlords. (For an extended discussion of the problem of nonbonafide conveyances, see Grebler, *Housing Market Behavior in a Declining Area,* pp. 199–200.)

The Interviewing Pattern
The Nature of the Instrument

The interview pattern which was decided on was a personally administered, structured one. There were thirty-one substantive questions plus an additional number of personal classification questions. It is obvious that securing reliable responses in sensitive areas is most difficult. In order to meet this problem, the pattern of the interview rotates relatively innocuous questions with the basic important ones, i.e. those concerning capacity and will to improve, given certain concessions. On such questions as vacancy rates and goals of property ownership, projective techniques were used, i.e. what do most owners do, etc.? A substantial degree of redundancy was introduced in order to check out difficult areas.

The interview instrument went through a number of permutations in dry runs conducted by the author among owners in other New Jersey municipalities, such as Jersey City and Hoboken, before being stabilized in the form in which it is presented in Appendix V on page 257. It can be observed there that a number of the questions are essentially open-ended. This provided the interviewer with an opportunity of jotting down the wealth of information that was often offered that would not have been encompassed in a completely structured instrument. A basic coding sheet was developed in the course of the pretests. All coding and checking were done by the same two-man team directed by Howard Nacht and the author.

The Interviewers

Sixteen individual interviewers worked on this project. However, four of them contributed nearly two-thirds of the total responses. Spot-checking by phone was conducted among those interviewed to assure the continuity of the performance. The interviewers had a variety of backgrounds with a majority being law school students at the Rutgers Law School. Several were social workers or teachers in the Newark area, and a number were elderly, retired individuals. In areas where the resident landlords typically were Negro, every effort was made to assure that the interviewer was also Negro. Interviews with Puerto Rican owners were done in Spanish by Miss Hilda Hidalgo. All interviewers, prior to doing any interviewing, went through training sessions under Mrs. Mildred E. Barry, who also supervised the field work. In addition, an interviewer's manual was prepared and the interviewers were tested on its contents. (A copy of the manual is in Appendix VI.) All interviews were checked in detail by Mrs. Barry with the individual interviewer. A typical interview lasted roughly one and one-half hours.

Finding the Owners

As mentioned earlier, the addresses given in title records are far from adequate for the purpose of finding slum tenement owners. Though cover letters indicating the nature of the project and alerting the owners to a forthcoming telephone call from the individual interviewer were sent out, nearly 40 percent of them were returned due to the lack of an appropriate address. Cooperation of the Newark tax authorities was secured for follow-up letters, based upon tax-record addresses, but even these were not completely adequate.

It was found necessary to do door-to-door investigation in a number of cases on the ownership of parcels. A substantial part of the success in this regard was due to the efforts of Lawrence Besserer, the chief field interviewer. Field researchers were unable to contact the owner in forty cases. This represents less than 8 percent of the total sample. In eight of these cases not even the name of the owner was secured. These cases were largely abandoned and vacant parcels. Eighty-seven of the parcels had owners who refused outright to cooperate. The accompanying summary of interview problems and refusals indicates their breakdown by area (Exhibit A–14 on page 58). The failure to secure interviews in the other cases was for a wide miscellany of reasons: deaths in the family, illness, inability to speak English, and so on. Twelve of the parcels were in the hands of owners who lived too far from the interview area to be contacted within the budget

EXHIBIT A-14
SUMMARY OF INTERVIEW PROBLEMS AND REFUSALS

Area	Unco-operative	Out of Town	Unable to Contact Owner	Incom-plete	Misc.	Total Missing Interviews	Total Number of Taxable Parcels in Sample (555)	Percent Missing Interviews to Total Taxable Parcels
1	35	5	9	6	2	57	183	31.1
2A	18	2	7	4	1	32	123	26.0
2B	7	1	4	2	2	16	53	30.2
3A	11	2	13	4	2	32	113	28.3
3B	16	2	7	1	2	28	83	33.7
Total All Areas	87	12	40	17	9	165	555	29.7
Percent of Grand Total of 566 Parcels	15.4	2.1	7.1	3.0	1.6	29.2	98.1	—

of the research project. Eleven of the five hundred sixty-six parcels were in tax-exempt hands, and in those cases no effort was made to secure interviews. In sum, therefore, three hundred ninety-two interviews were secured and one hundred sixty-five were not secured, with three of the latter partially secured.

Respondents vs. Nonrespondents

Is there any skew in the nonrespondents distribution which would make generalizations dangerous? Can these generalizations be made on the basis of the 70 percent of the sample who permitted themselves to be interviewed as to the conduct and attitudes of the nonrespondents? This is a difficult question to answer.

Based upon interviewers reporting on their failures, the nonrespondents are perhaps weighted in the direction of elderly owners, typically of immigrant stock. There is no one single group that can be isolated from the nonrespondents. Two of them, for example, were Black Muslims who refused to cooperate with Negro interviewers who were "lackies of the whites." One of the nonrespondents who owned eight parcels in the sample group is one of the major owners of slum tenements in Newark. The interviewer finally gained admission into his real estate office by camping outside of it for an entire day. The owner, however, still refused to cooperate substantially with the questionnaire.

The bulk of the nonrespondents, however, were not multiple owners of parcels within our sample area. In asking major real estate dealers who were the significant owners of parcels, none of the persons mentioned, with the exception of the one noted above, were in the nonrespondent group.

One area of skew, however, was the owners of vacant parcels. As noted earlier, considerable difficulty was experienced in finding these owners. Frequently, when found, the interviewers were unable to secure adequate interviews. On the whole, however, it is the author's opinion that reasonable generalizations for the whole sample can be made on the basis of the 70 percent successful interviews secured. Exhibit A–15 on page 60 compares the maintenance of parcels with landlord interviews vs. those without.

As stated earlier, essentially complete interviews were secured with the owners of three hundred ninety-two parcels. This does not mean, however, that there were three hundred ninety-two individual interviews. In a number of cases there were owners who had more than one parcel in the sample.

EXHIBIT A–15

PARCELS WITH AND WITHOUT INTERVIEWS, BY CONDITION OF PARCEL

Parcels	Reasonably Kept		Poorly Kept		Well Kept		Totals	
	Num-ber	Per-cent	Num-ber	Per-cent	Num-ber	Per-cent	Num-ber	Per-cent
With interview	240	61.2	69	17.6	83	21.2	392	100.0
Without interview	114	64.4	37	20.9	26	14.7	177	100.0
Total sample	354		106		109		569*	

* Includes three tax-exempt parcels.

Figures in Exhibit A–16 indicate the extent of this. There was one owner who owned eleven parcels within the sample number. In the interview the owner indicated that his total holdings were in excess of two hundred parcels within Newark. The other multiples included one owner of five parcels, one who owned four, five who owned three, and thirty-five who owned two parcels each. The total number of multiple sample parcel holders were forty-three and these made up one hundred five of the total parcels in the

EXHIBIT A–16

NEWARK—MULTIPLE OWNERSHIP

NUMBER OF PARCELS	× NUMBER OF OWNERS	= PRODUCT
11	1	11
5	1	5
4	1	4
3	5	15
2	35	70
	43	105

Total interviews	392
− Multiples	105
= Individual sample parcel owners	287
+ Multiple owners	43
= Total property owners interviewed	330

sample. Thus, there were three hundred thirty property owners who were interviewed in the course of this study.

Multiple-parcel owners were asked about their parcels individually. The answers that are tabulated in this work are weighted in proportion to the three hundred ninety-two parcels owned.

Chapter 3

THE TENANTRY

Before turning to the operations of buying and selling of slum tenements, it is essential to have some feeling for the characteristics of the tenants. This chapter centers initially on the socio-economic characteristics of the tenantry: race, education, income levels, and capacity, as well as will to pay higher rents for more housing amenities. The focus then turns to rent discrimination in housing and to the tenants' effect on parcels.

Racial Mix

Exhibit 3–1 on page 63 presents an analysis of the response given by landlords in the several subsets of the research area to the question: "Do you have Negro or white tenants at (address)?" The answers indicate the dominance of nonwhite groups. There is a substantial variation, however, within the several areas. In Area 3B, for example, 47.1 percent of the parcels are occupied solely by whites. In Area 3A, which is of equivalent housing characteristics, only 12.7 percent are solely white-occupied. In Area 1 the figure is 7.9 percent.

Notice that there are comparatively few "mixed" buildings. Holders of slum tenements repeatedly made the point that they found it difficult to maintain balanced buildings. "If you are going to turn a building, you might as well go all the way; you're not going to keep the whites there for very long in any case," said one major professional holder.

The proportion of parcels occupied by nonwhites is directly proportional to the scale of the landlords holdings as shown in Exhibit 3–2. This is largely

EXHIBIT 3-1

Do You Have Negro or White Tenants at [ADDRESS OF PARCEL]?

	AREA 1		AREA 2A		AREA 2B		AREA 3A		AREA 3B		TOTAL	
	Num-ber	Per-cent	Num-ber	Per-cent	Num-ber	Per-cent	Num-ber	Per-cent	Num-ber	Per-cent	Num-ber	Per-cent
Negro	106	83.4	71	79.8	23	62.2	61	77.2	14	27.4	275	71.8
White	10	7.9	11	12.4	10	27.0	10	12.7	24	47.1	65	17.0
White-Negro	9	7.1	5	5.6	4	10.8	4	5.1	5	9.8	27	7.0
Puerto Rican	—	—	—	—	—	—	—	—	1	2.0	1	0.3
Negro-Puerto Rican	1	0.8	1	1.1	—	—	2	2.4	2	3.9	6	1.6
Puerto Rican-White	—	—	1	1.1	—	—	1	1.3	2	3.9	4	1.0
All three	—	—	—	—	—	—	1	1.3	2	3.9	3	0.8
Vacant parcel	1	0.8	—	—	—	—	—	—	1	2.0	2	0.5
Total	127	100.0	89	100.0	37	100.0	79	100.0	51	100.0	383	100.0
NA/DK	1	—	2	—	—	—	6	—	—	—	9	—

EXHIBIT 3-2

Do You Have Negro or White Tenants at [Address of Parcel]?

| | NA/DK | | Other | | Size of Holdings | | | | | | | | | | Total | |
					Over 12		7–12		4–6		2–3		1			
	Number	Per cent	Number	Per cent	Number	Per cent	Number	Per cent	Number	Per cent	Number	Per cent	Number	Per cent	Number	Per cent
Negro	3	75.0	—	—	54	88.6	28	90.3	33	80.5	59	71.1	98	60.1	275	71.8
White	1	25.0	—	—	1	1.6	2	6.5	2	4.9	16	19.3	43	26.4	65	17.0
White-Negro	—	—	—	—	2	3.3	1	3.2	6	14.6	3	3.6	15	9.2	27	7.0
Puerto Rican	—	—	—	—	—	—	—	—	—	—	—	—	1	0.6	1	0.3
Negro-Puerto Rican	—	—	—	—	1	1.6	—	—	—	—	1	1.2	—	—	2	0.5
Puerto Rican-White	—	—	—	—	1	1.6	—	—	—	—	1	1.2	4	2.5	6	1.6
All three	—	—	—	—	2	3.3	—	—	—	—	1	1.2	1	0.6	4	1.0
Vacant parcel	—	—	—	—	—	—	—	—	—	—	2	2.4	1	0.6	3	0.8
NA/DK	—	—	—	—	—	—	—	—	2	—	1	—	6	—	9	—
Sub-N	4		—		61		31		43		84		169		392	
Live sample	4		0		61		31		41		83		163		383	

a function of large-owner dominance in Area 1, as well as white small-owner prejudice.

The sample probably understates the proportion of Puerto Ricans living in slum areas of Newark. It is, however, roughly characteristic of the racial mix of tenantry and agrees reasonably well with the data presented in Exhibit 2–8 on page 32, *Proportion of Housing Units Occupied by Nonwhites by Group and Subgroups as a Percentage of the Total Occupied Units*. A substantial proportion of the white tenantry represents the newer immigrant strains that have passed through Newark from southern and eastern Europe. Italians dominate, closely followed by people of Polish and Russian extraction. These national origins have considerable significance in determining the degree of mobility of whites out of certain marginal housing areas.

Education

There are pitifully few statistical aids with which to categorize the slum tenement dweller as against the bulk of the city's population. For example, in terms of median school years completed by persons twenty-five years of age or more, shown in Exhibit 3–3 on page 66, it can be seen that the study area's inhabitants, in terms of schooling, lag behind the balance of the city, though substantial gains have been made over the past twenty years.*

Income Levels

Income levels are undoubtedly an even better criterion of the characteristics and potential of the tenantry. In Exhibit 3–4 there is a comparison of the income levels by tract grouping in 1950 and 1960 for "families and unrelated individuals," as well as data for "families only" in 1960. Again the picture is one of improvement over time within the several groups. Equally obvious, however, is the fact that in terms of the city total for all tracts, the slum areas have far to go. Notice that income levels vary roughly in proportion to housing characteristics, with an internal shift based on Negro or

---

* In this and other exhibits based upon census data, the information given is for the entire area, including resident owners as well as tenantry outside our housing category. The tenement dweller undoubtedly ranks somewhat lower than shown by the overall data; however, the data does give a reasonable indication of the basic discrepancies among the residents of the several tract groups.

EXHIBIT 3–3

MEDIAN SCHOOL YEARS COMPLETED OF PERSONS ≥25 YEARS OF AGE

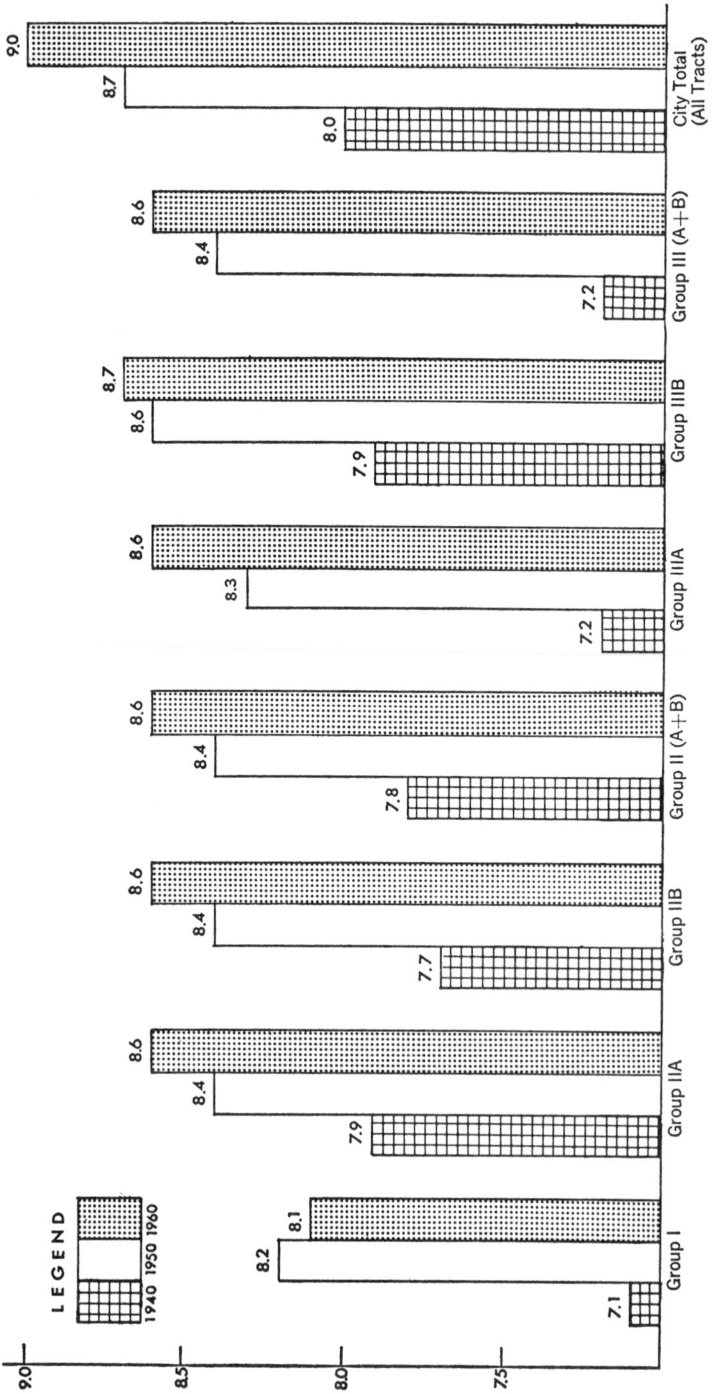
LEGEND
1940
1950
1960
9.0
8.5
8.0
7.5
7.1
8.2
8.1
Group I
7.9
8.4
8.6
Group IIA
7.7
8.4
8.6
Group IIB
7.8
8.4
8.6
Group II (A+B)
7.2
8.3
8.6
Group IIIA
7.9
8.6
8.7
Group IIIB
7.2
8.4
8.6
Group III (A+B)
8.0
8.7
9.0
City Total
(All Tracts)

Source: *U. S. Census:* 1940, 1950, 1960.

EXHIBIT 3-4

INCOME LEVELS

AVERAGE OF THE MEDIANS OF EACH GROUP OF TRACTS—FAMILIES AND
UNRELATED INDIVIDUALS (1950 & 1960) AND FAMILIES ONLY (1960)

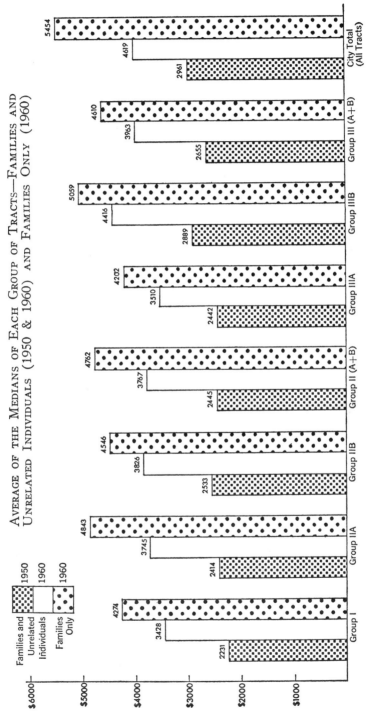

Source: *U. S. Census*: 1940, 1950, 1960.

white dominance in the areas. Later in this chapter the question of capacity to pay will be discussed. For the moment, however, it should be mentioned that the income levels of slum dwellers are substantially below the city-wide average.

In Exhibit 3–5 unemployment rates are presented by tract group. The absolute level of unemployment, though it certainly has improved since 1940, is obviously very high. For Group 1, for example, at 12.8 percent it is more than one and a half times the city total. The difference between A and B groups in unemployment is most clear-cut, with the Negro areas hardest hit. To the degree that these figures give a rough indication of the tenantry, what do they mean? Obviously, *they indicate a potential rent payer of relatively low income, of limited education, primarily nonwhite, with relatively high unemployment and concomitantly, irregular income levels.*

Will to Pay Higher Rent

The question of whether the rehabilitation of slum tenements can be accomplished without boosting rent levels, and its complement, the question of whether slum tenement dwellers can pay higher rents, has attracted considerable literature. According to Nash,[1] the basic hard core of low income families can only be aided by more rapidly rising incomes or some form of public assistance. Fisher,[2] on the other hand, in his analysis of 1950 census data, pointed to the fact that "nearly three out of every ten primary families and individuals renting substandard housing inside standard metropolitan areas could have paid the median gross monthly rent of $50.50 for standard housing without committing more than one-fifth of their 1940 incomes for rent." Without raising the question of priority of expenditures other than housing, even in Fisher's analysis, seven out of ten of these primary families and individuals could not have paid that one-fifth figure.

The question of whether, even given the means, the typical slum tenement dweller is willing to pay for upgrading, is beyond the scope of this study. There is considerable question on this point however, as Grebler, Blank, and Winnick state:

> There is impressive evidence that housing has moved downward in the consumer's scale of preferences. Newer consumer goods and services have been more successful in the competition for a place in the family budgets.[3]

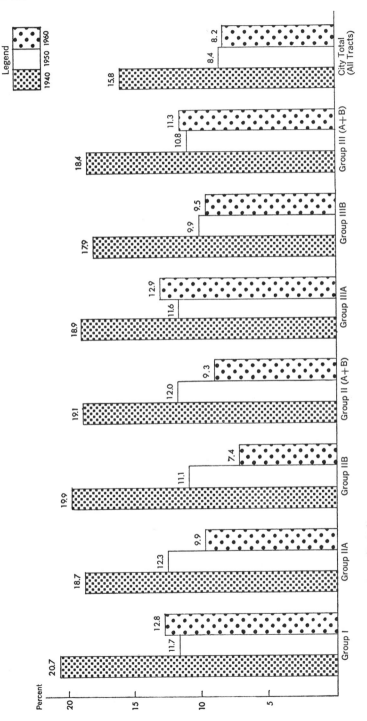

EXHIBIT 3-5

UNEMPLOYMENT RATES BY CENSUS TRACT GROUPS

Source: *U. S. Census*: 1940, 1950, 1960.

Certainly in the responses of the landlords there is an obvious feeling that the capacity and/or willingness of tenants to pay higher rents is marginal at best. For example, among owners, when asked about the installation of central heat in reward for a tax or mortgage deal, the response typically was that they simply could not get their investment back. Certainly in terms of the usual rate of return required by owners of tenements, this is perhaps the case. There is an obvious discontinuity between the tenant who rents for $40 a month and the tenant who pays $70 a month. If the owner feels it incumbent upon himself to repay his central heat expenditure within two years, this is the rent gap that must be bridged.* The question of whether there is enough "fat" in present returns on slum tenements to make enforced rehabilitation practicable without rent boosts will be raised in a later chapter. It should be noted here, however, that there is considerable question of the tenants' capacity or desire to pay higher rents in exchange for middle-class amenities.

Rent Discrimination in Housing

Complicating the question of the capacity to pay is the question of whether Negroes and other declassed groups have to pay more for equivalent housing than do whites. Certainly this attitude is felt strongly by Negroes themselves. Seventy-three percent of the Negroes interviewed in a broad scale survey of Newark attitudes felt that members of their race had to pay more for the same kind of apartments than do whites. Only 20 percent said that rent and race are unrelated matters. Most of the Negroes who believe they pay premium rents talk in very general terms about the reasons for this situation. However, in one way or another, it is clear that they are talking about discrimination by whites, and that they place the blame directly on the white property owners. It is interesting to note that 3 percent of the Negroes said spontaneously, without any special questioning on the matter, that Negro landlords themselves do this to other Negroes.[4]

---

* For an example of a well-meaning effort to move into extremely dilapidated tenements and bring them up to standard under private, low-return aegis, see the semicomical tale of Laurence Rockefeller's efforts on the Lower East Side, which ended with Mr. Rockefeller being sued by a number of the tenants discontented by rent boosts. See *The New York Times*, April 12, 1963, p. 29.

In Exhibit 3–6 is presented an attempt to derive the gross monthly rent for the study tract groups for whites and nonwhites, as well as all units. *For every one of the tract categories the nonwhites pay significantly more than do whites.*

There are obviously a number of limitations to this type of analysis. Foremost is the quality of the housing. Are Negroes, perhaps, renting either better units or larger units (which is not unlikely in terms of larger family unit size) in the same tracts? The situation is further distorted by the fact that a number of the most significant national origin groups among the whites frequently have members of their families living as tenants together in one multiple dwelling. (This is most common among people of Italian and Polish background, the most prevalent national origin stocks of Newark's white slumdwellers.)

In part, also, the discrepancy is a function of the fact that the poor pay more. For example, in the field sample there are two adjoining identical properties. One of them is unfurnished. It has four-room apartments in excellent condition renting for $90 a month. Its identical neighbor has furnished apartments; these latter rent with a few sticks of furniture for $35 a week. To the degree that the very poor are largely Negro, and are more attracted by the advantages of weekly rent payments and furnished apartments, they will obviously pay more for otherwise equivalent accommodations.

More basic, however, is the dual nature of the market. In a number of cases there were white resident landlords in areas that were largely Negro. In at least a few of these cases the tenantry in the building was also white. The owners seemed to indicate that they maintain their rents at a very low level for their present tenants for fear of losing the remaining white tenantry and having to take in Negroes.

Perhaps statements of a sixtyish, widowed postal worker of Italian descent typifies this reason for the difference between Negro and white rental payments. The parcel in question is one in which the owner had lived prior to the last several years. The parcel contains four apartments and, according to our interviewer, it is very well maintained. The tenantry is white, although the area as a whole is largely Negro.

> The tenants we have now won't pay higher rents because the neighborhood doesn't warrant it. If I raised rents from $75 to $100, tenants would move to Vailsburg (a largely white middle-class neighborhood on the fringe of Newark) where $100 is worth it for the neighbor-

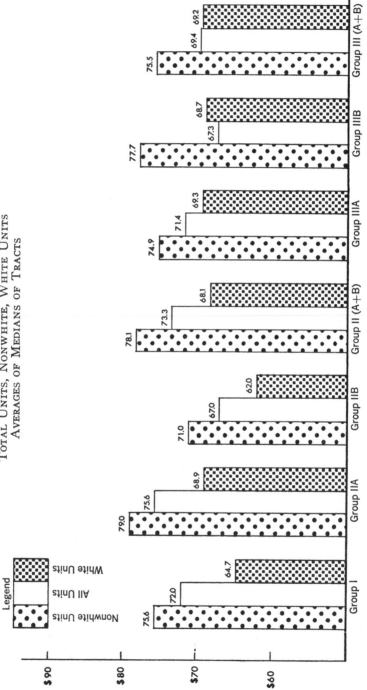

EXHIBIT 3-6
GROSS MONTHLY RENT
TOTAL UNITS, NONWHITE, WHITE UNITS
AVERAGES OF MEDIANS OF TRACTS

Source: *U. S. Census*: 1960.

hood. Negroes would pay $100 a month, but within a year the build-
ing wouldn't be worth a nickel because it is hard to screen Negro
tenants to get decent ones who would take care of the house.

Regardless of whether or not this attitude is justified, obviously it accounts
for a substantial rental differential.

The implication of these comments is that there are two housing markets. If the landlord wants to maintain white tenants in otherwise undesirable areas, the relatively hard-to-get prospective tenant must be given a
bonus in terms of relatively low rent payments. On the other hand, the
Negro population is growing, at least in many of the tracts. They are at
least willing to meet the market and frequently to do more than that. *The
owner of a "white" builing has to forgo a proportion of his rent in order to
maintain its racial characteristics while usually he demands a bonus for
switching tenancy.*

The Future of Racial Rent Differentials

Will this dichotomy in rents continue as the nonwhite population of Newark
finds greater housing choice? A former schoolteacher, now an owner of six
tenements in Jersey City, made the following comments:

> Negroes formerly paid more than whites for equivalent accommoda-
> tions. This is leveling off. The earlier condition existed because there
> were vacancies and higher vacancy rates in 'white' buildings, and
> therefore, landlords lowered the rents there, whereas 'Negro' buildings
> had relatively high occupancy. When the owners of white buildings
> capitulated and put Negroes in, they automatically converted to a Ne-
> gro building *per se.* This has gone on at such a rate as to make the
> vacancy rate in white and Negro buildings pretty much equivalent
> where I am. Therefore, the price pressure in order to secure white
> tenants is no longer higher than the equivalent for Negro buildings.

This individual owns both "Negro" and "white" buildings.

The Tenants and Maintenance

The landlords complain, and sometimes with cause, that Negro tenants
typically have more children and are more casual in the care and maintenance of housing facilities. It is very rare that landlords can successfully
prosecute tenants for damages. A typical comment was:

Tenants who willfully, or otherwise, damage the real estate are generally judgment-proof and are seldom, if ever, prosecuted by public agencies for violations of the Multiple Dwelling Law.

(It is significant in this connection that in New York the Rent Commission has granted rent reductions for failure of a landlord to repair a refrigerator that is deliberately damaged by the tenant—150 Holding Corporation vs. Temporary State Housing Rent Commission, N.Y.L.J., December 14, 1955, p. 7.)[5]

The problem is complicated by the existence of "the multi-problem tenant family." Based on an experience in Philadelphia in rehabilitation, the following comment was made:

> They [destructive tenants] afford reluctant property owners a talking point for doing nothing and they virtually assure that, even if every house is brought up to the highest possible standard, dilapidation will recur.[6]

The unfamiliarity of newcomers to the city with the urban way of life is not at all uncommon. And certainly, landlord complaints about garbage in the hallways, children running wild, and so on, are not without merit. (For example, see *The New York Times*, July 20, 1962, p. 2, on a program of the Neighborhood Conservation Program in that city.)

It is difficult to distinguish whether these are problems of the antipathy between landlord and tenant, or are essentially the concomitants of poverty and ignorance. The largest, single tenement owner in Newark, for example, prefers Negro tenants. He said, "If I rent to whites in the area that I own in, I get the worst drug addicts, pimps, and general no-goods. I get a much better Negro tenant." Interestingly enough, two youthful Puerto Ricans who are the new owners of a tenement made this comment about their white tenants: "They lived here when we bought the place; we wish they'd move because they are not clean." (Case 432—this latter interview was translated from Spanish.)

Certainly the questions of family size and relative youth of children should not be overlooked. The Negro household in the older slum areas typically has far more young children than does its white equivalent. As will be examined later in more detail, the whites typically are much older than Negro residents in these areas. The physical structure of tenements, aged, usually frame buildings without neighborhood play areas, are not the most resistant of housing. Some of the slum tenements are well maintained at the cost of not admitting large families. From the viewpoint of society, if not of the landlord, this may be too high a price to pay.

In addition, there is the factor of great turnover of tenantry. To the normal mobility of the American family are added all the causes which make the poor change addresses with great rapidity. Rent skips are far from uncommon. (Most landlords figure a minimum of 2 percent or 3 percent loss on this basis.) Typically, cold-water flats may be vacated during winter months by doubling up in heated facilities. All of these elements complicate the problem of maintenance and rehabilitation.

Without diminishing the importance of the factors cited, *there is no question that the basic alienation of absentee landlord* (frequently white) *and nonwhite tenant plays a major role. Physical rehabilitation which does not take this into account can only be transitory in its effect.*

In sum, the vast majority of slum tenement tenantry of Newark is Negro; the whites are largely first or second generation, eastern and southern European in origin. Income levels are relatively low, particularly for the Negro group. Substantial unemployment is commonplace, with rates running 50 percent higher than the city average. Rents, though on an absolute level perhaps not as high as in other older cities, are still substantially discriminatory, with nonwhites bearing the brunt of the burden. Frequency of moves, poverty, inability to pay rent consistently, and perhaps a basic retaliatory attitude toward landlords, all add to the difficulty of securing an adequate housing environment.

REFERENCES

1 See for example, Nash, *Residential* . . . , Chapter 4 and Grigsby, *Housing Markets* . . . , p. 275.
2 Fisher, *Twenty Years* . . . , p. 48.
3 Leo Grebler, *et al., Capital Formation in Residential Real Estate* (Princeton: Princeton University Press, 1956) p. 131 and also Lewis G. Watts *et al., The Middle Income Negro Family Faces Urban Renewal* (Waltham, Mass.: Brandeis University, 1965). A recent survey of research on expenditure patterns as a function of race is in Raymond Bauer *et al.,* "The Marketing Dilemma of Negroes," *Journal of Marketing,* (July, 1965).
4 See *MPC II,* and for more details see *MPC I,* pp. 34, 36, and appended tables.
5 See the Association of the Bar of the City of New York, Special Committee on Housing and Urban Development, *Memorandum 305/63/9,* p. 3.
6 Philadelphia, *Partnership for Renewal,* pp. 76–8.

Chapter 4

SLUM OPERATIONS
AND PROFITABILITY

How profitable is the operation of slum tenements? What kinds of rates of return can be expected in this type of property? What are the risk factors, such as vacancies and housing code enforcement, which shape the landlord's attitude? Are rents collected personally, or by intermediaries?

Operating Ratios of Slum Properties

There is considerable difficulty in securing reasonably reliable expense data for slum tenements. Previous efforts have been made using income tax returns as a source of information on repairs, maintenance, and profitability. These returns, when analyzed over a period of years, frequently indicate arithmetic errors and substantial misstatements.[1] Data gathered by the New York State Temporary State Housing Commission in the course of the Upper West Side Renewal Project would seem to indicate total operating expenses before depreciation and debt service of somewhere between 50 percent and 60 percent. (See Exhibit 4–1.)

In a somewhat similar study of the West Side urban renewal area of New York City by Chester Rapkin, the estimate of the ratio of net operation income to gross is cited as "somewhere in the vicinity of 40 percent to 50 percent on the average—a proportion that compares favorably with return on other rental property in New York City."[2] As Exhibit 4–2 indicates, real estate taxes are the number one expense of good-condition and poor-condition buildings. Net operating income is actually lower for poor-

EXHIBIT 4-1

EXPENSE ITEMS AS A PERCENT OF GROSS INCOME*
(MEDIANS)

| | Apartment Buildings Owned by | | Single-Room-Occupancy Buildings |
	Institutions	Others	
Real estate taxes	17.5	18.0	16.3
Utilities	3.2	3.3	3.9
Fuel	7.8	6.3	5.3
Insurance	3.1	2.4	2.1
Repairs and painting	11.2	7.6	7.4
Wages	11.2	8.4	11.6
Other	6.8	6.0	5.5
Total operating expense	60.9	52.1	52.0

* Data for estimates are based on 126 usable accounts from records of the City Tax Department between 1954 and 1956.
Source: N. Y. S. Temporary State Housing Rent Commission, *Prospects for Rehabilitation*, p. 89.

EXHIBIT 4-2

CONSOLIDATED OPERATING STATEMENT FOR OLD-LAW TENEMENTS (WALK-UPS)

BY QUALITY OF STRUCTURE AND MAINTENANCE AND INCOME

	Good-Condition and Well-Maintained Percent of Gross	Poor-Condition and Poorly-Maintained Percent of Gross
Real estate taxes	20.8	15.0
Utilities	3.5	5.1
Fuel	11.0	11.4
Insurance	4.0	7.3
Repairs and painting	10.6	12.6
Wages	5.3	6.4
Other	6.6	6.0
Total oper. expense	61.8	63.8
Net oper. income	38.2	36.2
Gross income	100.0	100.0

Source: Rapkin, *The Real Estate Market in an Urban Renewal Area*, p. 72.

condition and poorly-maintained parcels than for those which are in good condition and are well maintained. (The validity of data presented in this table is dependent upon the honesty of the landlords in compiling it, and the adjustments made by the researcher.)

For the purposes of this study, the researchers were fortunate enough to have available to them the complete records of a major tenement management company. Using the service of a firm of certified public accountants, the one hundred fifty parcels for which data of varying completeness was available were reduced to thirty-two parcels, all within the study areas and possessing complete documentation. Expense analyses were then developed for these parcels as shown in Exhibit 4–3. The results agree closely with the

EXHIBIT 4-3

OPERATING RATIOS OF 32 SLUM PROPERTIES

Category	Percent Expense to Income	
	Median	Interquartile Range
Management	13.33	9.82–16.13
Utilities	5.73	3.79–11.30
Services and fees	2.81	1.72– 4.77
Repairs and maintenance	18.15	12.62–28.27
Taxes	21.02	16.31–33.12
Sum of the medians	61.04	

Expense Breakdown

Management
1. Superintendent
2. Insurance
3. Management (7% usually)
4. Plans for bath

Utilities
5. Electricity
6. Water
7. Fuel

Service and Fees
8. Advertising
9. Accounting
10. Legal
11. Constable
12. ⎰Patent security
    ⎰Accident
    ⎱Miscellaneous
13. Services
14. Rental fee
15. Returned security
16. Returned deposit
17. Fire permit
18. Inspection fees

Repairs and Maintenance
19. Exterminator
20. Central maintenance
21. Hardware supplies
22. Painting
23. Plumbing—allowance boiler
24. Cleaning
25. Other repairs
26. Glass
27. Electric fixtures
28. Hall lights
29. Stove—gas heater
30. Garbage cans
31. Ceiling plastering

experience reported in New York. The sum of the medians of expenditure, for example, is 61 percent of gross income. Taxes are 21 percent of gross, closely followed by repairs and maintenance at 18.15 percent. The management figure shown here includes 7 percent for management fees.

There is a considerable range of variation in total expense percentages. As will be noted later in more detail, this range of variation is indicative of the risk factors which surround the operating of slum properties. In turn, they obviously limit the number of people interested in going into high risk areas and, as a complement of this, increase the rate of return required.[3]

Trends

Have these expense ratios increased over the last several years? There seems to be substantial evidence that this has been the case.

Leo Grebler, in his study, *Real Estate Investment Experience*, (Columbia University Press, 1955) has developed data for walk-up apartments from the 1920–24 period through 1945–49. These data would indicate that net income as a percentage of gross income has dropped by one-half from 59 percent to 28 percent. The *Journal of Property Management* in a 1964 study of walk-ups of twelve to twenty-five units which were built before 1920, indicated that the average ratio of expenses to gross rent collections was around 60 percent, and that this percentage has increased sharply because of static gross income in the face of increasing costs.[4]

Return on Investment

The profitability of investment in slum properties is as much a function of financial leverage as the percentage of return on gross income. In the next chapter tenement trading and financing are discussed in more detail, but it is worthwhile noticing here, for example, that if a tenement was purchased for four times its gross rent roll, a fairly generous multiplier, the yield before depreciation and financing charges based on the data presented would be 10 percent, i.e. 40 percent of 25 percent. If, instead of paying cash, the investor were able to secure a mortgage for 50 percent of the purchase price at a 6 percent interest figure, the yield would go up to 14 percent on his cash investment. Rapkin[5] estimates that old-law tenements return 9.3 percent on the total consideration in the West Side Urban Renewal Project. Brownstones return an estimated 10.7 percent and all types of elevator apartments combined return 9.3 percent.

Sporn,[6] conducting a study of one hundred twenty-three parcels in Milwaukee, showed an average rate of return on *equity* of 19.8 percent. (This does not take into account the owners' activity and/or wages in regard to personal labor and collections, etc.)

The actual return on investment figures obviously varies enormously, depending in substantial measure on the financing available. An example is the history of Parcel 553 in our study area, a six-family, three-story apartment in Area 3B. This was sold in October, 1962 for $16,500, with a savings and loan association taking back a $13,500 mortgage. In August, 1964 the mortgage was refinanced with another savings and loan association with the understanding that central heating equipment would be installed. This new mortgage was for $20,000. The owner made the improvements but the cost of central heat was less than the increment in the new financing and, therefore, his initial cash investment of $3,000 was essentially returned to him. The apartments are six-room flats, and rents now are between $90 and $100 per month for a gross rent roll of $6,000 per year, with interest charges of $1,200 and taxes of $1,100. Assuming all other costs including heat probably run no more than $1,000, the return is about $2,700 per year before depreciation and amortization on essentially no cash investment. (In justice to the owner, it should be pointed out that this is a very well-maintained and well-run parcel. The low expense figures which have been imputed are a function of the modernization and basic care with which the parcel has been handled.)

Cash-Flow Accounting

In appraising return on real estate investments, the basic consideration used by nearly all the landlords in this study were those of *cash flow*. Amortization, therefore, is considered an expense while depreciation charges are not. Given the relatively short-term nature of financing available for tenement purchase and improvements, the effects of this type of accounting on the rates of return demanded is all too clear.

Typical Returns on Value

To determine the return on the total value of tenement parcels required some method of assessing the value. In Exhibit 4–4, based on the thirty-two parcels examined in Exhibit 4–3, two approaches to this problem are pre-

EXHIBIT 4-4
RETURN ON TOTAL PRICE OF THIRTY-TWO SLUM TENEMENTS

Parcel No.	VALUE FIGURE		CONTRIBUTION TO FINANCING AS A PERCENT OF VALUE	
			Contrib. Fin.	Contrib. Fin.
	Tax Figure × 100/6.6	4 × Gross Income	Tax Figure × 100/6.6	4 × Gross Income
A1	$18,500.00	$20,872.00	11.4%	10.1%
2	20,606.00	12,952.00	3.0	4.8
3	20,394.00	15,172.00	10.6	14.3
4	2,606.00	11,220.00	54.5	12.7
5	19,606.00	24,156.00	8.6	7.0
6	16,394.00	16,176.00	8.7	8.8
7	11,697.00	18,324.00	47.2	30.1
8	14,697.00	15,628.00	8.0	7.5
9	14,803.00	19,460.00	—	—
10	10,697.00	17,680.00	—	—
11	13,803.00	24,552.00	12.1	6.8
12	14,000.00	19,760.00	7.7	5.4
13	33,606.00	62,324.00	10.8	5.8
14	28,000.00	16,612.00	5.4	9.1
15	28,000.00	9,188.00	—	—
16	17,394.00	12,632.00	10.2	14.1
17	10,394.00	18,780.00	17.6	9.7
18	10,803.00	19,212.00	4.0	2.3
19	5,500.00	8,900.00	4.6	2.8
20	14,803.00	23,544.00	6.6	4.1
21	17,303.00	18,572.00	10.3	9.6
22	17,394.00	19,760.00	4.7	4.1
23	6,500.00	9,556.00	22.8	15.5
24	18,000.00	12,820.00	5.5	7.7
25	12,106.00	16,204.00	14.0	10.4
26	14,394.00	17,960.00	12.5	10.0
27	18,894.00	15,060.00	—	—
28	14,500.00	20,120.00	8.1	5.8
29	14,303.00	17,948.00	7.0	5.6
30	20,394.00	24,668.00	6.1	5.1
31	15,000.00	18,840.00	6.1	4.8
32	13,606.00	24,732.00	9.0	4.9
Average	15,897.00	18,856.00	12.04	8.53
Interquartile Range			6.10–11.75	5.00–10.05
Median			8.65	7.25

sented. The first uses the assessment value which is nominally 100 percent; the second uses a multiplier of four times gross income, which in terms of the current market is undoubtedly high. On the former base the thirty-two parcels, which were examined earlier, yield an average return of 12.04 percent and a median of 8.65 percent; on the latter basis the equivalent figures are 8.53 percent and 7.25 percent. Again it should be noted that there is a wide range within the interquartile figure.

Service Elements

In part, the range of variation shown in Exhibit 4–4 is a function of the vagaries of the market; but it is also caused by the variation in service elements offered by the landlord. More than 10 percent of the three hundred ninety-two parcels in the field sample were other than purely unfurnished. (See Exhibit 4–5.) As was noted in the last chapter, furnished apartments typically rent for a premium far above the value of the furnishings. Another variation is in the rent collection procedure. As shown in Exhibit 4–6, a substantial proportion of the interviewed landlords indicated that rent is collected other than monthly in the parcels within the sample areas. While only 6 percent of the parcels have clearly defined weekly collections, over 15 percent collect either partly by the month, partly by the week, or just nominally monthly.

That last description requires some elucidation. The answer given by landlords is that though rents are not normally charged on a weekly basis, it behooves the landlord to collect weekly if he is to avoid major rent losses While the value of these "services" may be questioned, they tend to increase the gross of a particular parcel. Most of the expenses of these procedures are essentially those which can only be imputed, such as rent collection. As Exhibit 4–7 indicates, the vast bulk of rents are collected by the owners.

Variation in Service by Landlord Size

Exhibits 4–7, 4–8, and 4–9 show that there is relatively little difference, either by area or by size of holdings, in type of service offered. The provision of furnished apartments is perhaps the outstanding exception. Of those parcels in the hands of two or three parcel owners, 12.2 percent are providing furnished accommodations in the parcels within the sample area as com-

EXHIBIT 4-5

Is [Address of Parcel] Furnished or Unfurnished?

	AREA 1		AREA 2A		AREA 2B		AREA 3A		AREA 3B		TOTAL	
	Number	Per-cent	Number	Per-cent	Number	Per-cent	Number	Per-cent	Number	Per-cent	Number	Per-cent
Furnished apt.	3	2.3	9	10.2	2	5.4	5	6.3	3	5.9	22	5.7
Unfurnished apt.	122	95.4	71	80.7	32	86.5	66	82.4	46	90.2	337	87.8
Mixed	3	2.3	5	5.7	3	8.1	4	5.0	2	3.9	17	4.4
Rooming house	—	—	1	1.1	—	—	4	5.0	—	—	5	1.3
Other	—	—	2	2.3	—	—	1	1.3	—	—	3	0.8
Total	128	100.0	88	100.0	37	100.0	80	100.0	51	100.0	384	100.0
NA/DK	—		3		—		5		—		8	

EXHIBIT 4-6

Do You Collect Your Rents Weekly or Monthly at [Address of Parcel]?

	AREA 1		AREA 2A		AREA 2B		AREA 3A		AREA 3B		TOTAL	
	Number	Per cent	Number	Per cent	Number	Per cent	Number	Per cent	Number	Per cent	Number	Per cent
Weekly	6	4.7	7	8.0	1	2.7	6	7.5	3	5.9	23	6.0
Monthly	96	74.9	65	73.9	33	89.2	58	72.4	45	88.1	297	77.3
Partly each	2	1.6	7	8.0	1	2.7	6	7.5	1	2.0	17	4.4
Other	—	—	1	1.1	—	—	1	1.3	—	—	2	0.5
Nominal monthly (must collect more frequently)	24	18.8	6	6.8	2	5.4	8	10.0	1	2.0	41	10.7
No tenants, but house partially occupied	—	—	2	2.3	—	—	1	1.3	—	—	3	0.8
Vacant parcel	—	—	—	—	—	—	—	—	1	2.0	1	0.3
Total	128	100.0	88	100.0	37	100.0	80	100.0	51	100.0	384	100.0
NA/DK	—		3		—		5		—		8	

EXHIBIT 4-7
Do You Use a Manager or Rent Collector for Your Properties?

	AREA 1		AREA 2A		AREA 2B		AREA 3A		AREA 3B		TOTAL	
	Number	Per cent	Number	Per cent	Number	Per cent	Number	Per cent	Number	Per cent	Number	Per cent
Manager	7	5.5	8	9.0	2	5.4	7	8.6	5	9.8	29	7.5
Rent collector	3	2.3	6	6.7	2	5.4	2	2.5	1	2.0	14	3.6
Self	107	83.7	65	73.1	27	73.0	69	85.2	43	84.2	311	80.7
Other	3	2.3	9	10.1	5	13.5	1	1.2	1	2.0	19	4.9
In part	4	3.1	—	—	—	—	—	—	—	—	4	1.0
Employee	—	—	—	—	—	—	—	—	—	—	—	—
Agent	1	0.8	—	—	—	—	1	1.2	—	—	2	0.5
Superintendent	3	2.3	1	1.1	1	2.7	1	1.2	1	2.0	7	1.8
Total	128	100.0	89	100.0	37	100.0	81	100.0	51	100.0	386	100.0
NA/DK	—		2		—		4		—		6	

EXHIBIT 4-8
Do You Use a Manager or a Rent Collector for Your Properties?

| | Size of Holdings | | | | | | | | | | | | | | | |
| | NA/DK | | Other | | Over 12 | | 7–12 | | 4–6 | | 2–3 | | 1 | | Total | |
	Number	Per cent	Number	Per cent	Number	Per cent	Number	Per cent	Number	Per cent	Number	Per cent	Number	Per cent	Number	Per cent
Manager	1	25.0	—	—	7	11.7	2	6.5	8	19.0	5	6.1	6	3.6	29	7.5
Rent collector	1	25.0	—	—	3	5.0	2	6.5	2	4.8	4	4.9	2	1.2	14	3.6
Self	1	25.0	—	—	43	71.6	22	70.9	29	69.0	66	80.5	150	89.8	311	80.7
Other	—	—	—	—	4	6.7	2	6.5	—	—	5	6.1	8	4.8	19	4.9
In part .	—	—	—	—	2	3.3	—	—	2	4.8	—	—	—	—	4	1.0
Employee	—	—	—	—	—	—	—	—	—	—	—	—	—	—	—	—
Agent	—	—	—	—	—	—	—	—	—	—	1	1.2	1	0.6	2	0.5
Superintendent	1	25.0	—	—	1	1.7	3	9.6	1	2.4	1	1.2	—	—	7	1.8
NA/DK	—	—	—	—	1	—	—	—	1	—	2	—	2	—	6	—
Sub-N	4		—		61		31		43		84		169		392	
Live sample	4		0		60		31		42		82		167		386	

EXHIBIT 4-9

DO YOU COLLECT YOUR RENTS BY THE WEEK OR MONTHLY?

Size of Holdings

	NA/DK		Other		Over 12		7–12		4–6		2–3		1		Total	
	Number	Per cent	Number	Per cent	Number	Per cent	Number	Per cent	Number	Per cent	Number	Per cent	Number	Per cent	Number	Per cent
Weekly	—	—	—	—	1	1.7	1	3.2	4	9.3	9	10.8	8	4.8	23	5.9
Monthly	3	75.0	—	—	44	73.3	22	71.0	27	62.8	58	70.0	149	88.6	303	77.9
Partly each	1	25.0	—	—	3	5.0	1	3.2	2	4.7	4	4.8	5	3.0	16	4.1
Other	—	—	—	—	—	—	—	—	—	—	1	1.2	1	0.6	2	0.5
Nominal monthly (must collect more frequently)	—	—	—	—	12	20.0	7	22.6	10	23.2	8	9.6	4	2.4	41	10.5
No tenants, but house at least partially occupied	—	—	—	—	—	—	—	—	—	—	2	2.4	1	0.6	3	0.8
Vacant parcel	—	—	—	—	—	—	—	—	—	—	1	1.2	—	—	1	0.3
NA/DK	—	—	—	—	1	—	—	—	—	—	1	—	1	—	3	—
Sub-N	4		—		61		31		43		84		169		392	
Live sample	4		0		60		31		43		83		168		389	

pared with an overall figure of 5.7 percent. The small holders seem to have the least nominal monthly collection procedure while only the larger holders use managers or rent collectors to any considerable degree.

Rent Collection Procedure

To give some feeling for the flavor of the rent collection procedure, it is worthwhile to describe the one used by the largest single tenement landlord in this study—an owner of more than two hundred tenement parcels in Newark.

All rents are due monthly at the landlord's office. If they are not paid by the tenth of the month, a note goes to the tenant. A dispossession notice is sent out on the twenty-seventh of the month. According to this owner, at least 75 percent of their rents are paid by check or money order and are received in the office. The other 25 percent are paid in person. In the course of an hour while the interviewer was in the office, at least eight people came in to pay the rent. Many of the tenants pay weekly even though the rents are ostensibly on a monthly basis. By this means they essentially budget their rent payments. Despite the brisk pace of warning and eviction notices, the landlord still finds that he gets stuck with a two-month-run bill on evictions, because of the time it takes for court proceedings to result in an official eviction notice.

In sum then, tenement parcels are returning, before debt service and depreciation, approximately 40 percent of the gross rentals received by the landlord. The actual return on investment in terms of the overall parcel value is clearly in the neighborhood of 10 to 12 percent. The range of variation both in expenses and in net return is considerable. A major factor affecting this is the variation of gross income as a function of the vacancy rates. It is the vacancy rate which determines a substantial part of the upward flexibility of the rent structure as well as the extent of gross rental. Let us examine this very significant function in detail.

Vacancy Rates

The basic fact of tenement ownership in hard-core Newark is that vacancy rates are very high. In 1950 only 0.7 percent of Newark's nonseasonal, sound-condition dwelling units were vacant. By 1960 this had increased to 4.1 percent; and in the author's opinion has substantially increased since then. The vacancy factor is concentrated in the hard-core slums.

The dynamics of this change are clear-cut. In the MPC attitude study cited earlier, Central Ward residents (roughly co-terminous with Area 1) indicated the most substantial pattern of forecasted intent to move out. At the time the area was cited in the study as having a vacancy rate of 4 percent, i.e. four out of every one hundred contacts of the survey interviewers proved to be empty dwelling units. Even at this time the vacancy rate in the Central Ward was double the overall figure for the entire city.[8]

That this trend has continued is indicated by Exhibits 4–10 and 4–11. These exhibits are basically the same in their content, the only variation being in the manner in which the question on vacancy rate was asked. In Exhibit 4–10 the question was: "In your opinion has the vacancy rate changed in the past several years in the general area of ——————?" In Exhibit 4–11 the phrasing was "Has the vacancy rate changed in your property at (address)?"

The answers in Exhibit 4–10 are perhaps more realistic evaluations of the situation; in either case, however, the trend is clear. *Vacancy rates are moving up and most forcefully in the hard-core slum area.* Notice that in Exhibit 4–10 there is a separate subset of *Yes—up, people moved to projects.* (As has been mentioned before, Newark has had a very substantial public housing development over the last decade.) To both questions it is Area 2, the recipient of much out-migration from Areas 1 and 3B and dominated by long-tenure immigrant stock, that has the greatest number of *no's.*

Variation in Vacancy Rates by Size of Landlord's Holdings

Does the vacancy rate affect all sizes of landlords, or is there a difference as a function of size of holding? Exhibits 4–12 and 4–13 present an analysis of the answers to the two questions as a function of number of parcels owned. As can clearly be seen in these exhibits, it is the small landlords who have been least affected by the vacancy rates. While, in part, this may be a function of large landlord holdings in the worst areas as well as of the diffidence of small owners in admitting that they are having renting difficulties, it probably indicates that it is the small owner, particularly the resident owner, who manages to maintain a parcel in such fashion as to secure tenantry.

The overall picture, however, is one of a substantial vacancy rate. The figure of 20 percent vacancies and rent skips combined (the latter in some cases running roughly 3 percent or 4 percent of gross rent) was often cited by larger landlords as the vacancy rate in their particular parcels.

EXHIBIT 4-10

In Your Opinion Has the Vacancy Rate Changed in the Past Several Years in the General Area of _____?

	AREA 1		AREA 2A		AREA 2B		AREA 3A		AREA 3B		TOTAL	
	Number	Per-cent	Number	Per-cent	Number	Per-cent	Number	Per-cent	Number	Per-cent	Number	Per-cent
Yes—up	72	60.5	31	41.3	15	45.5	36	54.5	20	42.6	174	51.2
Yes—up, people move to projects	10	8.4	8	10.7	1	3.0	5	7.6	5	10.6	29	8.5
Yes—down	2	1.7	3	4.0	1	3.0	2	3.0	3	6.4	11	3.2
No	35	29.4	33	44.0	16	48.5	23	34.8	19	40.4	126	37.1
Total	119	100.0	75	100.0	33	100.0	66	100.0	47	100.0	340	100.0
NA/DK	9		16		4		19		4		52	

EXHIBIT 4-11

Has the Vacancy Rate Changed in Your Property at [Address]?

	AREA 1		AREA 2A		AREA 2B		AREA 3A		AREA 3B		TOTAL	
	Number	Per-cent	Number	Per-cent	Number	Per-cent	Number	Per-cent	Number	Per-cent	Number	Per-cent
Yes—up	67	52.7	28	31.8	6	17.6	33	40.8	14	27.5	148	38.8
Yes—down	3	2.4	3	3.4	1	2.9	4	4.9	3	5.9	14	3.7
No	57	44.9	57	64.8	27	79.5	44	54.3	34	66.6	219	57.5
Total	127	100.0	88	100.0	34	100.0	81	100.0	51	100.0	381	100.0
NA	—		2		—		4		—		6	
DK	1		1		3		—		—		5	

EXHIBIT 4-12

HAS THE VACANCY RATE CHANGED IN THE PAST SEVERAL YEARS IN THE GENERAL AREA OF _____?

Size of Holdings

	NA/DK		Other		Over 12		7-12		4-6		2-3		1		Total	
	Number	Per-cent	Number	Per-cent	Number	Per-cent	Number	Per-cent	Number	Per-cent	Number	Per-cent	Number	Per-cent	Number	Per-cent
Yes—up	3	75.0	—	—	35	61.3	15	57.7	29	69.0	27	37.4	65	46.7	174	51.2
Yes—down	—	—	—	—	3	5.3	1	3.8	—	—	4	5.6	3	2.2	11	3.2
No	1	25.0	—	—	5	8.8	6	23.1	10	23.9	37	51.4	67	48.2	126	37.1
People move to projects	—	—	—	—	14	24.6	4	15.4	3	7.1	4	5.6	4	2.9	29	8.5
Unclassifiable—other	—	—	—	—	—	—	—	—	—	—	—	—	—	—	—	—
NA	—	—	—	—	1	—	—	—	—	—	—	—	3	—	4	—
DK	—	—	—	—	3	—	5	—	1	—	12	—	27	—	48	—
Sub-N	4		—		61		31		43		84		169		392	
Live sample	4		0		57		26		42		72		139		340	

EXHIBIT 4-13

HAS THE VACANCY RATE CHANGED IN YOUR PROPERTY IN THE LAST COUPLE OF YEARS?

| | Size of Holdings | | | | | | | | | | | | | | |
| | NA/DK | | Other | | Over 12 | | 7–12 | | 4–6 | | 2–3 | | 1 | | Total | |
	Number	Per cent	Number	Per cent	Number	Per cent	Number	Per cent	Number	Per cent	Number	Per cent	Number	Per cent	Number	Per cent
Yes—up	1	25.0	—	—	39	63.9	18	60.0	25	58.1	28	34.1	37	23.0	148	38.8
Yes—down	1	25.0	—	—	5	8.2	—	—	2	4.7	2	2.4	4	2.5	14	3.7
No	2	50.0	—	—	17	27.9	12	40.0	16	37.2	52	63.5	120	74.5	219	57.5
Unclassifiable—other	—	—	—	—	—	—	—	—	—	—	—	—	—	—	—	—
NA	—	—	—	—	—	—	1		—	—	1		5		6	
DK	—	—	—	—	—	—			—	—	1		3		5	
Sub-N	4		—		61		31		43		84		169		392	
Live sample	4		0		61		30		43		82		161		381	

A check of nearly six hundred dwelling units—owned by one individual and scattered throughout Newark's slum areas—was undertaken. The vacancy rate, as of April, 1965, was nearly 18 percent. This rate prevailed at a time when the season was mild enough to reverse the doubling-up in heated units during the winter.

The Effect of High Vacancy Rates

The effect of high vacancy rates is much more complex than might be thought at first glance. As yet, for example, they have rarely resulted in rent *reductions*. As Grebler[9] pointed out, a substantial exposure to high vacancy rates over time is required before the market adjusts price to meet the decreased demand. On the other hand, the high vacancy rate certainly inhibits rent increases. The fear of raising rents in a weak market is compounded of two elements; the possibility of ending up with substantial vacancies, and, perhaps even more significantly, the fear that in order to secure tenants at the increased rates the landlord must take in lower categories of tenantry.

One Negro owner stated: "The only man who can afford the increased rates around here would be the man without roots, a drifter, and they're no good." *The availability of housing for Negroes in better areas of Newark, as well as in the surrounding suburbs, limits the number of people with capacity and willingness to pay high rents in the slum areas. The willingness of tenement owners to make improvements, therefore, is substantially inhibited by the feeling that there would be limited demand for better, i.e. higher rent, apartments.* The controller of a small hospital who owns two parcels in our sample area typified the attitude when he claimed:

> Any increase in rents immediately results in vacancies even with the improvements; that's why the tenants are willing to stay in cold-water flats. This type of tenant cannot afford the increase in rents to offset taxes for improvements. The financial economy of the people don't permit it. They're big families with little or no employment.

The fear of losing the tenants one knows for the tenants one doesn't know, upon raising rents, also serves as an inhibitor. The attitude of a fifty-nine-year-old Portugese resident-owner and construction worker was representative of a substantial number of landlords. He said; "I couldn't raise the rents because I would get bad tenants, and that's the worst thing you can have." Faced with reassessment on this particular parcel and a lid on rents, this owner maintains the place but is very loath to put money into it.

Vandalism

In the face of a weak market, the fear of vacancies is a compound not only of the fear of loss of rent, but also, and perhaps equally, the fear of vandalism that goes with vacancy. A major real estate holder said:

> Some tenants might appreciate certain improvements and, therefore, might pay some additional rents, whereas other tenants wouldn't care or couldn't pay more, and as a result some might move out. I wouldn't want to take the chance of vacancy. Vacancies lead to vandalism and looting. It's better business to be fully rented at the expense of getting top dollar.

Subsequent chapters will examine the effect of the poor rental market as an inhibitor of improvements despite tax and/or mortgage easements. It should be noted here, however, that the landlord's fear of substantial vacancies is a very real one. A fairly typical process is for the landlord of a six-family house to lose two or three tenants at once. Either he rents to undesirable tenants and thus drives out the balance of his tenantry, or he runs the risk of a group of delinquents moving into one of the vacant apartments by breaking through a window or by kicking down a door and proceeding to vandalize the premises. It is not uncommon to find that bathroom fixtures and piping are removed to be sold to junk dealers. Lighting fixtures and other elements of value are often removed also. The end result frequently is a vacant parcel with little residual value.

An example in point is a parcel currently assessed at $1,600 for land and $7,000 for building in the hard-core area. The classic pattern of several tenants moving out at once developed. Vandals got into one of the empty apartments and the remaining tenants then moved out. The building was boarded up and shortly thereafter was gutted by the neighborhood teenagers. It was sold in 1963 for $4,500, half its prior cost. This sale was accomplished only by means of a purchase money mortgage of $4,000.

The prevalence of vacant parcels, which was noted in an earlier chapter, has an enormously deleterious effect on surrounding land values as well as upon the overall neighborhood as a place in which to live, and these abandonments do not disappear from the scene. The reasons for this longevity of vacant parcels are indicated in Grebler's study of housing market behavior.

> In the removal of slums the action of market forces alone appears to be related not so much to physical or economic depreciation, as to alternative uses for the land, particularly the rate of which nonresidential can replace residential land use. This rate is dependent upon the speed and locational pattern of urban growth.[10]

These observations of Grebler, based upon his study of a fifty-year period in the life of slums in New York's Lower East Side, indicate that unless the basic areas of slums in Newark regain some of their lost vitality, these blotches will die slowly at best. The land, with no improvement upon it, has literally no use and no value. Certainly, high tax rates levy a penalty against the owners of such unproductive shells, but this is relatively minor compared with the realization of loss which would accompany the shell's removal. As noted in Chapter 2, municipal policy enforcement of those sections of the housing code which call for demolition of vacant parcels is far from rigorous.

Risk and Return

It is the risk factor, typified by the vacant parcel, which raises the required threshold of return on investment in slum properties. In a sense, the very weakness of the market has increased the rewards which potential buyers of slum tenements require in return for their investment. The risks also, as shall be seen again and again in the following chapters, limit the *kind* of investor who is attracted to slum tenements. Both of these limitations are increased by the fear of housing inspection. One observer put it very aptly:

> Landlords may suddenly be confronted with enthusiastic, if often short-lived, campaigns to enforce long dormant occupancy in building codes. Such campaigns are not inherently undesirable, nor is the rental market unable to adjust to consistent standards of code enforcement. But sporadic drives, together with the wide gulf that exists between the standard recited in statutory codes and actual enforcement, create many uncertainties; uncertainty is a notoriously uncongenial climate for investors.[11]

The high rate of current return demanded by investors in slum tenements can be summarized as a compound of the fear of costly code crack-

downs; the basic weakness of the market, both in terms of rental increases and securing full tenancy; the risk of outright loss through the complete abandonment of a parcel; and in substantial part, the pejoratives which society heaps upon the "slum lord." All of these combine to shape the nature of the trading market in slum tenements—the buying and selling, the maintenance and will to rehabilitate, the very characteristics of the landlords who become involved in tenements—all are closely shaped and defined by the realities of the market.

In sum, high vacancy rates have been looked forward to by urban planners who have felt strongly that the major inhibitor to appropriate code enforcement and rehabilitation efforts was the lack of housing for those displaced. While this potential is now being made available through the actions of the market, the landlord's will and desire to upgrade his parcels, with some exceptions discussed, are being eroded by the relative lack of profitability of those parcels. Faced with a weak market, the entrepreneur can do one of three things:

1. Sell out, or

2. Do as little as possible in terms of new investment and wait for "better times," or

3. Upgrade his holdings so as to attract either higher paying or a more stable tenantry.

Which shall the landlord choose?[12]

The chapter which follows concerns tenement trading; the buying and selling of parcels. In chapter 6 attention will focus on the question of who owns the slums and what factors affect their actions.

REFERENCES

1 Arthur D. Sporn, "Empirical Studies in the Economics of Slum Ownership," *Land Economics*, (Nov., 1960), p. 340.
2 Chester Rapkin, *The Real Estate Market in an Urban Renewal Area* (N.Y.C. Planning Commission, 1959), p. 65.
3 The expenses indicated by this analysis are roughly corroborated by a study by Louis Winnick, *Rental Housing* . . . , p. 279, which presents the distribution of gross rent income for 201 FHA 608 projects for areas as of 1955. For New York walk-ups, for example, operating costs, plus real estate taxes, were 51.1%. This did not include any officers' salaries or management costs. If the 7% figure which has been indicated in this operating ratio data was included, it would increase the total to 58.1%.

4 *Exchange of Rental Income and Operating Expense Data,* Journal of Property Management (Chicago: Institute of Real Estate Management of the National Association of Real Estate Boards, 1964), p. 7.

5 Rapkin, *Real Estate,* p. 67.

6 Sporn, "Empirical . . . ," p. 338.

7 Frieden, *The Future* . . . , p. 161.

8 MPC I, p. 25.

9 Leo Grebler, *Experience in Urban Real Estate Investment* (N. Y.: Columbia University, 1955), pp. 182–183.

10 *Ibid.,* p. 15.

11 Winnick, *Rental Housing* . . . , p. 102.

12 Several thousand dwelling units are shortly to be removed from the market because of new highway construction. While this undoubtedly will tighten the housing situation, its effect will be transitory. The basic market realities as sketched here will dominate landlord investment policies.

Chapter 5

TENEMENT TRADING:
THE BUYING AND SELLING
OF SLUM TENEMENTS

Turnover Rates

One of the more familiar statements about the problem of maintenance and rehabilitation of slum tenements is the platitude that this type of realty is characterized by a very high turnover rate. A former mayor of Milwaukee stated:

> One of the great problems of slum ownership is the fact that slum properties have changed hands many times during their life and each person is expected to make a profit from the sale. The tendency, therefore, is to raise the price of the building and to seek ever-increasing rents at the same time the physical value of the building is deteriorating. As a building gets older and the price the latest owner pays for it represents more and more profit taking and successive sales, the latest owner must crowd more and more tenants in a dying building to meet his costs, thus hastening its debilitation. . . . The latest owner may possess what is little more than a pile of bricks and kindling wood. He presumes the building has a high residual value. If he is lucky, the local government will come along and buy him out at an inflated price for some public work or slum clearance project.[1]

While this statement is undoubtedly descriptive of many slum parcels, how general is the high rate of turnover upon which it is predicated? The limited data which is available would tend to disagree substantially with this thesis.

98

For example, in Grebler's study of a sample of nine hundred fifty-eight parcels whose titles were analyzed during the period 1900 to 1949, only 4.5 percent changes per parcel were noted.[2] Grebler pointed out, however, that:

> This picture of low average velocity is compatible with rapid turnover and short duration of ownership of some parcels, as is illustrated by the wide dispersion in the frequency distribution of conveyances.

This low rate of conveyances is confirmed by a somewhat similar study done by Chester Rapkin on New York's West Side. (See Exhibit 5-1, *Number and Rate of Conveyances by Type of Property 1938–1955*.) The old-law

EXHIBIT 5-1

NUMBER AND RATE OF CONVEYANCE BY TYPE OF PROPERTY, 1938–1955

Type of Property	Number of Conveyances	Number of Properties	Conveyances per Property
Old-law tenement (walk-up)	258	267	.97
Old-law tenement (single-room occupancy)	36	37	.97
New-law tenement (walk-up)	8	4	2.00
Brownstone, 1- and 2-family	94	79	1.19
Brownstone, multi-family	342	158	2.16
Brownstone, rooming house	710	428	1.66
Old-law tenement with elevator	26	14	1.86
New-law tenement with elevator	61	28	2.18
Post-1929 elevator building	26	22	1.18
Nonresidential structure	58	71	2.82
Total	1,619	1,108	1.46

Source: Rapkin, *The Real Estate Market in an Urban Renewal Area*, pp. 21.

tenements, mentioned earlier in this report, actually have the lowest rate of conveyances. The highest rate of turnover, that of multiple family non-elevator, was little more than two times in the seventeen-year period analyzed. In a study of turnover rates and slum properties in Milwaukee, similar data is presented. Of the one hundred twenty-three parcels which were studied over the period 1929–1958, the average number of qualified conveyances was only 2.3.[3]

EXHIBIT 5-2
AGE OF TITLE

	AREA 1		AREA 2A		AREA 2B		AREA 3A		AREA 3B		TOTAL	
	Num-ber	Per-cent	Num-ber	Per-cent	Num-ber	Per-cent	Num-ber	Per-cent	Num-ber	Per-cent	Num-ber	Per-cent
Less than 2 years	26	14.7	15	11.9	8	14.8	10	8.8	11	13.4	70	12.7
2–4 years	20	11.3	14	11.1	10	18.5	20	17.5	13	15.9	77	13.9
5–6 years	17	9.6	8	6.3	3	5.6	3	2.6	8	9.7	39	7.0
7–10 years	28	15.8	16	12.7	11	20.4	17	14.9	8	9.7	80	14.5
11–15 years	22	12.4	25	19.8	4	7.4	14	12.3	10	12.2	75	13.6
16–20 years	28	15.8	19	15.1	4	7.4	17	14.9	13	15.9	81	14.6
More than 20 years	36	20.3	29	23.0	14	25.9	33	28.9	19	23.2	131	23.7
Total	177	100.0	126	100.0	54	100.0	114	100.0	82	100.0	553	100.0
No data available	—	—	—	—	—	—	—	—	—	—	13	—

In order to check this factor in the field sample, analysis was made of the age of title in the five hundred sixty-six parcels studied. Data was obtained on this point for five hundred fifty-three. In Exhibit 5–2, data is presented by area. Notice that there is a surprising consistency throughout the several areas. Overall, just a little over a quarter of the titles dated from the last four years. They were nearly matched in number by those of twenty or more years of duration. The average title was more than ten years old. Again, it should be pointed out that this does not mean that within this sample grouping there are not many parcels which change hands with considerable frequency, but the fact is undeniable that the overall rate of turnover has popularly been overestimated.

Accelerated Depreciation

A corollary of the turnover hypothesis has been that lack of maintenance of slum properties was the result of tax treatment under Federal income tax laws. This provided for accelerated depreciation of real estate investment until fairly recently.[4] For example, the Internal Revenue Code of 1957 permitted owners of rental housing the right to use the declining balance method at a rate of not more than 150 percent of the applicable straight-line rate provided this resulted in a reasonable allowance.

The thesis continues that people of high income would buy slum tenements and then take advantage of accelerated depreciation to provide a write-off against current income. When the cream of the depreciation had been skimmed off, the owner would sell the tenement to yet another high income individual, who would repeat the process. Obviously, this would encourage investment in tenements as a tax shield and would not provide the kind of seasoned real estate operation and maintenance which they so desperately required.

> To the extent that the maintenance and operation of housing in a substandard or deteriorating condition is financially attractive, such a state of affairs impedes the effectiveness of slum clearance efforts along legal lines of attack. It will be seen that the remarkable feature of the income tax depreciation allowance under our present rules is that the effect is not merely to undercut the forces of a tax area in this general manner. By increasing the overall profitability of operating slum housing, its counteracting effect upon such attacks is heightened by two further specific influences that it exerts: first, it increases the

profitability of operating such housing in the most irresponsible, slum-producing manner, and in addition it decreases the relative profitability of replacing the same with new facilities.[5]

Regardless of whether accelerated depreciation provides the kind of effect indicated, an effect which has been questioned by at least some authorities,[6] the rate of turnover which has been described here would tend to dispute the prevalence of this "high depreciation equals high turnover thesis."*

This author believes that the basic thesis assumes a "rational" behavior upon the part of landlords for which there is little evidence. Few of our major landlords, for example, admit to using accelerated depreciation. A conversation with two of the major tenement management houses and two firms which specialize in local real estate accounting corroborates this statement. In any case, the 1964 law on accelerated depreciation would certainly offset most of the rapid depreciation tax advantages.

In summary, most tenements are not beset by the kinds of high turnover rates that have often been presumed. On the other hand, on the basis of condition of parcel as a function of acquisition date, tenure of ownership in and of itself is not enough to insure the maintenance of the properties. The reverse is frequently the case. For example, parcel 219 in the sample group has been in the same family for forty years. It has no mortgage on it whatsoever. The son of the original owner admits the fact that, "There hasn't been a dime put into it in the past ten years." The parcel is in dreadful condition, and half of it is vacant. The owner, when questioned on his attitude toward improving the parcel, said, "I am waiting for the city to buy it. I have been losing money on it for five years." He claimed, "The city told the tenants that the parcel would be bought within a year. Now it's five years later, the good tenants moved out and the city still hasn't bought the property." The owner, desperate to insure himself of some tenants, has let four apartments in a single "wholesale" deal to one sub-landlord and has permitted the bulk realtor to rent to whomever he likes. "The tenants who remain are 'winos.' They are the only ones who cannot live in the projects." Once again, to restate the obvious, lengthy tenure of ownership does not necessarily equate with good maintenance of parcel.

---

*Interestingly enough, Sporn, the advocate of this connection, in a later publication entitled *The Economics of Slum Ownership*, pp. 335–336, studied income tax returns on one hundred twenty-three slum properties in Milwaukee and discovered that the average depreciation rate was only 3.8 percent—scarcely evidence of accelerated depreciation.

Slum Rent Multipliers

The purchase price of slum property is most usually evaluated as a multiple of the gross rent. To a substantial degree the vigor of capital gains potential, the changing expense elements, the degree of difficulty and risk in owning and managing such parcels, and not infrequently the social stigma attached to ownership of this type of realty are all mirrored in this multiplier. In two group sessions, the first with savings and loan representatives and investors in slum tenements and the second with five of the major individual tenement owners in Newark, the judgment of participants was that the multiplier on slum tenements had fallen to no more than three and one-half to four times gross rent.

This is not unique to Newark, as indicated by Rapkin.[8] For all the parcels in the area studied by him on New York's West Side, the gross rent multiplier was 4.27 percent, with elevator apartments running at a somewhat higher multiple, and walk-ups running lower. In a recent study of housing values in which some four thousand parcels were analyzed, including hotels, multi-story unfurnished apartments, walk-up buildings, apartment buildings, etc., slum properties were always capitalized at by far the lowest multiple.[9]

There is evidence to indicate that over the long run there has been a substantial decline in the multiplier extended to tenements. For example, Grebler developed the analysis, shown in Exhibit 5-3, for the gross rent multiplier at bench mark dates from 1890 to 1949.* As the table indicates, tenements have had their multipliers decreased by nearly half over the fifty years studied. Obviously, the total rent roll over this half century has been far from static. Has the increase in rent roll offset the decrease in the multiplier extended to that rent roll? The data seems very clear on the capital gains potential of tenement parcels purchased in the early Forties. It is not uncommon for parcels currently valued at $10,000 to have been sold for as little as $4,000 in that period.

Declining Tenement Prices

In more recent years, however, the situation may well have changed. In order to assess this possibility, the 1964 assessment of parcels has been used

---

* For an appraisal of this data see Louis Winnick, "Long-Term Changes in Evaluation of Residential Real Estate by Gross Rent," *Appraisal Journal* (October, 1952).

EXHIBIT 5-3

THE GROSS RENT MULTIPLIER AT BENCH-MARK DATES, 1890–1949

	Single-Family	Tenement	Apartment House	Other
1890–1892	14.1	9.5	10.1	—
1900	12.5	9.1	—	—
1905	11.1	—	—	—
1912	11.0 11.1	10.5	10.6 9.9	—
1913	12.1	—	9.0	—
1919	9.8	—	—	—
1923	—	—	6.2	—
1925	—	7.1	6.4	—
1936	8.3	—	—	—
1937	—	—	7.5	—
1937–1938	8.3	—	—	—
1937–1940	—	4.5	—	6.3
1939	7.4	—	—	—
1940	—	—	7.2	—
1940–1941	8.6	—	—	—
1941	7.9	5.1	4.1	6.5
1941–1942	—	—	5.5	—
1942	—	5.1	—	6.6
1943	—	3.2	4.8	—
1948	10.1	—	8.3	—
1949	—	4.6	5.6	—

Source: Grebler—*Capital Formation in Residential Real Estate*, p. 411.

as a base-line deflator of sales by year and area. In this manner an admittedly crude but perhaps adequate common denominator for sales of different parcels at different times was secured, (Exhibit 5-4). Based on this analysis, sales in the mid- and early-Forties were at little more than half current assessment. This ratio increased until by the mid- to late-Fifties the ratio for assessment to sales had reached roughly a one-to-one form. This relationship was relatively stable into the early Sixties, but there is some evidence that in the last year or two the ratio has been decreasing once again, indicating lower price levels.

The data presented here is, at best, a very rough guide; however, it is corroborated by the lack of landlord optimism as to future slum tenement capital gains potential.

Financing and Sale Price

Assessment ratio analysis such as this is also complicated by the question of financing. For example, one case involves a tenement on what is perhaps

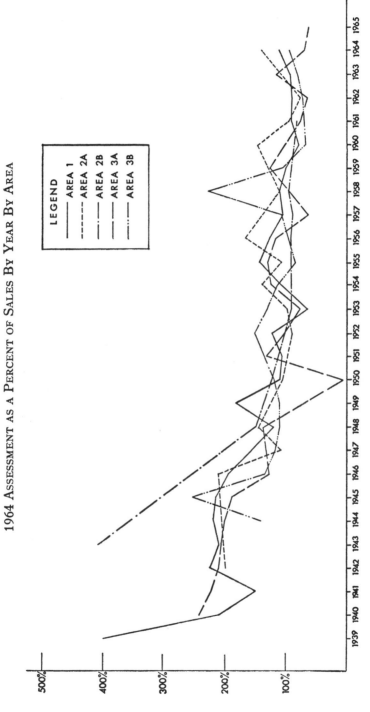

EXHIBIT 5-4

1964 Assessment as a Percent of Sales By Year By Area

LEGEND
AREA 1
AREA 2A
AREA 2B
AREA 3A
AREA 3B

the worst street in the city. A number of the houses on the block are semi-abandoned or in a state of advanced decay. In this case there were two separate sales of the same parcel consummated within several months of each other. The first involved the parcel in a purchase by Principal A at a cost of $13,500, of which $9,000 was in cash, with the seller taking back a $4,500 purchase money mortgage. Within a two-month period, Purchaser A sold the parcel to present Holder B for $17,000, which included the mortgage of $4,500. In addition, Purchaser A took back a $10,000 mortgage on a bond. In the first transaction Owner A put up $9,000 in cash, and in the second transaction $2,500 in cash was returned to him, thus reducing his cash investment to $6,500, for which he received a $10,000 mortgage. The new owner acquired the parcel for an ostensible $17,000. His cash investment, however, unlike Owner A, is only $2,500. From the viewpoint of the professional real estate dealer, there may be considerable question as to whether the position of Owner A, initially having paid $13,500 for a parcel and having $9,000 in equity in it, is to be envied over that of Owner B, who has paid $17,000 for the parcel and only has $2,500 of equity in it. Notice that all the transactions described here are among professionals. While this type of inflated purchase price, as a function of financing, certainly makes assessment/sales ratio most treacherous, the latter does provide an overall guide.

The effect of lowered capital gains potential in slum tenements obviously means that in order to secure equity investments, a higher current rate of return is required. In past generations the confidence in urban realty was so very strong as to its ultimate inflation in price that people were willing to take relatively lower rates of yield in exchange for the possibility of a substantial capital gain in the future. With a lowering of confidence in the future of slum realty in places like Newark or older cities generally, in order to secure any investors substantial current income must be assured.[10]

In essence then, the very weakness of the whole market produces a requirement for higher rates of return on new investment. Given a relatively weak rent structure, i.e. a relative inflexibility of rentals per unit, landlords will invest only when assured a very high rate of return. The effects of this market structure on determining the maintenance and rehabilitation strategies of landlords will be examined in more detail later.

Obviously, one of the major determinants, both of cash flow and of return on equity from slum properties, is the type of financing which is available.[11]

Financing the Slum Tenement

The *"Black List"*—the concept of areas which are black listed by potential lenders—is very common. The underlying basis of long-term financing is stability of prospects over an equivalent period of years. Areas, therefore, in transition (in character, or in racial composition, or in all the elements which provide continuity with past-appraised values) are suspect to the potential investor. The writer believes that the question of race is actually subordinate to economic risk; though undoubtedly significant racial prejudice still exists among certain lenders.

Lenders, therefore, have to be lured into these areas of change through the medium of relatively short-term mortgages, as well as by high rates of return. To the extent that usury or banking laws inhibit the latter, lenders can only be secured by owner payments of more or less dubious legality, typically through bonuses; and society succeeds in reversing most of its efforts by limiting potential lenders to those who are willing to take the risk of legal prosecution in return for very high rates of return.

In an extreme case, the owner of a slum property in a black-listed area can sell either at very low cash prices only or by taking back a purchase money mortgage. In turn, the potential new buyers are limited in number by the fear of being "locked into" a property on purchase. Obviously, this tends to depress the selling price of slum parcels. How serious is this problem in Newark?

In Exhibits 5–5, 5–6, and 5–7, are shown sources of first mortgages by year and area. The trends are obvious in Area 1, where the banks have disappeared from the scene completely. While savings and loans are still significant, the number of mortgages written by them in Area 1 is little more than half those written by private sources. Area 2* is very similar. Only two out of the forty-nine mortgages noted between 1960–1965 were written by banks, nineteen were written by savings and loans, eleven by mortgage companies, and thirteen by private sources. Area 3 represents a more "normal" picture. Savings and loans have grown in mortgage source dominance over the twenty-six-year period shown, while banks have diminished in importance. The ratio of private sources to savings and loans is nearly reversed from that of Area 1. In Exhibit 5–8 this data is summarized for the period 1960–1965. The minor significance of banks for the areas as a whole is indi-

---

* There was so little variation between A and B Areas in Groups 2 and 3 that they have been combined.

EXHIBIT 5-5

FIRST MORTGAGE BY YEAR AND SOURCE, 1939–1965

AREA 1

SOURCE	1939–1944		1945–1949		1950–1954		1955–1959		1960–1965		Totals
	Num-ber	Per-cent	Num-ber	Per-cent	Num-ber	Per-cent	Num-ber	Per-cent	Num-ber	Per-cent	
Savings and loan	—	—	5	23.8	10	50.0	9	26.5	14	28.0	
Private source	6	50.0	8	38.1	4	20.0	21	61.8	25	50.0	
Mortgage Company	—	—	—	—	1	5.0	—	—	4	8.0	
Commercial and savings banks	4	33.3	3	14.3	2	10.0	—	—	—	—	
Other— (Realty and construction companies and those who didn't know source of their mortgages)	2	16.7	5	23.8	3	15.0	4	11.7	7	14.0	
Total first mortgages	12	100.0	21	100.0	20	100.0	34	100.0	50	100.0	137
No mortgage shown											19
Total sales											156

Source: Title Records.

EXHIBIT 5-6

FIRST MORTGAGE BY YEAR AND SOURCE, 1939–1965

AREA 2

SOURCE	1939–1944		1945–1949		1950–1954		1955–1959		1960–1965		Totals
	Number	Per-cent	Number	Per-cent	Number	Per-cent	Number	Per-cent	Number	Per-cent	
Savings and loan	5	55.6	2	12.5	11	40.7	15	57.7	19	38.8	
Private source	2	22.2	8	50.0	12	44.4	8	30.8	13	26.5	
Mortgage company	—	—	1	6.3	1	3.7	1	3.8	11	22.4	
Commercial and savings banks	1	11.1	2	12.5	3	11.2	2	7.7	2	4.1	
Other— (realty and construction companies and those who didn't know source of their mortgages)	1	11.1	3	18.7	—	—	—	—	4	8.2	
Total first mortgages	9	100.0	16	100.0	27	100.0	26	100.0	49	100.0	127
No mortgage shown											20
Total sales											147

Source: Title Records.

EXHIBIT 5-7

FIRST MORTGAGE BY YEAR AND SOURCE, 1939–1965

AREA 3

SOURCE	1939–1944		1945–1949		1950–1954		1955–1959		1960–1965		Totals
	Number	Per cent	Number	Per cent	Number	Per cent	Number	Per cent	Number	Per cent	
Savings and loan	6	33.3	6	25.0	7	41.2	13	46.4	29	59.2	
Private source	7	38.9	11	45.8	4	23.5	10	35.7	12	24.5	
Mortgage company	—		3	12.5	1	5.9	4	14.3	5	10.2	
Commercial and savings banks	3	16.7	3	12.5	5	29.4	—		1	2.0	
Other—(realty and construction companies and those who didn't know source of their mortgages)	2	11.1	1	4.2	—	—	1	3.6	2	4.1	
Total first mortgages	18	100.0	24	100.0	17	100.0	28	100.0	49	100.0	136
No mortgage shown											27
Total sales											163

Source: Title Records.

EXHIBIT 5-8

FIRST MORTGAGES BY SOURCE AND AREA, 1960–65

SOURCE	AREA 1		AREA 2		AREA 3		TOTAL	
	Number	Percent	Number	Percent	Number	Percent	Number	Percent
Savings and loan	14	22.6	19	30.6	29	46.8	62	100.0
Private source	25	50.0	13	26.0	12	24.0	50	100.0
Mortgage company	4	20.0	11	55.0	5	25.0	20	100.0
Commercial and savings banks	—	—	2	66.7	1	33.3	3	100.0
Other— (realty and construction companies and those who didn't know source of their mortgages)	7	53.8	4	30.8	2	15.4	13	100.0
Total first mortgages	50	33.8	49	33.1	49	33.1	148	100.0

Source: Title Records.

cated by the fact that only three of the total of one hundred forty-eight first mortgages were written by them, while sixty-two were written by savings and loans, and fifty by private sources.

In summation, buyers and sellers residing in the poorest area, Area 1, had trouble obtaining mortgages from public sources, probably because they were considered a poor risk, and, therefore, had to seek aid in financing their purchases from private sources. On the other hand, landlords in Area 3, the best area, had relatively little trouble in securing mortgages from public sources as is evidenced by Exhibit 5–7.

Is there a racial bias behind this difficulty in securing public source financing? The answer to this is a most complicated one. Some data is available through the MPC I study mentioned earlier in which the question was asked both of white and Negro households whether they had found difficulty in securing a source of financing for their homes. In Exhibit 5–9

EXHIBIT 5–9

RESPONDENTS CLAIMING TO HAVE HAD DIFFICULTY IN FINDING
A SOURCE OF FINANCING THEIR HOUSES
(BY RACE)

Claimed Difficulty	White Households		Negro Households	
	Number	Percent	Number	Percent
Yes	11	9	6	8
No	90	78	67	89
No Answer (refused)	15	13	2	3
Total	116	100	75	100

Source: *MPC I*, Table A–7.

are presented the collated responses. There is little difference between the white and Negro responses. For both groups, however, it should be noted that the respondents are those who have been *successful* in securing mortgages. With more than 85 percent of all the conveyances that were viewed in the course of this study accompanied by mortgages, the importance of this data is unmistakable. *Real estate trading is dependent upon financing. In the absence of adequate financing, this trading, in turn, must suffer.* Even when financing is available, the terms are often prohibitive.

Lender Concentration

In Grigsby's study of racial shifts in West Philadelphia,[12] "legitimate" sources of financing, although heavily concentrated, predominated by far. The eight most active institutions provided 52 percent of the loans. There is no similar concentration of financing institutions in the Newark sample area. More than thirty different institutions were listed over the years, with no great shift observable over the period of years studied. Obviously, the concept of a very few institutions dominating slum tenement financing is not valid in Newark.

Longevity of Mortgages

In the New York State Upper West Side Study,[13] the median term of years for new mortgages was six, with a substantial number under five years in length. In conferences with landlords and savings and loan institutions during the Newark research, the consensus was that when mortgages were available in the hard-core slum areas of Newark, they were written for an eight- to ten-year period at best.

Equity as a Percentage of Consideration

Possibly one of the reasons for the lack of appeal of slum mortgages to institutional sources is the low proportion of equity to purchase price which characterizes them. In Exhibit 5–10 is presented the first mortgage to purchase price by area for Newark. While there is a considerable range of variation, it is quite evident that the average is higher in the very poorest area

EXHIBIT 5–10

FIRST MORTGAGE TO PURCHASE PRICE

	NEWARK		
	Area 1	Area 2	Area 3
Number of usable Transactions	112	110	99
Median percent	78	72	71
Interquartile range (percent)	62–88	58–87	63–81

at 78 percent, going down to 71 percent in Area 3. The interquartile ranges presented in the Exhibit agree with this statement. *The worse the area, the less is the equity as a percentage of sales price.* Tenement ownership is highly leveraged; given high mortgage ratios and relatively short repayment schedules, there is an obvious stringency in the cash flow generated by properties. The availability, therefore, of cash derived from the property itself as a source of funds for rehabilitation is limited.

Interest Rates

Actual interest rates upon new mortgages are very difficult to determine. Mortgage indentures do not reflect the discounts charged by lenders. The usual deal, currently reported by a number of major landlords as well as savings and loan authorities, is for the mortgage to have anywhere from a 3 percent to 7 percent discount off the face, and to be written at 6 percent interest. Difficult properties, i.e. those in areas where it is difficult to secure mortgages, may involve discounts of up to 25 percent. As will be noted later, there is an infinite number of variations in this regard.

Second Mortgages

Given the low ratio of equity to total consideration that results from the substantial first mortgages, it is not particularly startling to discover that only 13.9 percent of the transactions studied were accompanied by a second mortgage within six months of the transfer. Interestingly enough, however, as Exhibit 5–11 shows, there is a substantial discrepancy between this proportion in Areas 2A and 3A as against 2B and 3B. This reflects the disproportionately high use of this vehicle by Negro buyers. Practically all the second mortgages were granted by individual grantees at the time of the transfer.

Given the high rate of return required for first mortgages, obviously, second mortgages will be even higher. New Jersey's usury laws, with their ceiling of 6 percent for individuals, are obviously unrealistic. The usual second mortgage loan deal involves the following formula: the borrower signs a note for $1,300 at 6 percent for a three-year term with straight line amortization; he receives $1,000 less legal fees. On a five-year basis, when avail-

EXHIBIT 5-11
SECOND MORTGAGE

	AREA 1		AREA 2A		AREA 2B		AREA 3A		AREA 3B		TOTAL	
	Num-ber	Per-cent	Num-ber	Per-cent	Num-ber	Per-cent	Num-ber	Per-cent	Num-ber	Per-cent	Num-ber	Per-cent
Yes	26	14.0	22	17.2	5	9.3	20	18.2	5	6.0	78	13.9
No	159	85.5	106	82.8	49	90.7	89	80.9	78	94.0	481	85.7
Third mortgage	1	0.5	—	—	—	—	1	0.9	—	—	2	0.4
Total	186	100.0	128	100.0	54	100.0	110	100.0	83	100.0	561	100.0
Data not available	—	—	—	—	—	—	—	—	—	—	5	—

Source: Title Records.

able, the usual face of the note is $1,500 or $1,600, with a net of $1,000 less legal fees.*

Inflated Sales

Obviously, the sale price of tenements is often ballooned to provide an umbrella for inflated financing charges. A great many of the new owners are relatively poor residents of the area. There are a few of these new owners like the two youthful Puerto Ricans who bought their parcel in December 1964. One said: "Since we got married we wanted to buy our own place. Finally our ship came in. We got a little money in the lottery—the Puerto Rican lottery—and decided that the time had come for us to own our place." Obviously, the number of lottery owners or their equivalent is rare. Much more common are case situations such as Number 579:

> Owner—Negro; age forty; an attendant at a VA Hospital. His parcel is assessed at $12,000. (Note that as shown in Exhibit 5–4 current sales of slum tenements cluster near 100 percent of assessment.) He paid $21,000, secured a first mortgage of $15,000 from a savings and loan and a second mortgage from the previous owner for $4,100. From an appraisal of the parcel in question, the advisability of the first mortgage is doubted, and certainly the second mortgage represents at least a 50 percent discount figure.

A somewhat similar transaction involves a forty-five-year-old Negro stretching machine operator who owns two parcels.

> In 1964 he purchased a parcel which was assessed at $10,000. It had been sold in 1961 for $13,000. He paid $13,500 subject to a $6,000 mortgage. Then the previous owner took back an $11,100 mortgage.

---

* Note that in Laurenti's study, *Property Values and Race* (Berkeley: University of California, 1960), p. 216, based on interviews in the San Francisco Bay area in 1955, most buying of second mortgages was done by individual investors as is the case in Newark. At the time of the study the usual figure for buying second mortgages was between 50 percent and 60 percent of the unpaid balance. The effect of unrealistic usury laws, in chasing out "legitimate" money and leaving a vacuum which only high cost money can fill, is obvious. The owner of slum tenements is isolated from reasonable capital markets by well-meaning but destructive social legislation. For a discussion of this point, see Harrell, Gordon M., "Mortgage Investments and the Usury Problem," *Cleveland-Marshall Law Review*, (May, 1961), p. 343, and Prathers, "Mortgage Loans and the Usury Laws," *The Business Lawyer*, (Nov., 1960). In the transactions involving mortgages, first and second mortgages combined form 91.5 percent, 88.0 percent, and 87.0 percent of the sales price in Areas 1, 2, and 3 respectively.

While the new owner "owns" his parcel for a nominal sum, the mortgage indebtedness is far over the probable cash market value of the entire parcel.

VA Mortgages

In some cases this overpayment feature is a function of discounts on VA mortgages. Case 478 is indicative of this approach:

> The purchaser is a forty-year-old Negro bartender with seven children. He bought the parcel in January 1964, which was assessed for $9,-600. He paid $18,500 for it from its previous owner who had bought it in 1944 for $5,000. A mortgage corporation gave an $18,400 mortgage based on a VA guarantee. The owner, who stated that he "looks at the purchase as a chance for advancement," figures that he paid $4,000 more than the house is worth. When asked if he would improve the property if given a long-term mortgage, he said, "I can't do anything with this house for at least five years until I pay down the mortgage."

A similar case involves a house sold in 1963 for $20,500 with the same mortgage company giving a $20,500 VA mortgage while the parcel was assessed at $13,300. The new owner is a Negro machine worker. Despite the overpayment, in this case the house is very well-maintained and substantial improvements have been made by the owner and his family.

These discrepancies between sales and assessments may be accounted for in part by normal variations in the relationship. Undoubtedly, however, they represent a tribute to the seller's capacity to secure financing. The buyer, in turn, is often enabled to buy an income-producing home which otherwise would have been out of reach.

While VA mortgage guarantees permit a much longer term of indenture than would be available otherwise, as well as less equity, the risks of overpayment leading to foreclosure are obvious.

> For example, in August 1952, a new owner bought a parcel in the 3B area. He paid $18,500 and was able to get a VA mortgage for $17,200. In December of 1952 he got a second mortgage from a heating company for a central heating plant for $1,729. In September of 1954 he got yet another small mortgage for $450 from a personal acquaintance. By December of 1954 there was a sheriff's sale of a parcel to the savings and loan which had originally written the first mortgage. In July of 1956 the deed reverted to the Administrator of Veterans Af-

fairs, and in December 1956, the parcel was sold for $10,500 by the
VA, with the latter taking back a $9,450 mortgage to a real estate
speculator who owns about forty other properties. The assessment was
$9,500.

It is apparent from interview 320 that the lack of financial sophistication
is not confined to Negroes.

The owner, a forty-two-year-old Italian handyman, bought a parcel
assessed at $10,900 in December 1963, paying $14,000 through a VA
guaranteed mortgage for a similar amount. The buyer did not have a
lawyer of his own present at the transaction, leaving the entire deal in
the hands of the mortgage company which arranged it. The owner
commented that he presently would like to borrow money to further
improve the parcel, but he is inhibited because the mortgage company "says I can't borrow money from anyone else."

Financing of Acquisition Costs
as an Inhibitor of Improvements

The effect of very heavy interest charges and mortgage payments, as well
as taxes, on potential improvements of slum tenements is all too clear. A
typical example would be the response of the owner of Parcel 590:

A white draftsman in his mid-thirties said, I paid too much for that
house in the first place. My only hope for getting my money back is
to hold on to the property, collect the rents, pay the mortgage, and
wait for property values to go up and/or for my equity to increase.
Under these circumstances I can't see my way clear to making any
substantial improvements.

A Puerto Rican factory worker stated the situation bluntly:

Until I pay off the mortgage, I cannot think of any major improvements. To buy this house took every penny I had. (Interview translated from Spanish.)

There is no question that the form of financing, particularly in the case
of small resident owners, has a great effect on the potential for rehabilitation of parcels owned by this category of landholder.

Refinancing at a Higher Level

The flattening out of resale prices prevents rolling over mortgages and thus
securing improvement money, unless the equity in the parcel has been in-

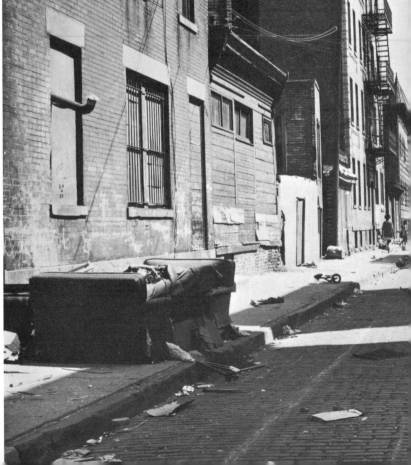

creased by years of amortization. Potential lenders are inhibited by the fear of being "locked into" a parcel on making a loan. The resale market is without question very weak. This is indicated by the most frequent answer to Question 15 of the personal interview—*Would you say that most owners of properties similar to* (address of parcel) *are looking for a return through rental or profit through sale?* The typical response was along the lines of— "It used to be for income, but now all they want to do is sell, but they can't because there are no buyers." In the course of the study a number of authentic cases of major hard-core owner-managers were discovered who were offered property without any cash downpayment, merely on the basis of their taking over existing mortgages. It should be noted that, at least in several cases, these "gifts" were refused. As will be shown later, the only real *cash* buyer of slum tenements is the public authority, either in the person of urban renewal or highway clearance.

Effect of Weak Resale Price

The significance of this relatively weak market (a market possessing very little in the way of capital gains potential; in which investment in a tenement may be completely inflexible, i.e. having no reasonable resale possibility) is hard to overestimate. Obviously, the type of professional trader who enters into this market is one who will demand very high rates of return in proportion to the risk and lack of flexibility of the investment. While slum tenement rent multipliers are low, the limited financing that is available for them contributes to the necessity of either high rent rolls and/or low maintenance expenditures. This is not to say that in the presence of more reasonable financing, landlords would necessarily prove to be maintenance conscious. (The question of how reversible the process is, is raised in a later chapter.) Slum properties in general are very highly leveraged. This is most true in the cases of new resident landlords. In these cases, with all the good will in the world, the cash flow on the property is frequently so thoroughly absorbed by the requirements of the initial financing as to preclude any reinvestment in improvements. *The weakness of the market encourages the sale of parcels to residents, facilitated either by government insured or purchase money mortgages. It increases the potential of massive transfer of slum ownership given facilitating legislation and a public desire to accomplish this end.*

THE TENEMENT LANDLORD

REFERENCES

1 Frank P. Zeidler, "Making Urban Renewal More Effective," cited in Schorr, *Slums* . . . , p. 93.
2 Grebler, *Housing Market* . . . , p. 80.
3 Sporn, *Economics* . . . , pp. 335, 336.
4 This loophole was largely closed in 1964.
5 Arthur Sporn, "Some Contributions of the Income Tax Law to the Growth and Prevalence of Slums," *Columbia Law Review*, (November, 1959), p. 1032.
6 See particularly, Walter J. Blum and A. Dunham, "Income Tax Law and Slums," *Columbia Law Review* (April, 1960).
7 See Commerce Clearing House, Inc., *Explanation 1964 Revenue Act*, pp. 71–72.
8 Rapkin, *Real Estate* . . . , p. 73.
9 Richard L. Nelson, *The Changing Composition of Capitalization Rates*, Monograph prepared from a speech by Mr. Nelson before the Southeastern Regional Conference of the Society of Real Estate Appraisers, May 1, 1964, Georgia State College.
10 On these points see Winnick, *Rental Housing*, chap. 5, and George Sternlieb, "Is Business Abandoning the Big City?" *Harvard Business Review*, (January, 1961).
11 An excellent introduction to this area is that of A. H. Schaaf, *Economic Aspects of Urban Renewal* (Berkeley: University of California, 1960).
12 William G. Grigsby, *The Residential Real Estate Market in an Area Undergoing Racial Transition* (unpublished doctoral dissertation, Columbia University, 1958), p. 96.
13 N. Y. S., *Prospects* . . . , p. 88.

Chapter 6

WHO OWNS THE SLUMS?
A PROFILE (I)
BASIC PARAMETERS

Introduction

In order to evaluate best the capacity of the various forms of governmental suasion in providing rehabilitation in slum areas, it is essential to know who owns the slums, why they own them, and what are the principal market factors which influence their behavior.

This chapter focuses on the characteristics of slum ownership and the form and concentration of holdings, with emphasis on the personal characteristics and attitudes of the slum owners themselves. The significance and salient characteristics of the single-parcel owner require a separate chapter. Following this, attention will be turned to the "whys" of purchase and the changes in these reasons over time. Then the presentation centers on the *who* and *why* of well-maintained and poorly-maintained tenements. The closing segments of this section analyze the ownership patterns of well-maintained parcels as against those of poorly-maintained parcels.

Form and Concentration of Holdings

The much-publicized popular concept of the "slum lord" relies on the supposition that there are a small number of individuals who own the bulk of slum tenements. While large owners are far from an insignificant proportion of total ownership, as the research presented here indicates, the degree of concentration is much overstated. This is far from unique to Newark. For example, in Grebler's study of ownership in New York's Lower East Side,[1] there is a strong indication that small holdings predominate. He states that, "If concentration is defined as a tendency for identical holders to own large numbers of parcels in the area, the records suggest that there is no widespread concentration of private ownership at the present time."

Similarly, in an earlier study done of ten thousand five hundred seventy-one land acquisitions from 1938 to 1941, under the 1937 U.S. Housing Act, fully a third of the parcels acquired in those "100 percent slum sites" were resident owned.[2] Over 40 percent of the Newark parcels, for which interviews were secured, are in the possession of landlords who own no other rental property. Less than a quarter are owned by landlords possessing over six parcels of this type.

There is a significant difference, as shown in Exhibit 6–1, between areas in the above categories. Area 1, for example, has the largest concentration of big-time owners by far. Even in this area, however, the comparatively small-time owners possess as many parcels as do the big-time operators. Areas 2B and 3B have far more resident owners than Areas 2A and 3A, which have similar housing characteristics but are largely nonwhite. Of the total sample, 42.8 percent have owners who own no other parcels, 21.6 percent own one or two more, 10.9 percent own more than three and up to six, 7.8 percent own more than six and up through twelve, and 15.8 percent are owned by those who are in possession of more than twelve parcels. In the course of more than three hundred individual interviews undertaken with landlords, there were at least six owners who owned more than forty parcels; two of this group owned approximately two hundred parcels.

Legal Forms of Ownership

The majority of tenements are held in individual form. Just under 20 percent are held by corporations, and a nearly equal number are held by partnerships of two or more individuals. (Notice that holdings by husband and wife are counted as individual.) The comparatively limited use of corporate holdings is undoubtedly largely a function of the fact that borrowing on parcels in the slums of Newark typically requires personal signatures. The corporate indemnity, therefore, is of no value.

EXHIBIT 6-1

I Assume You Own Other Rental Properties than the One at [Address]?

	AREA 1		AREA 2A		AREA 2B		AREA 3A		AREA 3B		TOTAL	
	Number	Per-cent	Number	Per-cent	Number	Per-cent	Number	Per-cent	Number	Per-cent	Number	Per-cent
No other	41	32.0	34	39.2	27	73.0	34	41.5	29	56.8	165	42.8
Other 1 or 2 more	32	25.0	27	31.0	4	10.8	14	17.1	6	11.8	83	21.6
3 to 6	16	12.5	8	9.2	—	—	16	19.5	2	3.9	42	10.9
7 to 12	13	10.2	7	8.0	3	8.1	4	4.9	3	5.9	30	7.8
Over 12	26	20.3	10	11.5	3	8.1	12	14.6	10	19.6	61	15.8
Used to own more than 2	—	—	1	1.1	—	—	—	—	—	—	1	0.3
Used to own another, but no more	—	—	—	—	—	—	2	2.4	1	2.0	3	0.8
Other	—	—	—	—	—	—	—	—	—	—	—	—
Total	128	100.0	87	100.0	37	100.0	82	100.0	51	100.0	385	100.0
NA/DK	—		4		—		3		—		7	

Area of Ownership

The typical slum owner concentrates his holdings in one city. (See Exhibit 6–2.) Only 8.3 percent have holdings in Newark and one or more of the other older New Jersey cities, while a trivial proportion own parcels in a wider geographical span. This geographical specialization was paralleled by the types of parcels owned.

Types of Parcels Owned

As shown in Exhibit 6–3, *the bulk of slum parcels are held by slum specialists.* Only 3.7 percent of the sample parcels are in the hands of owners who indicate that the bulk of their holdings are not slums; 6.3 percent indicate that there was a fifty-fifty range; 12 percent own largely slums with some others, while 33.9 percent indicate that all their holdings are of the same order. (Note that the last percentage excludes the 44.1 percent who own no other type of parcel.) *Owning slums, therefore, is a relatively specialized occupation. The investor in this type of property typically is not party to other areas of real estate investment.* Slum ownership is a distinct subset of real estate ownership in general with little crossing over into the broader area. Government programs which might appeal to the latter may have no effect on slum owners and vice versa.

Degree of Involvement with Slum Parcels

In Exhibit 6–4 is presented the response to the question: "Then you make (or don't make) your living from real estate holdings?" More than half of the parcels are owned by people to whom real estate represents a trivial supplement to income. Only 19.5 percent are in the possession of people who think of themselves as securing three-quarters or more of their income from real estate holdings. To a considerable degree this reflects the comparatively amateur kind of holder who predominates in the market. The significance of this factor from the viewpoint of securing rehabilitation should not be overlooked. Many of the owners interviewed in the course of this study are owners by default rather than by purpose; are owners by inheritance; or by lack of purchasers to buy unwanted properties; or by a relatively trivial investment which is not too meaningful in terms of overall capital or income. Shaking these owners loose from their lethargy and

EXHIBIT 6-2

AREA OF OWNERSHIP

	AREA 1		AREA 2A		AREA 2B		AREA 3A		AREA 3B		TOTAL	
	Number	Per cent	Number	Per cent	Number	Per cent	Number	Per cent	Number	Per cent	Number	Per cent
Owns no other	41	32.0	35	40.7	27	73.0	36	43.9	30	58.8	169	44.0
Newark solely	61	47.8	48	55.8	9	24.3	40	48.8	13	25.5	171	44.5
Newark plus other old N.J. central cities	19	14.8	2	2.3	1	2.7	3	3.7	7	13.7	32	8.3
Wider geographical spread	4	3.1	—	—	—	—	2	2.4	—	—	6	1.6
None Newark	3	2.3	1	1.2	—	—	1	1.2	1	2.0	6	1.6
Total	128	100.0	86	100.0	37	100.0	82	100.0	51	100.0	384	100.0
NA	—		4		—		3		—		7	
DK	—		1		—		—		—		1	

EXHIBIT 6–3

TYPE OF PARCEL OWNED

	AREA 1		AREA 2A		AREA 2B		AREA 3A		AREA 3B		TOTAL	
	Number	Per cent	Number	Per cent	Number	Per cent	Number	Per cent	Number	Per cent	Number	Per cent
Owns no other	41	32.3	35	39.8	27	73.0	36	43.9	30	61.3	169	44.1
All same (i.e. slums)	39	30.7	40	45.5	6	16.2	35	42.7	10	20.4	130	33.9
Great bulk slums—												
some other	24	18.9	9	10.2	1	2.7	5	6.1	7	14.3	46	12.0
50—50	17	13.4	3	3.4	1	2.7	2	2.4	1	2.0	24	6.3
Bulk not slum	6	4.7	1	1.1	2	5.4	4	4.9	1	2.0	14	3.7
Not usable	—	—	—	—	—	—	—	—	—	—	—	—
Total	127	100.0	88	100.0	37	100.0	82	100.0	49	100.0	383	100.0
NA	1		2		—		2		1		6	
DK	—		1		—		1		1		3	

EXHIBIT 6-4

THEN YOU MAKE (OR DON'T MAKE) YOUR LIVING FROM REAL ESTATE HOLDINGS?

	AREA 1		AREA 2A		AREA 2B		AREA 3A		AREA 3B		TOTAL	
	Number	Per cent	Number	Per cent	Number	Per cent	Number	Per cent	Number	Per cent	Number	Per cent
Full-time real estate owner ($\frac{3}{4}$ income or more)	28	22.0	11	12.4	6	16.2	16	19.8	14	27.5	75	19.5
Substantial ($\frac{1}{3}$ to $\frac{3}{4}$)	32	25.2	11	12.4	3	8.1	14	17.3	6	11.8	66	17.1
Minor supplement	57	45.0	58	65.1	21	56.8	39	48.1	21	41.1	196	50.9
No income, self sustaining	5	3.9	7	7.9	5	13.5	7	8.6	4	7.8	28	7.3
Claims loss on operation	5	3.9	2	2.2	2	5.4	5	6.2	6	11.8	20	5.2
Total	127	100.0	89	100.0	37	100.0	81	100.0	51	100.0	385	100.0
NA	—		1		—		4		—		5	
DK	1		1		—		—		—		2	

making them aware of possible governmental programs for aiding rehabilitation is perhaps much more difficult than doing the equivalent for the full-time real estate owner. The latter may well be a "hard case," but since he derives his living from real estate there may well be less inertia to overcome. *Programs may more easily be explained and more easily sold to the professional than to the amateur.*

There are a significant number of small holders who depend on rental income substantially (Exhibit 6–5). Not infrequently these are elderly, retired, or disabled individuals with no capacity for investment either in cash or sweat. In the face of a weak market their policy tends to be one of conservatism to the point of immobility.

Occupation of Slum Owners

What are the occupations of slum tenement owners? The wide diversity of response is indicated in Exhibit 6–6. The largest single occupational classification is nonhouse-oriented craftsmen. (There are two categories of craftsmen in the table.) Real estate brokers and real estate managers together are second in importance, owning some eighty-two out of the three hundred eighty-nine parcels for which this information was secured. Lawyers, who are often thought of as major investors in slum real estate, are much less important than might have been anticipated. Only twenty of the parcels were owned by this occupational category.

There is a substantial variation between areas of owner categories. In Area 1, for example, real estate brokers and managers owned more than a quarter of the parcels. Interestingly enough, the same formidable disproportionment is indicated for Area 3B. The professional owners are most significant in the "worst" and perhaps the "best" of the subsets. As shown in Exhibit 6–7, the large-scale owners are largely professional real estate people with lawyers and housecraft-oriented businessmen trailing behind.

There is a wide diversity of occupations among those people who own only a single parcel. The largest proportion are nonhouse-oriented craftsmen, while a substantial number, 16.9 percent, are retired. No other occupational category contains as much as 9 percent of the total group.

Age of Owner

There is little variation in age of owner by area (Exhibit 6–8). In the absolute, however, there are a substantial number of elderly owners. More than

EXHIBIT 6-5

You Make (Or Don't Make) Your Living from Real Estate Holdings?

| | Size of Holdings | | | | | | | | | | | | | | | |
| | NA/DK | | Other | | Over 12 | | 7–12 | | 4–6 | | 2–3 | | 1 | | Total | |
	Number	Per cent	Number	Per cent	Number	Per cent	Number	Per cent	Number	Per cent	Number	Per cent	Number	Per cent	Number	Per cent
Full-time real estate owner (¾ or more) income from real estate	1	25.0	—		41	68.3	13	41.9	8	18.6	7	8.4	5	3.0	75	19.5
Substantial (⅓ to ¾) income from real estate	—		—		12	20.0	8	25.8	18	41.9	8	9.6	20	12.2	66	17.1
Minor supplement to income	3	75.0	—		7	11.7	9	29.0	14	32.5	53	64.0	110	67.1	196	50.9
No income, self sustaining	—		—		—		—		3	7.0	8	9.6	17	10.4	28	7.3
Claims loss on operation	—		—		—		1	3.3	—		7	8.4	12	7.3	20	5.2
NA	—		—		1		—		—		—		4		5	
DK	—		—		—		—		—		1		1		2	
Sub-N	4		—		61		31		43		84		169		392	
Live sample	4		0		60		31		43		83		164		385	

EXHIBIT 6-6

OCCUPATION

	AREA 1		AREA 2A		AREA 2B		AREA 3A		AREA 3B		TOTAL	
	Number	Per-cent	Number	Per-cent	Number	Per-cent	Number	Per-cent	Number	Per-cent	Number	Per-cent
Housewife	5	3.9	6	6.8	3	8.1	2	2.4	1	2.0	17	4.4
Lawyer	4	3.1	10	11.4	1	2.7	4	4.7	1	2.0	20	5.1
Real estate broker	23	18.0	5	5.7	2	5.4	7	8.2	8	15.7	45	11.6
Real estate manager	12	9.4	5	5.7	5	13.5	9	10.6	6	11.8	37	9.5
House-oriented craftsman	6	4.7	1	1.1	3	8.1	1	1.2	3	5.9	14	3.6
Craftsman, other	24	18.7	28	31.7	11	29.8	27	31.8	18	35.2	108	27.7
Other professions and managerial	8	6.3	10	11.4	5	13.5	7	8.2	3	5.9	33	8.5
Retired	16	12.5	13	14.8	3	8.1	13	15.3	4	7.8	49	12.6
NA—Interviewer's observation, unskilled	1	0.8	2	2.3	2	5.4	7	8.2	—	—	12	3.1
Small businessman	15	11.7	6	6.8	1	2.7	4	4.7	5	9.8	31	8.0
Housecraft businessman	11	8.6	2	2.3	—	—	4	4.7	2	3.9	19	4.9
Big businessman	3	2.3	—	—	1	2.7	—	—	—	—	4	1.0
Total	128	100.0	88	100.0	37	100.0	85	100.0	51	100.0	389	100.0
NA	—		3		—		—		—		3	

half of the owners are over fifty; and a quarter of them are more than sixty. (The significance of this age factor, which is in part a function of the ethnic distribution of ownership, will be discussed more fully in a later chapter.) Only 15 percent of all the sample parcels are owned by people under the age of forty. *The typical parcel, therefore, is owned by people of late middle-age.* Certainly one of the inhibitors of investment in the uncertainties of rehabilitation must be accepted as the age of the owner.

Residents

As might be surmised by the prevalence of single-parcel owners, 36.6 percent of the parcels in the sample areas are lived in by their owners. An additional 10.2 percent of the parcels are owned by people who live within the study areas, but not within the specific parcel sampled. Fully 35 percent of all parcels are owned by people who live outside of Newark, though within a twenty-mile radius. A relatively trivial proportion live outside this radius. (While this proportion may be somewhat understated by the difficulties of contacting absentee landlords who live at considerable distances from the city, as Appendix I on Methodology indicates, the understatement is not significant.)

Area 1, with its many multi-parcel owners, has the smallest proportion of resident owners. (See Exhibit 6–9.) There is a substantial difference between the A categories and the B categories in Areas 2 and 3, respectively. In both B categories more than half of the parcels are lived in by their owners, while in the A equivalents the proportion is under 40 percent.

In Exhibit 6–10 the same data is analyzed by size of parcel holdings. Few of the major holders live within either the study area or, for that matter, Newark itself. Nearly 90 percent of them live outside Newark. The proportion within this category descends as the size of holdings decreases. The vast bulk of the owners of single parcels live in the house which they own. Typically, those who do not, formerly did.

Race

Exhibit 6–11 details parcel ownership by area and by race. More than a third of the three hundred eighty-six parcels for which data was secured on this point are owned by Negroes. There is considerable variation from Area to Area in this regard. Area 1, for example, has only 27.3 percent of its

EXHIBIT 6–7

Occupation By Size of Holding

Size of Holdings

	NA/DK		Over 12		7–12		4–6		2–3		1		Total	
	Num-ber	Per-cent	Num-ber	Per-cent	Num-ber	Per-cent	Num-ber	Per-cent	Num-ber	Per-cent	Num-ber	Per-cent	Num-ber	Per-cent
Housewife	—	—	—	—	—	—	2	4.8	6	7.1	9	5.4	17	4.4
Lawyer	1	25.0	6	9.8	—	—	9	21.4	4	4.8	1	0.6	20	5.1
Real estate broker	1	25.0	24	39.4	13	40.6	4	9.5	1	1.2	2	1.2	45	11.6
Real estate manager	—	—	17	27.9	4	12.5	5	11.9	2	2.4	8	4.8	37	9.5
House-oriented craftsman	—	—	—	—	1	3.1	1	2.4	3	3.6	9	5.4	14	3.6
Craftsman, other	—	—	—	—	4	12.5	4	9.5	24	28.5	76	45.9	108	27.7
Other professions and managerial	1	25.0	2	3.3	2	6.3	6	14.3	8	9.5	14	8.4	33	8.5
Retired	1	25.0	—	—	1	3.1	4	9.5	15	17.9	28	16.9	49	12.6
NA—Interviewer's observation, unskilled	—	—	1	1.6	2	6.3	—	—	3	3.6	6	3.6	12	3.1
Small businessman	—	—	2	3.3	1	3.1	6	14.3	13	15.4	9	5.4	31	8.0
Housecraft businessman	—	—	6	9.8	3	9.4	1	2.4	5	6.0	4	2.4	19	4.9
Big businessman	—	—	3	4.9	1	3.1	—	—	—	—	—	—	4	1.0
NA	—	—	—	—	—	—	—	—	—	—	3	—	3	—
Sub-N	4		61		32		42		84		169		392	
Live sample	4		61		32		42		84		166		389	

EXHIBIT 6-8
AGE OF OWNER

	AREA 1		AREA 2A		AREA 2B		AREA 3A		AREA 3B		TOTAL	
	Num-ber	Per-cent	Num-ber	Per-cent	Num-ber	Per-cent	Num-ber	Per-cent	Num-ber	Per-cent	Num-ber	Per-cent
Minor	—	—	—	—	—	—	—	—	—	—	—	—
21 to 30	2	1.6	2	2.3	1	2.7	1	1.3	1	2.0	7	1.9
31 to 40	17	13.5	11	12.5	6	16.2	8	10.5	8	15.7	50	13.2
41 to 50	30	23.8	25	28.4	9	24.3	25	32.9	16	31.4	105	27.8
51 to 60	43	34.1	26	29.5	13	35.1	18	23.7	17	33.3	117	30.9
61 to 70	25	19.8	18	20.4	8	21.6	15	19.7	4	7.8	70	18.5
Over 70	9	7.1	6	6.8	—	—	9	11.8	5	9.8	29	7.7
Total	126	100.0	88	100.0	37	100.0	76	100.0	51	100.0	378	100.0
NA	—		—		—		—		—		—	
DK	2		3		—		9		—		14	

EXHIBIT 6-9
RESIDENCE OF OWNER

	AREA 1		AREA 2A		AREA 2B		AREA 3A		AREA 3B		TOTAL	
	Num-ber	Per-cent	Num-ber	Per-cent	Num-ber	Per-cent	Num-ber	Per-cent	Num-ber	Per-cent	Num-ber	Per-cent
Same house	31	24.2	32	37.2	20	55.6	29	35.4	28	54.9	140	36.6
Within study area	13	10.2	10	11.6	1	2.8	12	14.6	3	5.9	39	10.2
Balance Newark	20	15.6	13	15.1	6	16.7	16	19.5	1	1.9	56	14.6
Within 20-mile radius Newark	63	49.2	27	31.4	7	19.4	22	26.9	15	29.4	134	35.0
Balance New Jersey	1	0.9	—	—	2	5.5	1	1.2	3	5.9	7	1.8
New York City	—	—	3	3.5	—	—	—	—	—	—	3	0.8
Elsewhere	—	—	1	1.2	—	—	2	2.4	1	1.9	4	1.0
Total	128	100.0	86	100.0	36	100.0	82	100.0	51	100.0	383	100.0
NA	—		2		—		3		—		5	
DK	—		3		1		—		—		4	

EXHIBIT 6-10

RESIDENCE OF OWNER

	Size of Holdings															
	NA/DK		Other		Over 12		7–12		4–6		2–3		1		Total	
	Number	Per-cent	Number	Per-cent	Number	Per-cent	Number	Per-cent	Number	Per-cent	Number	Per-cent	Number	Per-cent	Number	Per-cent
Same house	1	33.3	—	—	—	—	—	—	4	9.8	18	21.4	117	70.5	140	36.6
Within study area	—	—	—	—	1	1.7	4	13.3	8	19.5	21	25.0	5	3.0	39	10.2
Balance Newark	1	33.3	—	—	5	8.5	7	23.3	9	22.0	19	22.6	15	9.0	56	14.6
Within 20-mile radius Newark	1	33.3	—	—	53	89.8	14	46.7	15	36.5	25	29.8	26	15.7	134	35.0
Balance New Jersey	—	—	—	—	—	—	4	13.3	2	4.9	—	—	1	0.6	7	1.8
New York City	—	—	—	—	—	—	1	3.4	2	4.9	—	—	—	—	3	0.8
Elsewhere	—	—	—	—	—	—	—	—	1	2.4	1	1.2	2	1.2	4	1.0
NA	—	—	—	—	2	—	—	—	2	—	—	—	1	—	5	—
DK	1	—	—	—	—	—	1	—	—	—	—	—	2	—	4	—
Sub-N	4		—		61		31		43		84		169		392	
Live sample	3		0		59		30		41		84		166		383	

EXHIBIT 6-11
Landlord Ethnicity by Area

	AREA 1		AREA 2A		AREA 2B		AREA 3A		AREA 3B		TOTAL	
	Number	Percent	Number	Percent	Number	Percent	Number	Percent	Number	Percent	Number	Percent
Negro	35	27.3	35	38.5	17	48.6	32	39.5	10	19.6	129	33.4
Puerto Rican	2	1.6	—	—	—	—	1	1.2	2	3.9	5	1.3
Other white	91	71.1	56	61.5	18	51.4	48	59.3	39	76.5	252	65.3
Total	128	100.0	91	100.0	35	100.0	81	100.0	51	100.0	386	100.0
NA/DK	—		—		2		4		—		6	

EXHIBIT 6-12
Landlord Ethnicity by Size of Holding

Size of Holdings

	NA/DK		Other		Over 12		7–12		4–6		2–3		1		Total	
	Number	Percent	Number	Percent	Number	Percent	Number	Percent	Number	Percent	Number	Percent	Number	Percent	Number	Percent
Negro	1	25.0	—	—	—	—	1	3.4	9	21.4	32	38.1	86	51.4	129	33.4
Puerto Rican, Cuban	—	—	—	—	—	—	—	—	—	—	1	1.2	4	3.0	5	1.3
Other white	3	75.0	—	—	60	100.0	28	66.6	33	78.6	51	60.7	77	45.6	252	65.3
NA/DK	—	—	—	—	1	—	2	—	1	—	—	—	2	—	6	—
Sub-N	4		—		61		31		43		84		169		392	
Live sample	4		0		60		29		42		84		167		386	

parcels owned by this group. Area 2A, by contrast, has 38.5 percent, and Area 2B is highest of all with 48.6 percent, while Area 3B is lowest with 19.6 percent. The reasons for this skewed distribution are obviously complex; however, there is considerable evidence to indicate that Negroes are no longer buying parcels in Area 1. Area 2B, which at the time of the 1960 census was largely a white area, is in the process of a very fast transition, while Area 3B is still substantially closed to Negro buyers.

As can be seen in Exhibit 6–12, there are no Negroes in the largest size holding category. Of the one hundred twenty-nine parcels owned by Negroes in the sample that were analyzable in this detail, only one is owned by an individual having six to twelve parcels, nine are owned by holders of three to six parcels, with nearly a quarter in the hands of owners of two or three parcels while the bulk of Negro owners own single parcels.

It will be helpful to examine more closely the various categories of landlords as a function of size of holdings.

The Big-Time Professional

Of the parcels whose owners were interviewed, 15.8 percent were held by owners of more than twelve properties. Who are these people? Typically they are white middle-aged businessmen, representing the earlier immigrant strains in Newark, substantially Jewish and Italian who now live in the upper middle-class suburbs which surround the city. The major proportion are professional real estate people. Their modular age is in the fifty-to-sixty bracket. With a few exceptions, the bulk of their holdings are in slum properties either in Newark or in other Northern New Jersey cities. They are essentially slum specialists. As such, they can afford an infra-structure which would be too costly for lesser holders. This refers to the fact that typically they employ full-time repair and maintenance people. Their parcels receive at least a minimal degree of maintenance. At the same time, however, they rarely own the best-maintained of parcels. Most of them have been in the rental real estate business for more than fifteen years, and as such they are seasoned operators, wary of doing more than is absolutely required in maintaining parcels.

Perhaps because of the skewed distribution of their holdings, with an oversized proportion being in Area 1 which is suffering most with vacancy rates, they answered the question: "Has the vacancy rate changed in the past several years in the general area of [Address]?" with the greatest degree of affirmation. (See Exhibits 4–12 and 4–13.) They are much less impressed by the problems of tax rates and reassessments than are smaller holders. Their major single complaint is the quality of the tenantry.

A frequent response to the question of "What source would you turn to if you needed financing?" among this category of owners was "personal resources." By and large, it is, as would be expected, a sophisticated group. Selling a rehabilitation program to owners in this category, assuming that it promised a high enough return, would probably be easiest of all of the landlord categories.

The Part-Time but Still Significant Holder

The owners of six to twelve parcels are a much more diverse group—13.3 percent of them live within the study area and 23.3 percent live in the balance of Newark. A little less than half of this category of landholders are not real estate brokers or managers by profession. There is a wide diversity of professions with craftsmen, housecraft-oriented businessmen, and, surprisingly enough, unskilled workers being the chief categories. When the question was asked: "Why did you buy the property at [address]? the answers of this group largely revolved around rental return, though 12.9 percent had inherited their holdings. It is this group, as will be shown in Chapter 8, which shows the greatest degree of disillusionment on the potential profitability of slum holdings. Typically they cannot afford the full-time services of repairmen which larger holders can secure. Only 25.8 percent of this category of holders give full time to rental properties. While a few holders in this category do the bulk of their own repair work and maintain their parcels uncommonly-well, they are exceptions.

How does this category of owners get started? There is no single answer. Perhaps a couple of brief profiles will define the general nature of the ambient. One landlord said:

> My husband was in the installment business and he decided, at the suggestion of a friend, to purchase some rental properties instead of expanding his business. We bought our first parcel about five years ago.

The couple now owns nine parcels with a total of forty-five apartments.

The function of tenement realty as an annuity for old age was probably the most common response. For example, a sixty-six-year old attorney pointed to the fact that he started buying properties some ten years before with the idea that ultimately, once he had paid off his mortgages, he would be able to subsist on the cash flow derived from the parcels in question. Another owner, a seventy-four-year old retired bricklayer, owns twelve parcels, most of them in Area 1. He said:

> I started out figuring on a small addition to my income while I was working, but now I have money and I am retired. I used to be a bricklayer. I saved my money. I invested in these properties. Now, besides my pension and my social security, I get a good income.

It is this category of owners who might be most difficult to move in any pattern which requires substantial reinvestment in parcels as long as the cash flow from their holdings provides a basic supplement in their income. *As long as the cash flow is satisfactory, there is little capacity or will to reinvest.*

The Impersonality of the Larger-Scale Owner

It is obvious that the substantial owner of slum real estate is not in business for altruistic purposes. The really active owner may buy and sell parcels at a considerable rate. As such, the individual parcel may have little meaning for him. It becomes an impersonal element in his business life, having no relationship to the fact that people live in it. For example, one of the major owners interviewed in the course of this study secured a parcel in Area 1 as part of a package deal involving six parcels. He told the interviewer:

> As soon as I bought the parcel; and I bought it as part of a package; I looked around to try to get rid of it. It was in lousy condition, and simply wasn't worthwhile keeping. It took me the better part of four years to sell the parcel in question. . . . It wasn't worth my while to improve the parcel since I planned on selling it.

In this particular case the parcel, for three or four years, just consistently degenerated.

At least on a number of occasions in the course of the interviewing, the phenomenon was found that the owner of record knew very little, if anything, about the parcel to which he held title. Case 48 is an example. This parcel in Area 1 is owned by a group of four. The owner of record is a prosperous lawyer. He is not sure of the number of units in the tenement since another one of the partners acts as manager. *There is an obvious gap between ownership and feeling of responsibility.*

A similar condition exists in the case of a forty-five-year old clerk at the county court who owns three parcels. She purchased them on her sister's recommendation—her sister being a professional real estate person. She has never seen two of the three parcels which she has owned for five years.

This degree of noninvolvement is often accentuated by the geographical gap between the living place of the owner and the parcel. Perhaps the most poorly-maintained parcel in the sample is in Area 3A. It is a parcel which can best be described in the words of our field surveyor: ". . . surrounded by garbage, stairs rotting, property in terrible shape." The owner, an engineer, inherited the property. He lives in another state; has an income level in the $11,000 to $20,000 bracket; and states his attitude towards the parcel very clearly: "I want to sell it; I'm not afraid of being reassessed because I'm not going to make any improvements." When asked what improvements he would make if he were sure of not getting a boost in taxes, he replied, "None, the parcel isn't worth it." The inheritance factor noted in the above case should not be underestimated as a source of poor maintenance. The recipient frequently has no involvement in the real estate business, no knowledge of proper maintenance procedures, and basically just tries to get out from under the parcel. Given a weak market, however, this may be a very lengthy process. For example:

> Mr. X and his sister inherited a parcel in Area 3A from their father, which at one time had been the family residence. Mr. X has no interest in the building other than to keep it standing until the city buys it for scheduled urban renewal project. He says he makes minor repairs to conform with building and health regulations, but he will not make major improvements. He complained bitterly that someone took out the copper pipes from a vacant apartment and that he had light bulbs taken from the hall. Also, fixtures and electric wires were tapped by the tenants for the tenants' personal use, etc. He finds the whole deal "a pain" and he just wants to get out.

Apparently, it is this type of owner, who has the least will to take advantage of any proposed self-help programs by the government for landlords.

In this uninvolved landlord subset should be incorporated the significant number of parcel owners who hold commercial facilities, typically street-floor stores. The owners of these parcels generally think of their resident tenants as being unpleasant incumbrances at best. Though, in general, the parcels receive reasonable maintenance, the landlords typically express no interest in significant rehabilitation of the residential parts of the parcels in question.

REFERENCES

1 Grebler, *Housing Market* . . . , p. 104.
2 National Housing Agency, *Who Owns the Slums? Where Does Money Spent for Slum Property Go?* (National Housing Bulletin 6, March, 1946) pp. 2–4.

Chapter 7

WHO OWNS THE SLUMS? (II)
THE SINGLE-PARCEL OWNER

THE single-parcel tenement owner's characteristics are quite distinct from those of larger holders. As was seen in Exhibit 6–10, the great bulk of single-parcel owners are residents. Who are these people? Eighty-nine of the one hundred thirty-nine for whom there is data are Negroes. Fifty are white. As was indicated earlier, few of the Negroes who are owners of parcels within the sample are multiple-parcel owners. In this analysis of Negro owners, they will be equated with Negro resident owners. Exhibits 7–1 and 7–2 give some feeling for the accession rate of Negro owners. Notice that this is increasing fastest outside of Area 1. While this is perhaps to be expected considering the low base of Negro ownership outside that area, it is Area 1 that has the highest proportion of relatively new white-owner titles. (Exhibit 7–3.) To restate: *The new Negro buyer is avoiding the old hard-core area. In his absence, it is the large holder who is the new purchaser. Negro buyers are leaving the hard core to the big time professional, preferring better areas for home ownership.*

While the overall age of single-parcel owners is younger than the equivalent for all owners, there is a substantial dichotomy in age distribution by race. In Exhibit 7–4 the ages of resident owners are given by race. More than half of all the white resident owners are over sixty; this contrasts with the equivalent data for Negro owners of less than one quarter. The average age of the Negro group is forty-nine and six-tenths years; for whites it is over fifty-eight years. The data indicates that the typical white resident-owner is relatively elderly; from other cross tabulations it can be seen that

EXHIBIT 7–1

DATE OF TITLE

NEGRO OWNERS AS PERCENT OF TOTAL

	AREA 1	AREA 2A	AREA 2B	AREA 3A	AREA 3B	TOTAL
Up to but not includ- ing 2 years old	15.4	40.0	50.0	20.0	36.4	28.6
2–4 years old	20.0	7.1	50.0	35.0	15.4	24.7
5–6 years old	35.3	37.5	66.7	33.3	12.5	33.3
7–10 years old	28.6	25.0	27.3	29.4	12.5	26.3
11–15 years old	27.3	52.0	0.0	50.0	20.0	32.9
16–20 years old	14.3	26.3	25.0	23.5	0.0	17.3
Over 20 years old	8.3	13.8	0.0	15.2	0.0	9.2
Total	18.8	28.6	27.8	27.2	12.2	22.6

he represents the earlier immigrant groups who settled and have since largely out-migrated from Newark. Given this data, combined with the cumulative percent by race of date of title which indicates increasing vigor of purchase by resident Negroes as against resident whites, the dynamics of the situation are clear-cut. *As white resident owners die out, they will in all probability be replaced, not by equivalent white single-parcel resident owners, but either by Negro residents or by white major real estate holders. A deciding role in this decision will be played by government legislation— or its absence.*

Why do Negroes buy tenements? The most consistent single answer is for the purpose of a home:

> . . . We couldn't find a nice place for the children. . . . We couldn't af- ford a one-family house. . . . We were raised in the neighborhood and we knew the people. . . . I bought the property because I wanted a comfortable place to live. . . . I thought it would be easier to pay off the mortgage if I could rent. . . . I tried to get into a white neighbor- hood but no one would sell to me. . . .

A forty-eight-year old Negro iron molder said:

> I always wanted to own a home. One time I started to buy one but I just couldn't get the money up. My younger brother started me when he got a home before I did. I got tired of paying rent, so I figure for a few more dollars I would own a home. I live right down the street . . . , so when I found out that this home was for sale I got it. I couldn't af-

EXHIBIT 7-2

DATE OF TITLE, CUMULATIVE PERCENT

	AREA 1		AREA 2A		AREA 2B		AREA 3A		AREA 3B		TOTAL	
	White	Negro	White	Negro	White	Negro	White	Negro	White	Negro	White	Negro
Up to 2 years old	15.5	11.4	10.0	16.7	10.3	26.7	9.6	6.5	9.7	40.0	11.5	15.7
2–4 years old	26.8	22.9	24.4	19.4	23.1	60.0	25.3	29.0	25.0	60.0	24.8	30.7
5–6 years old	34.5	40.0	30.0	27.8	25.6	73.3	27.7	32.3	34.7	70.0	30.7	40.9
7–10 years old	48.6	62.9	43.3	38.9	46.2	93.3	42.2	48.4	44.4	80.0	44.3	57.5
11–15 years old	59.9	80.0	56.7	75.0	56.4	93.3	50.6	71.0	55.6	100.0	57.3	79.5
16–20 years old	76.8	91.4	72.2	88.9	64.1	100.0	66.3	83.9	73.6	100.0	72.7	90.6
Over 20 years old	100.0	100.0	100.0	100.0	100.0	100.0	100.0	100.0	100.0	100.0	100.0	100.0

EXHIBIT 7-3

DATE OF TITLE, NUMBER

	AREA 1		AREA 2A		AREA 2B		AREA 3A		AREA 3B		TOTAL	
	White	Negro	White	Negro	White	Negro	White	Negro	White	Negro	White	Negro
Up to 2 years old	22	4	9	6	4	4	8	2	7	4	50	20
2–4 years old	16	4	13	1	5	5	13	7	11	2	58	19
5–6 years old	11	6	5	3	1	2	2	1	7	1	26	13
7–10 years old	20	8	12	4	8	3	12	5	7	1	59	21
11–15 years old	16	6	12	13	4	—	7	7	8	2	57	28
16–20 years old	24	4	14	5	3	1	13	4	13	—	67	14
Over 20 years old	33	3	25	4	14	—	28	5	19	—	119	12
Total	142	35	90	36	39	15	83	31	72	10	436	127
No Data Available	—	—	—	—	—	—	—	—	—	—	—	3

EXHIBIT 7–4

RESIDENT OWNERS' AGE BY RACE

	NEGRO		WHITE	
AGE	Number	Percent	Number	Percent
21–30	—	—	1	2.0
31–40	15	16.9	4	8.0
41–50	39	43.8	11	22.0
51–60	16	18.0	8	16.0
61–70	17	19.1	13	26.0
70 plus	2	2.2	13	26.0
Total	89	100.0	50	100.0
NA/DK	—		2	
Approximate average age	49.6 years		58.4 years	

ford to own a one-family home. Some day I will be able to build me a home out somewhere, but I will live here until it is built.

In summation, these answers are not very different from the response that would probably be secured from an equivalent group of low-income whites. In a number of cases the resident Negro owners had very large families and had experienced considerable difficulties in finding landlords who would rent them appropriate facilities. In most cases, the rental income from the tenement made it possible for relatively poor families to purchase property which otherwise would be out of the question.

Overpayment Factor—Financing

In this area, as in many others, the poor pay more. Largely, this overpayment factor is a function of financing. An iron molder paid $16,000 for his four-family tenement. He was able to secure a $15,900 first mortgage through a mortgage company. The assessment on the parcel is $8,400, and a cash sale value of the parcel is probably no more than $12,000. The situation is similar in the case of one parcel in another hard-core area with an assessment of $7,000. The parcel was purchased by its present Negro owner in 1960 for $12,500 from a major holder; the previous owner took back a first mortgage of $10,000 and a second mortgage for $1,500. There is an obvious inflationary element in this type of low-cash transaction.

Overpayment Factor—Anti-Negro Prejudice

Aside from this price discrimination on the basis of credit facilities, is there price discrimination in terms of Negroes purchasing homes? This is a question which has been debated in a number of areas. Rapkin in his study of group relations in Newark, stated:

> There appear to be two housing markets—one for whites and another for Negroes. When a Negro acquires a dwelling in a white neighborhood, he is usually required to pay a price higher than that which existed prior to his entry. Thus, in an area in which dwellings previously sold for $20,000 on the average, a Negro will pay between $22,000 and $24,000. On the other hand, should the dwelling in the same area be sold to a white purchaser, the price would most likely be $16,000 to $17,000.[1]

Is this true of areas in which substantial immigration of Negroes is an accepted fact? Exhibit 7–5 undertakes to show Negro versus white purchases by year by purchase price as a percentage of 1964 assessment. At best, this kind of data can serve only as a rough guide. The vagaries of assessments as well as loaded prices for financing are obviously major variables. In addition, the white purchaser is increasingly a professional looking for bargains. The Negro buyer, on the other hand, is usually an amateur looking for a home. The difference in will to buy is clear. Given these stipulations, however, *there is remarkably little difference in the ratios which are shown by area for white purchases and for equivalent purchases by Negroes in recent years.*

The very substantial proportion of Negroes in Newark may mean that the battle for exclusion is no longer being fought through the price mechanism. Indeed, some of the strongest statements against new Negro buyers were made by some of their more fortunate peers. This statement from a thirty-five-year old owner and occupant of a substantial rooming house in Area 2A is fairly typical:

> Negroes have ruined the property on [Name] Avenue. We are just not ready! My family were the first Negroes on this block; there were nice lawns, etc., and the property was well kept. Now those who try to keep yards nice are fighting a losing battle with the children and grownups.

Newark then, at least in the bulk of its tenement areas, may be at a much later stage of progression than are other older American cities where the

EXHIBIT 7-5

COMPARISON OF MEDIANS

ASSESSED VALUE 1964 TO SALES BY YEAR BY AREA

NEGRO VS. WHITE

	AREA 1 Medians		AREA 2A Medians		AREA 2B Medians		AREA 3A Medians		AREA 3B Medians	
	Negro	White	Negro	White	Negro	White	Negro	White	Negro	White
1945	—	2.156	—	22.063	—	—	—	1.911	—	2.458
1946	—	1.980	—	2.057	—	—	—	1.318	—	1.466
1947	1.695	1.580	—	1.075	—	—	—	1.320	—	1.130
1948	1.033	1.247	—	1.418	—	1.482	—	1.472	—	1.115
1949	—	1.925	1.054	—	—	—	—	—	—	—
1950	1.105	1.362	—	—	—	—	—	.098	—	1.214
1951	1.025	1.370	2.013	.863	—	—	1.136	1.460	—	1.540
1952	.998	1.997	—	.979	—	—	—	—	—	—
1953	—	.640	—	1.339	—	.911	—	.800	—	.982
1954	—	—	—	1.200	—	—	—	1.200	—	.748
1955	.752	1.520	.870	1.650	—	—	—	1.281	—	—
1956	.930	1.285	—	—	—	—	—	1.154	—	1.155
1957	1.011	1.276	—	1.062	—	.963	—	.681	—	—
1958	—	1.102	—	1.260	—	.970	—	.952	2.280	—
1959	1.106	1.011	1.461	—	—	—	—	1.260	—	.944
1960	.683	.904	—	.942	—	—	—	—	—	.700
1961	1.012	.887	—	.793	.787	—	—	.806	—	.751
1962	.829	1.022	—	—	—	—	.700	.722	—	—
1963	1.389	.895	—	1.317	—	—	—	1.060	—	.842
1964	.869	1.244	—	—	—	—	—	.694	—	.929
1965	—	—	—	—	—	—	—	.651	—	—

ownership segregation battle is still hard fought. It may provide an insight into the future of those cities.

The Aged Owner

Even if purchases by Negro owners, largely for their own homes, provide a new, more youthful ownership group for slum tenements, there still remains a very substantial number of aged owners. The factor of age of owner as an inhibitor of improvement is quite clear. In the heart of Area 1 a resident owner, when asked about improvements, replied:

> "I am eighty-four and I'm not interested in making any improvements; I just want a comfortable place to live in." Although the building with its eight cold-water flats is in reasonably good condition, Mr. X was the first to point out that possibly a younger man might want to make some improvements and conceivably would "make out" if he did so.

A significant modular type of white resident owner is the widow, typically of immigrant stock, who remains in an area that has largely changed in character. Case 9 is representative of this:

> Mrs. X, of Italian parentage, lives in one parcel in Area 1 and owns another several streets away. The former she has lived in since 1923; the latter was purchased fifteen years ago for income. Both her home and the rental parcel have cold-water flats. Her expenses are largely taken care of by her son who lives with her. When asked what source she would turn to if she needed money to make improvements she said, "I am seventy-one-years old and the bank or the home finance company would never lend me money."

Taxes are her number-one problem. This is not, however, in terms of reassessment, but rather in terms of their increased level, in contrast to the relatively static or degenerating rent roll.

> A similar case was that of an elderly spinster of seventy-four who was living on social security. She inherited the three-unit tenement in Area 3B, in which she presently lives, from her father who, in turn, had owned it since the 1920's. She likes the area because it is quiet and most of the people are elderly Italians, similar to herself. While the housekeeping of the parcel itself is immaculate, it has no central heat and is in need of a major overhaul.

The absolute age of a tenement owner does not necessarily preclude improvement. In the course of this study many exceptions were found. The typical case, however, is one of "end game" with the owner basically trying to reduce any commitment to the parcel, either financial or in terms of personal effort. Where there are problems of racial transition the attitude is reinforced. This was expressed vividly by a seventy-seven-year old widow of Italian extraction who said, "I just want to sell and get out." The parcel in question used to be the residence of the owner, but now it is very poorly-maintained and the owner obviously has just lost all interest in it.

The problems of the aged owner are obviously not confined to whites alone. In the case of Negroes, they are often compounded by obvious poverty.

> For example, Parcel 143 in Area 1 is owned by a sixty-one-year old Negro woman in poor physical condition. The three-family parcel needs extensive exterior repairs. The interior, however, is maintained in a very clean condition. There is no central heat; Mrs. X, the owner, bought it in 1953 as a place to live. Her sister lives upstairs and when working pays $10 rent per week. When the third floor is rented, she gets $50 per month. It has been vacant for three months. The income from the parcel is the owner's only income. She keeps a couple of boarders in her own apartment. She is not on welfare; her sister and grandchildren help her pay expenses and she does babysitting once in a while. When asked what source she would turn to if she needed money to make improvements on the property, she replied, "The bank, but if I have to make improvements I would have to move out because I can't afford to pay for them." In response to our question on income, she indicated an income level of under $3,000 and said, "Gee, I could just live wonderfully on $3,000 and really could do much for the place."

As will be noted in the chapters on the potential of financing and tax aid, the response of the elderly to either of these stimuli ran along the lines of this answer of a seventy-year-old Negro owner presently retired and living in a parcel which is in very poor condition: "I'm too old to worry about money now. I am retired and cannot afford to pay a lot of taxes and interest on money."

The Poverty Stricken Owner

Poverty is not a monopoly of aged owners. The owning of real estate particularly by Negroes is not always a function of their having regular jobs. A number of the Negro owners basically are unemployed. As such, they have little means and less initiative with which to repair their homes. It is for this reason perhaps that taxes rank very high in their thinking. Given a limited income from parcel ownership, the pinch of taxes is most acute. For some of the poorer owners, their homes, even though initial financing may have been repaid, serve as collateral for borrowing from loan companies and a variety of high interest sources.

> For example, Case 555, a Negro woman in her middle sixties who has never had a permanent job, has owned her present residence, a three-family house, since 1943. She lives in one apartment and the proceeds from the other two apartments are her only resources. Within the last five to ten years there have been two mortgages taken out on the parcel from different sources. Her original mortgage was paid off, but the house is now heavily encumbered. "I have always borrowed from loan companies; I wish I hadn't because they sure ride you."

This lack of cash flow, either from work or from the parcel ownership itself, is often a function of the inflated financing. The case of one of the few Puerto Rican owners interviewed in this study is indicative of the point. The parcel was purchased by its present occupant in November, 1963, and was assessed in 1964 at $4,400. The owner paid $15,000 and got a $14,400 mortgage from the seller, a mortgage company. The sale pattern of the parcel indicates something of the nature of the present owner's problem. In 1953 the parcel was sold for $3,500; in 1961 there was a nominal transfer to another individual who in turn sold it again through the form of a nominal transfer to the mortgage company. The present owner, Mr. X, is a forty-year-old factory worker whose reasons for purchasing the property were:

> I figured that it was cheaper than paying rent. I have been trying to better myself and my family. This way I make a little extra money. I have this apartment house for a little over a year. I do not like to have debts. It is like an ax hanging over your head, so it bothers me to owe so much money on the house and it's going to be a long time before I am able to pay it off.

When asked about taxes, he said:

> You know I don't understand too much about taxes. I make monthly payments to the bank and that includes everything. They have the brain to figure everything out.

When asked about improvements he said:

> At present I'm not planning to make any. I don't have the money and I don't want to borrow more. (This interview was translated from Spanish.)

The problems of age, the problems of poverty and the problems of "gyp" repair companies feasting on the ignorance of new landowners—all are obvious inhibitors of efforts at rehabilitation within the present context of efforts in that regard. The vacuum of government policy in aiding the single-parcel slum owner is all too evident.

REFERENCES

1 Rapkin, *Group Relations* . . . , p. 38.

Chapter 8

WHO OWNS THE SLUMS? (III)

Reasons for Purchase and Attitudes Toward Rehabilitation

WHY did the owners of parcels within the sample area acquire them? In Exhibit 8–1 are presented the answers to this question. There is a wide variation from area to area. In Area 1, for example, "home" and "home plus income" equals only 21.8 percent of the response. It is closely followed in this regard by Area 2A with 37.4 percent response. In the other areas the responses are close to the 50 percent mark. The responses grouped under the heading of speculation (all answers indicating hope for profit through resale) are few in number. While undoubtedly there is a ritualistic inhibition about a positive response to this question, it is indicative of the relative weakness of the resale market.

Inheritance

More than 11 percent of the parcels in the sample were secured through inheritance. The importance of this factor should not be underestimated. Frequently, the owner by inheritance has little information and less interest in his parcel than the owner by deliberate purchase. As has been noted, some of the poorest maintained parcels were secured by this means.

Foreclosures

In Exhibit 8–2 the responses are analyzed by size of landlord holdings. Observe that mortgage foreclosures as a source of acquisition by major owners is a frequent tribute to high purchase money mortgages extended by them.

EXHIBIT 8-1
WHY DID YOU BUY THE PROPERTY AT [ADDRESS]?

	AREA 1		AREA 2A		AREA 2B		AREA 3A		AREA 3B		TOTAL	
	Number	Per-cent	Number	Per-cent	Number	Per-cent	Number	Per-cent	Number	Per-cent	Number	Per-cent
Home	14	10.9	22	24.2	11	29.7	24	28.9	20	40.0	91	23.4
Rental return	77	60.1	35	38.4	11	29.7	34	41.0	14	28.0	171	43.9
Speculation	1	0.8	1	1.1	—	—	1	1.2	1	2.0	4	1.0
Inheritance	13	10.2	10	11.0	4	10.8	10	12.0	6	12.0	43	11.1
Debt	—	—	—	—	—	—	—	—	—	—	—	—
Commercial purpose	7	5.5	6	6.6	1	2.7	1	1.2	4	8.0	19	4.9
Home plus income	14	10.9	12	13.2	8	21.7	12	14.5	3	6.0	49	12.6
Other	2	1.6	2	2.2	—	—	—	—	—	—	4	1.0
Mortgage foreclosure	—	—	3	3.3	2	5.4	1	1.2	2	4.0	8	2.1
Total	128	100.0	91	100.0	37	100.0	83	100.0	50	100.0	389	100.0
NA/DK	—		—		—		2		1		3	

EXHIBIT 8-2

WHY DID YOU BUY THE PROPERTY AT [ADDRESS]?

| | Size of Holdings | | | | | | | | | | | | | | | |
| | NA/DK | | Other | | Over 12 | | 7–12 | | 4–6 | | 2–3 | | 1 | | Total | |
	Number	Per-cent	Number	Per-cent	Number	Per-cent	Number	Per-cent	Number	Per-cent	Number	Per-cent	Number	Per-cent	Number	Per-cent
Home	2	50.0	—	—	—	—	—	—	—	—	9	10.7	80	48.3	91	23.4
Rental return (investment)	2	50.0	—	—	56	91.8	21	67.7	32	74.4	40	47.6	20	12.0	171	43.9
Speculation	—	—	—	—	—	—	2	6.5	1	2.3	1	1.2	—	—	4	1.0
Inheritance	—	—	—	—	1	1.6	4	12.9	5	11.6	13	15.5	20	12.0	43	11.1
Debt	—		—		—		—		—		—		—		—	
Commercial purpose	—	—	—	—	—	—	1	3.2	2	4.7	9	10.7	7	4.2	19	4.9
Home plus income	—	—	—	—	—	—	1	3.2	3	7.0	11	13.1	34	20.5	49	12.6
Other	—	—	—	—	—	—	—	—	—	—	1	1.2	3	1.8	4	1.0
Mortgage foreclosure	—	—	—	—	4	6.6	2	6.5	—	—	—	—	2	1.2	8	2.1
NA/DK	—	—	—	—	—	—	—	—	—	—	—	—	3	—	3	—
Sub-N	4		—		61		31		43		84		169		392	
Live sample	4		0		61		31		43		84		166		389	

Rental vs. Resale

In a later stage of the interview (question 15), the subject of goals was returned to with the question rephrased: "Would you say that most owners of properties similar to [Address] are looking for return through rental or profit through sales?" Again the bulk of the response to this projective question revolved around rentals. In Area 1 and in Area 2A, however, a substantial group of responses centered around profit from resale either mainly or exclusively. (See Exhibits 8–3 and 8–4 on pages 156–157.) When the owners were asked the following question directly, "Would you differ with this opinion?" the same general pattern was indicated. In addition, a substantial number of owners, particularly in Areas 1 and 2, said in effect, "I'd love to sell, but there are no buyers. I'm locked in and it's going to have to be rental." (For present attitudes of parcel owners, see Exhibits 8–5 and 8–6 on pages 158–159.)

Changes in Attitude

In gauging landlords' morale, it is interesting to follow the changes, if any, from acquisition motives to present attitudes. Exhibits 8–7 and 8–8 present the responses by area and size of holding, respectively, to the question: "Is this still your reason(s) for keeping property?" Notice that the "want to sell" responses are broken down into several subsets. Even if the number of owners who have not listed their parcels currently with a broker is discounted, the picture does not speak well of market vigor. Exhibit 8–9 presents a matrix showing the shifts from original goal to present attitude. The problem of reducing the pessimism indicated by these exhibits to the point of inducing investment for rehabilitation is evident—its cure not at all clear. Chapters 10, 11, and 12 will consider this question more fully.

Effect of Area on Landlords' Willingness to Improve

The point was repeatedly made that it was essential not to improve a parcel beyond the value of limitations implicit in the area itself. In a number of cases when owners were asked, "What source would you turn to if you needed money to make improvements on your property?" they replied, "To the bank, but a bank wouldn't make a loan in our area." The attitude of the

EXHIBIT 8-3

WOULD YOU SAY THAT MOST OWNERS OF PROPERTIES SIMILAR TO [ADDRESS] ARE LOOKING FOR RETURN THROUGH RENTAL OR PROFIT THROUGH SALES?

	AREA 1		AREA 2A		AREA 2B		AREA 3A		AREA 3B		TOTAL	
	Number	Per-cent	Number	Per-cent	Number	Per-cent	Number	Per-cent	Number	Per-cent	Number	Per-cent
Rental (exclusively)	55	49.1	33	42.9	21	60.0	41	64.1	26	57.8	176	52.9
Profit from resale (rental mainly)	7	6.3	6	7.8	—	—	3	4.7	4	8.9	20	6.0
Fifty-fifty	12	10.7	6	7.8	6	17.1	3	4.7	7	15.6	34	10.2
Profit from resale (mainly)	14	12.5	16	20.8	2	5.7	8	12.5	3	6.7	43	12.9
Profit from resale (exclusively)	12	10.7	7	9.1	1	2.9	2	3.1	1	2.2	23	6.9
Other	12	10.7	9	11.7	5	14.3	7	10.9	4	8.9	37	11.1
Total	112	100.0	77	100.0	35	100.0	64	100.0	45	100.0	333	100.0
NA	1		3		—		1		2		7	
DK	15		11		2		20		4		52	

EXHIBIT 8-4

WOULD YOU SAY THAT MOST OWNERS OF PROPERTIES SIMILAR TO [ADDRESS] ARE LOOKING FOR RETURN THROUGH RENTAL OR PROFIT THROUGH SALES?

| | Size of Holdings | | | | | | | | | | | | | | | |
| | NA/DK | | Other | | Over 12 | | 7–12 | | 4–6 | | 2–3 | | 1 | | Total | |
	Num-ber	Per-cent	Num-ber	Per-cent	Num-ber	Per-cent	Num-ber	Per-cent	Num-ber	Per-cent	Num-ber	Per-cent	Num-ber	Per-cent	Num-ber	Per-cent
Rental (exclusively)	1	33.3	—	—	39	66.1	19	65.5	20	50.0	35	50.7	62	46.7	176	52.9
Profit from resale (rental mainly)	1	33.3	—	—	1	1.7	—	—	4	10.0	6	8.7	8	6.0	20	6.0
Fifty-fifty	—	—	—	—	5	8.5	—	—	1	2.5	8	11.6	20	15.0	34	10.2
Profit from resale (mainly)	—	—	—	—	9	15.2	5	17.2	8	20.0	10	14.6	11	8.3	43	12.9
Profit from resale (exclusively)	—	—	—	—	3	5.1	2	6.9	7	17.5	5	7.2	6	4.5	23	6.9
Other	1	33.3	—	—	2	3.4	3	10.4	—	—	5	7.2	26	19.5	37	11.1
NA	—	—	—	—	—	—	—	—	—	—	—	—	7	—	7	—
DK	1	—	—	—	2	—	2	—	3	—	15	—	29	—	52	—
Sub-N	4		—		61		31		43		84		169		392	
Live sample	3		0		59		29		40		69		133		333	

EXHIBIT 8-5

WOULD YOU DIFFER WITH THIS OPINION?

	AREA 1		AREA 2A		AREA 2B		AREA 3A		AREA 3B		TOTAL	
	Num- ber	Per- cent	Num- ber	Per- cent	Num- ber	Per- cent	Num- ber	Per- cent	Num- ber	Per- cent	Num- ber	Per- cent
Rental (exclusively)	60	48.3	43	49.4	21	60.0	47	61.0	31	60.8	202	53.9
Profit from resale (rental mainly)	8	6.5	7	8.0	2	5.7	4	5.2	7	13.7	28	7.5
Fifty-fifty	13	10.5	2	2.3	1	2.9	4	5.2	—	—	20	5.3
Profit from resale (mainly)	10	8.1	10	11.5	2	5.7	3	3.9	1	2.0	26	7.0
Profit from resale (exclusively)	16	12.9	7	8.0	1	2.9	6	7.8	2	3.9	32	8.6
Waiting for U. R.	2	1.6	—	—	—	—	1	1.3	—	—	3	0.8
Rental and place to live	5	4.0	4	4.6	1	2.9	—	—	—	—	10	2.7
Other	10	8.1	14	16.1	7	20.0	12	15.6	10	19.6	53	14.2
Total	124	100.0	87	100.0	35	100.0	77	100.0	51	100.0	374	100.0
NA/DK	4		4		2		8		—		18	

EXHIBIT 8-6

WOULD YOU SAY THAT MOST OWNERS OF PROPERTIES SIMILAR TO [ADDRESS] ARE LOOKING FOR RETURN THROUGH RENTAL OR PROFIT THROUGH SALES? WOULD YOU DIFFER WITH THIS OPINION?

| | Size of Holdings | | | | | | | | | | | | | | | |
| | NA/DK | | Other | | Over 12 | | 7–12 | | 4–6 | | 2–3 | | 1 | | Total | |
	Num-ber	Per-cent	Num-ber	Per-cent	Num-ber	Per-cent	Num-ber	Per-cent	Num-ber	Per-cent	Num-ber	Per-cent	Num-ber	Per-cent	Num-ber	Per-cent
Rental (exclusively)	1	25.0	—	—	39	65.0	12	38.6	25	58.1	48	60.0	77	49.3	202	53.9
Profit from resale (rental mainly)	1	25.0	—	—	3	5.0	3	9.7	6	14.0	3	3.8	12	7.7	28	7.5
Fifty-fifty	—	—	—	—	6	10.0	3	9.7	3	7.0	4	5.0	4	2.6	20	5.3
Profit from resale (mainly)	—	—	—	—	6	10.0	2	6.5	4	9.3	7	8.7	7	4.5	26	7.0
Profit from resale (exclusively)	—	—	—	—	4	6.7	9	29.0	4	9.3	6	7.5	9	5.8	32	8.6
Waiting for U. R.	—	—	—	—	—	—	2	6.5	—	—	—	—	1	0.6	3	0.8
Rental and place to live	—	—	—	—	—	—	—	—	—	—	2	2.5	8	5.1	10	2.7
Other	2	50.0	—	—	2	3.3	—	—	1	2.3	10	12.5	38	24.4	53	14.2
NA/DK	—	—	—	—	1	—	—	—	—	—	4	—	13	—	18	—
Sub-N	4		—		61		31		43		84		169		392	
Live sample	4		0		60		31		43		80		156		374	

EXHIBIT 8-7

Is This Still Your Reason(s) for Keeping Property?

	AREA 1		AREA 2A		AREA 2B		AREA 3A		AREA 3B		TOTAL	
	Num-ber	Per-cent	Num-ber	Per-cent	Num-ber	Per-cent	Num-ber	Per-cent	Num-ber	Per-cent	Num-ber	Per-cent
Yes	76	59.4	58	66.0	28	77.8	44	54.3	41	80.4	247	64.3
Want to sell—no broker	21	16.4	13	14.8	2	5.6	11	13.6	2	3.9	49	12.8
Want to sell—listed with broker	8	6.3	4	4.5	2	5.6	11	13.6	2	3.9	27	7.0
Want to sell—no buyers	3	2.3	—	—	—	—	1	1.2	1	2.0	5	1.3
Want to sell—no use, no buyers	6	4.7	4	4.5	—	—	4	4.9	1	2.0	15	3.9
Income	9	7.0	5	5.7	2	5.6	5	6.2	2	3.9	23	6.0
Income plus cap. apprec.	—	—	—	—	2	5.6	—	—	—	—	2	0.5
Waiting for U. R.	5	4.0	4	4.5	—	—	5	6.2	2	3.9	16	4.2
Total	128	100.0	88	100.0	36	100.0	81	100.0	51	100.0	384	100.0
NA/DK	—		3		1		4		—		8	

EXHIBIT 8-8

IS THIS STILL YOUR REASON(S) FOR KEEPING PROPERTY?

	Size of Holdings															
	NA/DK		Other		Over 12		7–12		4–6		2–3		1		Total	
	Number	Per-cent	Number	Per-cent	Number	Per-cent	Number	Per-cent	Number	Per-cent	Number	Per-cent	Number	Per-cent	Number	Per-cent
Yes	2	50.0	—	—	41	68.2	8	27.7	26	61.9	52	64.3	118	70.2	247	64.3
Want to sell—not listed with broker	1	25.0	—	—	10	16.7	7	24.2	5	11.9	9	11.1	17	10.1	49	12.8
Want to sell—listed with broker	—		—		3	5.0	3	10.3	4	9.5	5	6.2	12	7.1	27	7.0
Want to sell—no buyers	—		—		1	1.7	1	3.4	1	2.4	1	1.2	1	0.6	5	1.3
Want to sell—no use, no buyers	—		—		4	6.7	4	13.8	—	—	4	4.9	3	1.8	15	3.9
Income	1	25.0	—		—		1	3.4	5	11.9	7	8.6	9	5.4	23	6.0
Income plus cap. apprec.	—		—		—		—		—		—		2	1.2	2	0.5
Waiting for U. R.	—		—		1	1.7	5	17.2	1	2.4	3	3.7	6	3.6	16	4.2
NA/DK	—		—		1	—	2	—	1	—	3	—	1	—	8	—
Sub-N	4		—		61		31		43		84		169		392	
Live sample	4		0		60		29		42		81		168		384	

EXHIBIT 8-9

CHANGES IN LANDLORD ATTITUDES

Why Did You Buy The Property at [Address]?		Are These Still Your Reasons For Keeping It?								
	Yes	Want to Sell, No Broker	Want to Sell, Listed w/Broker	Want to Sell, No Buyers	Want to Sell, No Use, No Buyers	Income	Income Plus Cap. Apprec.	Waiting for Urban Renewal	Total	NA/DK
Home	66	6	6	—	1	10	—	2	91	1
Rental return (investment)	115	25	10	3	8	—	—	7	168	4
Speculation	1	1	—	—	—	1	—	—	3	1
Inheritance	16	5	4	1	3	9	—	5	43	—
Debt	—	—	—	—	—	—	—	—	—	—
Commercial purpose	11	4	1	—	1	1	—	1	19	—
Home plus income	37	4	3	—	—	2	—	1	47	2
Other	3	1	—	—	—	—	—	—	4	—
Mortgage fore-closure	—	2	2	1	2	—	—	—	7	1
Total	249	48	26	5	15	23	—	16	382	9
NA/DK	—	1	—	—	—	—	—	—	1	—

professional landlord towards improving in bad areas was typified by an owner of more than one hundred parcels in Newark. In the past year he has put central heating into twelve parcels, some of which are in Area 3. When asked about holdings in Areas 1 and 2 he said, "I won't touch them!"

This attitude was far from confined to major holders. For example, the son of a ninety-one-year old Italian owner clearly indicated the importance of area in determining the advisability of putting in improvements when he said, "We wouldn't do a thing in this area for we couldn't get our money back, but if we were in a better area, I would probably put on at least new aluminum siding. It pays."

The man in question, a sheet-metal worker, indicated the only reason that the parcel has not been sold is that his father still views it as their original home. After the father's death, it was indicated that the parcel would be sold. Prior to that time, however, certainly no repairs are to be expected regardless of any governmental inputs. While the bulk of these unsolicited comments were evoked in interviews concerning parcels in Area 1, they were consistently espoused, as will be shown in the later chapters on financing and tax impact, by owners in Areas 2 and 3.

The defeatism of landlords who own parcels in hard-core slum areas is exemplified by an interview with an absentee owner of a parcel in Area 1. Though aware of FHA Title I financing, he said: "There is no financing in an area as bad as the one I'm in." When questioned about the effect of building and health inspectors, he said, "They make me improve the parcel and I'll never get my money back."

While from a societal point of view this approach can be disparaged and the question raised as to whether the landlord has responsibilities to his tenants as well as to his profit statements, but from a realistic point of view the lack of positive behavior implicit in this attitude must be accepted by the worker for rehabilitation. *With the bulk of Newark now open to depressed socio-economic groups for housing, the hard-core areas are centers for individuals who cannot afford or would not be permitted into desirable housing.* The major part of landlord complaints centers on this facet. Complaints about the character of the population moving into the hard-core areas are not confined to white owners alone. For example, a resident owner in Area 1, a Negro drill press operator, said, "It's getting so that you can't walk the streets safely." While the statement may be exaggerated, it was voiced so frequently in one form or another that it cannot be ignored.

The Effect of Urban Renewal

As Exhibit 8–10 indicates, the bulk of the respondents were reasonably sure that if their property were taken for urban renewal, they would be able to get back the investment made by making improvements. There were, however, substantial variations by area, in part reflective of variations in size of land holdings. Less than 30 percent of the parcels are held by owners who thought that in case of urban renewal, they would not get appropriately reimbursed upon urban renewal landtaking. Exhibit 8–11 analyzes the response by the number of parcels owned. *Plainly, it is the large owners who have the greatest degree of faith in the equitable settlements involved in the program, while contrarily the small owners exhibit the least degree of equanimity at the prospect.*

Reasons for Fear

What reason do owners who feel that they will not be treated properly have for this attitude? Of the eighty-seven negative respondents, ten referred specifically to the time lag between urban renewal announcement and actual landtaking. One of the major landowners put it this way:

> They come around and start doing their survey, and before you know it, tenants are scared and move out. Then the property goes to hell and you're left without income for three years before they make a settlement.

This type of worry was frequently stated by some of the small storekeepers in areas threatened by renewal. For example, Mrs. X, a middle-aged Negro woman, has two small grocery stores in an area that has been largely cleared for urban renewal. She finds that not only has the number of her customers diminished, but also that there has been such a long lag between the announcement of urban renewal and actual landtaking, that she has lost a number of her tenants without being able to replace them with others because of fear of ultimate landtaking. She said: "I won't do a thing with my parcels until I know which way the city is going."

Again and again, the small landowners expressed this ignorance of the basic urban renewal program and its actual limitation in Newark. This was voiced most eloquently by a Mr. Y, an eighty-two-year old handy man for a hotel:

EXHIBIT 8-10

IF YOUR PROPERTY IS TAKEN FOR URBAN RENEWAL, WILL YOU BE ABLE TO GET BACK THE INVESTMENT YOU MADE BY MAKING IMPROVEMENTS?

	AREA 1		AREA 2A		AREA 2B		AREA 3A		AREA 3B		TOTAL	
	Number	Per-cent	Number	Per-cent	Number	Per-cent	Number	Per-cent	Number	Per-cent	Number	Per-cent
Yes	65	57.0	41	53.9	9	34.6	33	47.1	21	51.2	169	51.8
Yes—but	6	5.3	7	9.2	2	7.7	14	20.0	6	14.6	35	10.7
Maybe	14	12.3	12	15.8	2	7.7	6	8.6	2	4.9	36	11.0
Probably not	6	5.3	6	7.9	4	15.4	3	4.3	5	12.2	24	7.3
Definitely not	23	20.2	8	10.5	8	30.8	13	18.6	7	17.1	59	18.0
Doesn't care— wants out	—	—	2	2.6	1	3.8	1	1.4	—	—	4	1.2
Total	114	100.0	76	100.0	26	100.0	70	100.0	41	100.0	327	100.0
NA	3		3		2		4		1		13	
DK	11		12		9		11		9		52	

EXHIBIT 8-11

If Your Property is Taken for Urban Renewal, Will You be Able to Get Back the Investment You Made by Making Improvements?

| | Size of Holdings | | | | | | | | | | | | | | | |
| | NA/DK | | Other | | Over 12 | | 7–12 | | 4–6 | | 2–3 | | 1 | | Total | |
	Number	Per-cent	Number	Per-cent	Number	Per-cent	Number	Per-cent	Number	Per-cent	Number	Per-cent	Number	Per-cent	Number	Per-cent
Yes	1	33.3	—	—	37	69.8	20	77.0	15	38.5	41	56.2	55	41.4	169	51.8
Yes—but	—	—	—	—	4	7.5	2	7.7	10	25.6	1	1.4	18	13.5	35	10.7
Maybe	1	33.3	—	—	3	5.7	—	—	6	15.4	12	16.4	14	10.5	36	11.0
Probably not	—	—	—	—	1	1.9	2	7.7	—	—	7	9.6	14	10.5	24	7.3
Definitely not	1	33.3	—	—	8	15.1	1	3.8	8	20.5	12	16.4	29	21.8	59	18.0
Doesn't care—wants out	—	—	—	—	—	—	1	3.8	—	—	—	—	3	2.3	4	1.2
NA	—	—	—	—	6	—	3	—	1	—	2	—	1	—	13	—
DK	1	—	—	—	2	—	2	—	3	—	9	—	35	—	52	—
Sub—N	4		—		61		31		43		84		169		392	
Live sample	3		0		53		26		39		73		133		327	

> They say they are going to take it (his one parcel in Area 2A) for the
> new highway, but they don't, and still they want me to fix it up. It's
> worrying me sick. I wish they would tell me what they're doing . . . the
> property ain't much good and I don't see no sense in spending money
> on it just to have it torn down. You can't charge people a big rent
> unless you give them something for it, and there ain't no sense in
> spending money on the place if they are going to tear it down.

The ignorance of the details of urban renewal revealed in some of the
responses to the question is sometimes a little startling. For example, a number of owners said, "If I don't get an adequate return from urban renewal I
won't sell."

It is the small owners particularly from whom this kind of response came:

> I don't think we will get it (a fair settlement on urban renewal land-
> taking) and I doubt it because my bargaining position is against that
> of the city. In addition, I don't think I could adequately prove the cost
> of my improvement especially in regard to labor costs because I did a
> lot of it myself.

This type of attitude was expressed not infrequently even by those people who were sure that on urban renewal landtaking they would get fair
awards. For example, in Area 1, the owner of a parcel in the heart of the
core slum area, with a reasonably successful fish market on the first floor and
four cold-water flats above, was asked whether he would improve the parcel if he were sure of not getting a boost in taxes. The response was:

> Since I am in an urban renewal area, I just won't do anything major;
> only necessary improvements. If there wasn't urban renewal coming,
> I think I would probably re-side the house. It sure needs it, and I'd
> put in central heating. It seems to improve the quality of the tenancy.

Interestingly enough, this particular parcel is not in an area which is presently slated for urban renewal.

Ignorance of Urban Renewal Scheduling

There is no question that some of the people who responded to the question about improvements by pointing to urban renewal as precluding them
were obviously taking the easy way out. It should not be assumed, however,
that this is true of all of them. The political exigencies in Newark, as in a

good many other cities, make for sweeping announcements of urban renewal development that precede their actuality, frequently by many years. There is a great degree of ignorance on just which areas are scheduled for urban renewal, and if so, when. This is complicated by the fear, on the part particularly of small landowners, of anything smacking of politics; a fear of the small man against the administrative monster. In general, however, there is a substantial degree of faith that urban renewal landtaking is equitable in its ultimate payments.

As related earlier, a substantial number of the major landowners look to urban renewal as the only means of cashing in their investments. It is interesting, however (Exhibit 8–12), that less than a quarter of all the parcels in the sample area were in defined renewal areas (identified by the address book of the Newark Renewal Authority as of the time of the interviews) while only 56.7 percent of the respondents were definitely sure they were not in urban renewal areas (Exhibit 8–13).

The responses of owners of parcels which are scheduled for urban renewal are tabulated in Exhibit 8–14. The wide range of answers indicates the need for better communication. While the difficulties in securing developers and of doing long-range planning in the face of a relatively weak demand market in Newark are obvious, the urban renewal program in the city obviously requires some clarification. In addition, there seems to be some possibility of misinformation derived from other landtaking programs.

> A case in point is the response of the owner of a parcel in Area 3B, an elderly retired Italian who owns two other parcels and lives in the parcel under investigation. When asked whether he would get back his investments in making improvements on land taken for urban renewal, he replied: "The state is going to build a highway and a representative from the state said I would lose 75 percent of any money spent for additional improvements."

There are substantial areas of Newark which cry out for urban renewal. The need for the program is unquestionable. There is an equal necessity, however, to clarify its timing and impact, particularly among smaller holders. The weakness of the Newark real estate market and a concomitant shortage of developers has required an opportunistic approach by authorities. This has led to further inhibition of landlord action.

In the midst of these general negative elements there is no consistency of upkeep by landlord. Which factors can be isolated as making for "good" or "bad" landlords?

EXHIBIT 8-12

PARCELS OFFICIALLY IN RENEWAL AREA

	AREA 1		AREA 2A		AREA 2B		AREA 3A		AREA 3B		TOTAL	
	Number	Per cent	Number	Per cent	Number	Per cent	Number	Per cent	Number	Per cent	Number	Per cent
In renewal area	37	19.9	42	32.8	—	—	49	42.6	4	4.8	132	23.3
Not in renewal area	149	80.1	86	67.2	54	100.0	66	57.4	79	95.2	434	76.7
Total	186	100.0	128	100.0	54	100.0	115	100.0	83	100.0	566	100.0

EXHIBIT 8-13

AREA SCHEDULED FOR URBAN RENEWAL?

	AREA 1		AREA 2A		AREA 2B		AREA 3A		AREA 3B		TOTAL	
	Number	Per cent	Number	Per cent	Number	Per cent	Number	Per cent	Number	Per cent	Number	Per cent
No	52	51.0	33	47.1	23	85.2	35	57.4	22	71.0	165	56.7
Yes, within 1 year	6	5.9	1	1.4	1	3.7	2	3.3	—	—	10	3.4
Yes, 1 to 5 years	14	13.7	10	14.3	1	3.7	10	16.4	3	9.7	38	13.1
Yes, 6 to 10 years	1	1.0	4	5.7	1	3.7	2	3.3	2	6.5	10	3.4
Yes, long term	18	17.6	13	18.6	—	—	7	11.5	3	9.7	41	14.1
Not sure	6	5.9	5	7.1	1	3.7	4	6.6	—	—	16	5.5
Other	5	4.9	4	5.7	—	—	1	1.6	1	3.2	11	3.8
Total	102	100.0	70	100.0	27	100.0	61	100.0	31	100.0	291	100.0
NA/DK	26		21		10		24		20		101	

EXHIBIT 8-14

PARCELS WHICH ARE IN AN URBAN RENEWAL AREA—ARE YOU
IN AN AREA SCHEDULED FOR URBAN RENEWAL?

	AREA 1		AREA 2		AREA 3		TOTAL	
	Num-ber	Per-cent	Num-ber	Per-cent	Num-ber	Per-cent	Num-ber	Per-cent
No	4	18.2	6	24.0	10	34.5	20	26.3
Yes, within 1 year	1	4.5	1	4.0	2	6.9	4	5.3
Yes, 1 to 5 years	9	40.9	4	16.0	8	27.6	21	27.6
Yes, 6 to 10 years	—	—	3	12.0	2	6.9	5	6.6
Yes, long term	5	22.7	10	40.0	6	20.7	21	27.6
Not sure	1	4.5	—	—	1	3.4	2	2.6
Other	2	9.1	1	4.0	—	—	3	3.9
Total	22	100.0	25	100.0	29	100.0	76	100.0
NA/DK	5		5		10		20	

Chapter 9

WHO OWNS THE SLUMS? (IV)
THE "BAD" AND "GOOD" OWNERS

THE characteristics of owners of exceptionally "bad" and exceptionally "good" parcels are considered in this chapter. Are there some pertinent generalizations that can be made here which have significance for rehabilitation efforts? From this question, the discussion turns briefly to the problems and potential of code enforcement.

The Owners of Dilapidated Parcels

Who owns the *really* dilapidated parcels? Why are they kept in this condition? What future, if any, is anticipated for these dilapidated parcels by the owner?

There is obviously no single answer to any one of these questions. Let us take one case study, for example, in the hard-core area. It is a six-family stucco house in very poor condition. The fire escapes are of dubious workability and porches are dilapidated and leaning to one side. The field surveyor's report reads "stucco patched with tar, whole building leans, woodtrim rotted. Back yard resembles garbage dump." The four-room apartments each rent for $40 per month; however, the house, which has no central heat, is half empty. The parcel was purchased in 1948 for $2,500; it is presently assessed at $7,900 with its original mortgage paid off and is now free and clear.

The parcel is owned by a moving contractor, who also owns another half-dozen parcels, most of which are in somewhat better condition, but all of which are in slum areas of Newark. The owner would like to sell it, but he claims that he cannot. He doesn't have it listed with a broker because "I wouldn't get anything back for it." His feeling is that the only way he can sell it is by taking back close to a 100 percent mortgage. While the rents are nominally collected monthly, he frequently has to go twice a week to collect from most of his tenants. He admitted that the vacancy rate in the parcel has gone up substantially in the last several years.

When asked whether the building could be made more profitable by fixing it up, he said:

> I would have to spend too much money to fix the parcel up and it takes too long to get the investment back. People don't pay rents so I have to evict them. I also have the problem of skips. This area is very bad and that keeps people away. Also, the tenants want central heat and have better properties for the same price.

When asked what improvements he would make if he could be sure of not getting a boost in taxes, the owner recited a long list of potential improvements, including central heat, hot water, new paint, etc., but then ended by saying, ". . . actually I would like to get financing to knock down the parcel and rebuild it." When asked if the resale market was such that he could get back the money invested in improvements, he said that he thought so, ". . . but I will have to take back a big mortgage and I don't want to do it."

When asked if he could get an improved rent roll, he said:

> No, I can get an increase in rent, but not enough to get an adequate return on the investment. I just improve to make parcels rentable. We leave them alone and they become vacant overnight and vandalized. So I just improve enough to keep it from being vacant.

The owner stated that he would have to pay 35 percent to 40 percent annual cost (by this the owner meant interest plus amortization) in order to secure a five-year loan.

> "No bank would lend on this property," he said. "I would have to go to a private source."

Since the owner's expenses are limited to taxes and trivial expenditures for maintenance, there being no mortgage, the property probably generates a small net cash flow.

Standards

Sometimes the basic problem is one of standards. For example, the interviewer's report for a parcel owned since 1943 by an unmarried Negro woman now in her mid-sixties stated:

> This is a run-down house in a run-down neighborhood. 'Vacancy' and 'For Sale' signs are common. In this house the doors were broken, the windows were broken, the railings were loose, and the front hall cluttered with old furniture. Mrs. —————'s apartment is dark, dirty, cluttered and cold. She explained that the furnace was broken. We talked in the kitchen which was warmed by the gas stove, but which was also dark and dirty and cluttered with broken furniture. My impression was that she was unaware of another mode of living. This was reinforced by insistence that nothing needed to be done to the property.

(Note—The interviewer in this case was a middle-aged Negro who lived in the same general area as this particular parcel.)

Abandonments

The path of very dilapidated parcels can frequently end in their virtual abandonment. This is not a problem merely of white owners. For example, Number 160, a substantial frame building, was purchased in 1960 by a Negro carpenter. It has been vacant for over six months. The owner lives in one of Newark's better suburbs. Despite his craftsman's background, the owner refused to make any repairs on the parcel. His reason is very simple —"The area is so run-down nobody wants to live there."

The Well-Kept Parcel

In the midst of parcels which are similar in description to those above, are some which are, by any standards, very well-maintained indeed. The ever-present garbage of the slums seems to disappear at their borders. Who owns them? The patterns again are diffuse. Not infrequently they are owned by resident landlords, who see their tenements as a pathway to wealth accumulation and ultimately better living conditions.

> For example, there is a Negro couple in their forties. Mr. X works at the post office; his wife works at Western Electric as an assembler.

The parcel which they presently occupy is their second house. The first was poorer than the present one. When this present parcel is paid off, they hope to sell it and in turn move to get a better home. The rentals make it possible for them to essentially carry the house on a minimal out-of-pocket cost; and to this degree *the tenement ownership is a path to upward mobility.*

A wide variety of cases could be presented here, without clarifying the undeniable complexity of the basic question: Who owns the good versus the bad parcel? Reports of rehabilitation efforts in other communities differ as to the degree of cooperation that can be secured from the several land-lord types. In Philadelphia, for example, considerable opposition was met from the multi-parcel landlords, while comparative cooperation was achieved with single-parcel owners and resident owners.[1]

Certainly the significance of ownership as a factor in maintenance is clear-cut. Expenditures by resident owners for maintenance purposes are larger than those for equivalent rental units.[2] Resident owners, however, not infrequently lack the means for rehabilitation efforts, and even with all the goodwill in the world, occasionally possess truly blighted parcels.

Note that with the methodology used in research presented here, parcel maintenance was determined in the course of the original field study. While it represents a cursory investigation of the outward elements of landlord repair: paint, steps, lighting, doorways; upon investigation exterior repair has tended to correlate highly with the interior maintenance of the dwell-ing units themselves. This part of the analysis was done without any knowl-edge of who owned the parcels. The latter element of the analysis was done completely independently.[3] Exhibit 9–1 shows the results of this analysis by area. Note that significant as is the effect of neighborhood, even Area 1 is far from bereft of well-maintained parcels, though it has the highest pro-portion of poorly-maintained holdings.

In Exhibit 9–2 the same data is presented as a function of size of land-lords' holdings. There are obvious and substantial differences in the results. The large landlords, interestingly enough, are second, if by a very large margin, only to the single parcel owners in the lowness of the proportion of poorly kept homes which they own. On the other hand, they have the lowest proportion of well-kept houses. As was commented earlier, because of possessing their own repair facilities, they attempt to achieve at least a reasonable degree of maintenance, while obviously not particularly inter-ested in "over improving" a parcel. The poorest record is that of the

EXHIBIT 9-1
QUALITY OF PARCEL MAINTENANCE

	AREA 1		AREA 2A		AREA 2B		AREA 3A		AREA 3B		TOTAL	
	Num-ber	Per-cent	Num-ber	Per-cent	Num-ber	Per-cent	Num-ber	Per-cent	Num-ber	Per-cent	Num-ber	Per-cent
Reasonably kept	113	60.8	78	60.9	36	66.7	79	68.7	43	51.8	349	61.6
Poorly kept	46	24.7	27	21.1	4	7.4	19	16.5	13	15.7	109	19.3
Well kept	27	14.5	23	18.0	14	25.9	17	14.8	27	32.5	108	19.1
Total	186	100.0	128	100.0	54	100.0	115	100.0	83	100.0	566	100.0

EXHIBIT 9-2
PARCEL MAINTENANCE AS A FUNCTION OF SIZE OF HOLDING

Size of Holdings

	NA/DK		Other		Over 12		7-12		4-6		2-3		1		Total	
	Num-ber	Per-cent	Num-ber	Per-cent	Num-ber	Per-cent	Num-ber	Per-cent	Num-ber	Per-cent	Num-ber	Per-cent	Num-ber	Per-cent	Num-ber	Per-cent
Reasonably kept	—	—	—	—	44	72.1	19	63.3	27	62.8	47	56.6	97	57.4	234	60.6
Poorly kept	—	—	—	—	13	21.3	9	30.0	10	23.3	21	25.3	16	9.5	69	17.9
Well kept	—	—	—	—	4	6.6	2	6.7	6	14.0	15	18.1	56	33.1	83	21.5
Sub-N	—		—		61		30		43		83		169		386	
Live sample	—		—		61		30		43		83		169		386	
No response	—		—		—		—		—		—		—		6	

six- to twelve-parcel owner. These owners rarely can afford more than one universal handyman, while the scale of holdings minimizes personal efforts. *It is the single-parcel owner who, by a very wide margin, has the smallest proportion of poorly-kept and the highest proportion of well-kept parcels.* The single-parcel owner's 9.5 percent figure for poorly-kept is less than half that of all the other size categories of landlords, with the reverse approximately the case for well-kept parcels.

Is this variation in maintenance of parcel a result of residence or a function of single parcel ownership? In order to answer this question, analysis was undertaken of resident versus nonresident landlords, both in terms of single-parcel ownership and in terms of multiple-parcel ownerships. The results in Exhibits 9–3 and 9–4 indicate *the great importance of residence and preferably resident single-parcel ownership in securing good landlord maintenance. Regardless of area, resident ownership is the keystone of good maintenance.* This factor will be returned to in Chapter 12.

Landlord Maintenance by Occupation of Owner

It is interesting to analyze the maintenance factor by occupation of owner as shown in Exhibit 9–5. The largest group of poorly-maintained parcels as a proportion of total parcels owned by occupational category is that of the housecraft-oriented businessmen. In a sense, there is substantial incongruity here. These are people who should have the skills with which to improve parcels.

Interviews with two representatives of this category, one a plumber and the other a roofer, give some insight into the reasons. In both cases, they became familiar with the general area of slum tenements by doing repair work on them. In both cases, the degree of equity in their parcels was trivial. They had accumulated their parcels largely by being approached by landlords who wanted to get out of the business and were willing to take back purchase money mortgages. They both expressed the intent to "ultimately" improve their parcels. Despite relative longevity of holding, there is little evidence of this type of activity. Note that this disappointing record is paralleled by the parcel maintenance of house-oriented craftsmen holders; again good intentions with little to show for them. Lawyers, who own 20 parcels in the sample, have similarly poor records. The "good" occupational categories are those most closely associated with the occupational categories of those people who live in the area.

EXHIBIT 9-3

QUALITY OF PARCEL MAINTENANCE FOR RESIDENT LANDLORDS BY AREAS

LANDLORDS' MAINTENANCE	AREA 1		AREA 2A		AREA 2B		AREA 3A		AREA 3B		TOTAL	
	Number	Per-cent	Number	Per-cent	Number	Per-cent	Number	Per-cent	Number	Per-cent	Number	Per-cent
Reasonably kept	16	51.6	19	59.3	11	55.0	15	53.6	13	46.4	74	53.3
Poorly kept	4	12.9	2	6.3	—	—	4	14.3	2	7.2	12	8.6
Well kept	11	35.5	11	34.4	9	45.0	9	32.1	13	46.4	53	38.1
Total	31	100.0	32	100.0	20	100.0	28	100.0	28	100.0	139	100.0

EXHIBIT 9-4

QUALITY OF PARCEL MAINTENANCE FOR RESIDENT LANDLORDS
AS A FUNCTION OF SIZE OF HOLDINGS

Size of Holdings

	Total		1		2–3		4–6		7–12		Over 12		Other		NA/DK	
	Number	Per-cent	Number	Per-cent	Number	Per-cent	Number	Per-cent	Number	Per-cent	Number	Per-cent	Number	Per-cent	Number	Per-cent
Reasonably kept	74	53.3	63	54.3	8	44.4	3	60.0	—	—	—	—	—	—	—	—
Poorly kept	12	8.6	9	7.8	2	11.2	1	20.0	—	—	—	—	—	—	—	—
Well kept	53	38.1	44	37.9	8	44.4	1	20.0	—	—	—	—	—	—	—	—
Sub-N	139		116		18		5		—		—		—		—	
Live sample	139		116		18		5		—		—		—		—	

EXHIBIT 9-5

QUALITY OF PARCEL MAINTENANCE
BY OCCUPATION OF OWNER

	QUALITY OF MAINTENANCE							
	POOR		REASON-ABLE		GOOD		TOTALS	
OCCUPATION	Num-ber	Per-cent	Num-ber	Per-cent	Num-ber	Per-cent	Num-ber	Per-cent
Housewife	2	11.8	10	58.8	5	29.4	17	100.0
Lawyer	6	30.0	13	65.0	1	5.0	20	100.0
Real estate broker	9	20.5	32	72.7	3	6.8	44	100.0
Real estate manager	5	13.5	27	73.0	5	13.5	37	100.0
House-oriented craftsman	3	21.4	8	57.2	3	21.4	14	100.0
Craftsman, other	12	11.1	61	56.5	35	32.4	108	100.0
Other profession and managerial	4	12.5	18	56.3	10	31.2	32	100.0
Retired	9	18.8	27	56.2	12	25.0	48	100.0
NA interviewer's observation, unskilled	3	25.0	6	50.0	3	25.0	12	100.0
Small businessman	7	22.6	19	61.3	5	16.1	31	100.0
Housecraft businessman	8	42.1	10	52.6	1	5.3	19	100.0
Big businessman	1	25.0	3	75.0	—	—	4	100.0
Totals	69	17.9	234	60.6	83	21.5	386	100.0
No response	—	—	—	—	—	—	6	—

The "Good" Maintainer — The Multi-Parcel Owner

One of the most important factors in good maintenance of a parcel is con-
trolling the type of tenancy. In the course of the research a number of
multi-parcel owners were interviewed; all of whom had parcels in excellent
condition. Without exception, these owners pointed to the key requirement
of good maintenance as requiring a strong rental policy. By this, they meant
personal interviewing of tenants and no overcrowding of apartment units.

It should be noted also that these owners typically had substantial
equities in their parcels. The owner who is highly leveraged, and faced
with the necessity of improving his parcel, frequently can only respond by
taking in the type of tenancy which he would not normally do. This is the
landlord who overcrowds his apartments and takes in families whose very

size would bring down the standards of the building, or who are of a cali-
bre which would ultimately hurt the maintenance of the unit.

Code Enforcement

The power of American municipalities to strongly regulate housing conditions is most substantial. The brief in Frank vs. Maryland, 359 U. S. 360,
(1959), states the basic foundation for the law perhaps as succinctly as can
de done.

> A man's home may be his castle, but that castle no longer sits on a hill
> surrounded by a moat. The modern castle is connected to a central
> water system, a sewerage system, a garbage collection system, and
> frequently houses on either side.[4]

Given this authority, the question may well be raised: "Why cannot adequate
housing standards be maintained simply by appropriate code enforcement?"
In substantial part, this is unquestionably a function of the sheer magnitude
of the job in most of our older cities. For example, the figures below reflect
the volume of activity of the New York Housing Court, 1961:[5]

Complaints Received	114,567
Complaints Acted Upon*	115,115
Inspection Made	448,928
Violations Filed	198,409
Violations Dismissed	222,586
Court Cases	21,787
Convictions	19,651
Fines Imposed	18,273
Amount of Fines	$420,041

* Action taken on the backlog of cases held over from the previous
year accounts for the seeming discrepancy in some of the numbers.

The time lags between complaints and appropriate enforcement of co-
ordinating the activities of inspectors and of maintaining the public inter-
ests, which is an indispensable part of enforcing a difficult program, are
made clear-cut in the same report. In describing the occasional success, one
authority used the following description:

> . . . the effects of these efforts read like accounts of guerilla war-
> fare. The enemy is never vanquished, but only pressed back. Eternal
> vigilance is required, and in most places it is lacking. . . . the excite-

ment that is generated around a handful of successful demonstration projects is a significant indication of the level at which codes are enforced, or fail to be enforced—generally.[6]

The areas in which code enforcement is most required are the hard-core slums in the city. These are far from safe. In a study of code enforcement for multiple dwellings in New York City, for example, the following description is given. Under normal conditions, a fully trained inspector works alone, but in some areas in the city the Department has had to double up on manpower as a protection to the men. There have been several cases of "muggings" of inspectors, and in some buildings, heavily "tenanted" by narcotics addicts, the risks of attack are so great that inspections are not made after about two o'clock in the afternoon, the hour when the addicts begin to be up and about. Doubling up, of course, decreases the number of inspections that can be made.[7]

The fines which housing courts typically exact were described by one municipal authority in Newark to the writer as "license fees for running slums." Not infrequently, they are the trivial or relatively trivial costs of doing a profitable business. The situation is further complicated by the fact that many of the poor parcels are in the hands of poor owners. Enforcement of the code may therefore, in essence, be confiscatory in those cases.[8]

The very codes themselves often are highly unrealistic. They may call for a variety of improvements which add little to the basic safety or amenities of the tenantry of the buildings, and this in turn inhibits their full utilization. And overshadowing this problem is the continual backsliding. After a dramatic beginning—the typical picture of the municipal authority looking at a rat hole in a tenement ceiling or floor, the cleanup drive which follows and attracts much newspaper publicity—there is all too frequently a relapse.

In Baltimore, for example, two years after the well-known Fight Blight movement was instituted, the city was described as reverting to its former conditions.[9] Philadelphia's Leadership Program in 1956–59 experienced the same problem.[10] Not infrequently, code enforcement, where successful, results in an upgrading of building standards and with it, an increase in rents. This in turn may cause, inadvertently, the very thing which code enforcement strives to do away with, the lessening of standards as tenants double up to pay increased rents.[11]

The very standards of the code may be completely inadequate in terms of the basic objective; improving the lifeways of the inhabitants of the buildings under enforcement. Code compliance, *per se,* at least as most codes are constructed presently, may be irrelevant to the latter.

For example, "A structure might be in a fallen-down condition, and yet not contain any enforceable code violation. On the other hand, the structure might be in excellent condition, while the dwelling units in it exhibited certain code violations."[12]

The landlord's attitude toward code enforcement is, in substantial degree, a compound of the condition of his parcel and his view of the market realities. Exhibit 9–6 analyzes the response to the question: "How have visits of building and health inspectors affected your property?" Less than 7 percent of the owners of only one parcel referred to these inspections as a continual problem—unreasonable. On the other hand, the larger owners were much more strongly negative in their response. Of the twelve-plus parcel owners, 30 percent responded along the lines of continual problem —unreasonable, the percentage actually increasing among those owners owning six to twelve and three to six parcels. This is in part reflective of the condition of parcels owned by these several ownership groups. Their response which essentially said that the building inspected was above criticism was influenced by the size of holdings.

The complaints by multiple-parcel owners about inspection were based on beliefs that the code, as administered, might impose improvements above the capacity of the market to pay for them, as well as some fear of inequitable application of the code.

Although favoritism was not an item in the interview schedule, 8.3 percent of the owners of twelve or more parcels brought it up (the number of such responses from small owners was insignificant). It was, of course, beyond the scope of this study to determine the extent to which such fears of inequitable enforcement were founded on actual experience. But one cannot ignore these owners' impression, well-founded or not, that some inspectors are not enforcing the law uniformly.

One owner who complained of favoritism said that he was in a sense doubly penalized. Not only did he have to maintain his parcels properly while his neighbors did not, but their actions tended to depreciate the value of the entire neighborhood, thus affecting his own property adversely.

There is no reason to believe that the housing inspectors of Newark are any less conscientious than those in other cities. The rates of pay, running essentially between $5,000 and $6,000 per year, the scale of the task, and the political realities of Newark as in any other large city, all make the job

EXHIBIT 9-6

HAVE VISITS OF BUILDING AND HEALTH INSPECTORS AFFECTED YOUR PROPERTY?

	Size of Holdings													
	NA/DK		Over 12		7–12		4–6		2–3		1		Total	
	Number	Per-cent	Number	Per-cent	Number	Per-cent	Number	Per-cent	Number	Per-cent	Number	Per-cent	Number	Per-cent
No effect—visits rare	2	66.7	3	5.0	8	25.8	4	9.8	34	40.5	57	35.5	108	28.4
No effect—building above criticism	—	—	11	18.3	4	12.9	6	14.2	11	13.1	49	30.4	81	21.3
Occasional— worthwhile nuisance	—	—	13	21.7	3	9.7	5	11.9	10	11.9	5	3.1	36	9.4
Occasional— good meaningless	1	33.3	4	6.7	3	9.7	9	21.3	5	6.0	24	14.9	46	12.1
Continual. problem—unreasonable	—	—	18	30.0	12	38.7	15	35.6	18	21.3	11	6.8	74	19.4
Significant factor	—	—	6	10.0	1	3.2	2	4.8	5	6.0	14	8.7	28	7.3
no value judgment	—	—	—	—	—	—	1	2.4	—	—	—	—	1	0.3
Reference to favoritism	—	—	5	8.3	—	—	—	—	1	1.2	1	0.6	7	1.8
NA/DK	1	—	1	—	—	—	1	—	—	—	8	—	11	—
Sub-N	4		61		31		43		84		169		392	
Live sample	3		60		31		42		84		161		381	

most difficult. As long as the market realities make it cheaper to evade code regulations, either by accepting fines or by other means, it is doubtful whether anything less than heroic efforts would suffice to make code enforcement in itself a truly dynamic factor in improving housing conditions in Newark. At present, it is the author's opinion that it serves very effectively at least as a stabilizing factor in housing conditions.[13]

Code enforcement, as has been noted in an earlier chapter, has all too often been associated with increases in rents, and as such, it has often been attacked by the people whom it is supposed to benefit. Tenants faced with a shortage of apartments at a low rental have had very little choice except to double up. Thus code enforcement has frequently brought about the very results which it is intended to do away with. Given the typical highly leveraged forms of financing, the demand for high cash flow payments, hastily conceived fix-up campaigns, with a stiff sode enforcement behind them, are most frequently met by either evasion or at the cost of rent boosts with a corollary frequently of more tenants per unit.

Is there some possibility that at even higher vacancy rates than now exist, landlords will be forced either to improve the quality of the accommodations that they offer, lower their rents, or close up their buildings? Could the very weakness of the market help to improve standards? As of the moment, present landlord attitudes must yield a negative answer to both these questions. The uncertainties of the market, as well as tax and mortgage difficulties, certainly provide little help. Rigorous code enforcement, in and of itself, currently is essential—but limited in its effectiveness. The problems of ownership are too complex to yield to any single treatment.

There are obvious differences in the types of stimuli, and in the types of problems which these several categories of landlords respond to and are affected by. In the next two chapters is presented an analysis of two of the most significant of these: the problem of financing and the problem of taxation.

REFERENCES

1 City of Philadelphia, *Partnership for Renewal—A Working Program* (Philadelphia: 1960), pp. 32–3.
2 See Grigsby, *Housing Markets* . . . , p. 236.
3 See Appendix 1 for details.
4 Cited in Robert F. Allnutt and G. Mossinghoff, "Housing and Health Inspection," *George Washington Law Review* (January, 1960). The article is a comprehensive guide to the legal background of code enforcement.

5 Committee on Housing and Urban Development, *Code Enforcement for Multiple Dwelling in New York City* (N.Y.: Community Service Society of New York, n.d.), p. 5.
6 Schorr, *Slums* . . . , p. 89.
7 *Code Enforcement* . . . , p. 6.
8 On this point see Millspaugh, *Human Side* . . . , p. 7.
9 Ibid., p. 21.
10 City of Philadelphia, *Partnership* . . . , pp. 16–22.
11 Nash, *Residential* . . . , pp. 113–14.
12 Schaaf, *Economic Aspects* . . . , p. 28.
13 For a good introduction to the problem of formulating and administering housing codes, see the three-volume study entitled *Housing Codes, The Key to Housing Conservation,* by the New York State Division of Housing in cooperation with the Housing and Home Finance Agency, New York, 1960. For additional information, see the *Action Report, Municipal Housing Codes in the Courts,* Action, New York City, 1956.

Chapter 10

FINANCING
REHABILITATION

In Nash's study of residential rehabilitation a half-dozen years ago, financing was pointed out as the major inhibitor of rehabilitation efforts.[1]

> If rehabilitation is going to alter the urban scene, it must be made an economically attractive business. To accomplish this, it must have access to credit on terms that are competitive with new construction. It is plain from this survey that this is not the case. The problem is essentially one of how to alter the investment situation so that rehabilitation can bid for funds on equal footing with new house builders.

This chapter will briefly survey rehabilitation financing; the emphasis will initially be on the governmental scene and the numerous programs that have been adopted to aid in the problem. From this analysis attention will be turned to the resources that the slum landlord currently has available to him for "repair money." The last section of the chapter focuses on the basic will to improve tenement parcels and the actual desire of landlords to invest funds regardless of their availability. Given the availability of funds, will the landlord improve?

Government Dominance in Real Estate Financing

The Government's role, both as a direct financing agency and perhaps even more importantly as a pacesetter for private realty financing, is indisputable. This function has largely centered around the acquisition of parcels rather than the financing of their repairs and rehabilitation. The reason for this difference is understandable. The original initiative in the Government realty financing was to serve as an initiator of new construction. This was defended as being part of the Government's accepted role in spurring on the economy. The precedence of New Deal legislation to encourage house construction in the years of the Depression was quickly pursued in postwar legislation to help cure the housing shortage and also take up the slack caused by the cessation of wartime production.

Though neither of these basic drives has disappeared, they have been joined by the desire for improving the existing supply of housing facilities. Although potential exceptions are possibly in the making, government rehabilitation financing has essentially relied on guarantees of privately initiated loans for the purposes of home improvement; essentially the same mechanism and the same channels which have proven to be so effective in new dwelling unit construction. Rehabilitation lending, unfortunately, has proven far more complex. The one-of-a-kind nature of home improvements, the relatively small scale of the individual loans required their lack of capacity to withstand the high cost of investigation and the question of the standards which are to be applied in both granting and administering loans, have all proven most difficult to overcome.

Legislative fear of "give away" programs has certainly played a role in limiting the types of return that financial institutions can typically secure for rehabilitation loans. The sheer multiplicity of programs in this area is perhaps a sufficient commentary on the effectiveness of any one of them. As one critic pointed out in 1960:

> To invoke Title I, the borrower's personal credit standing and income must constitute him an 'acceptable credit risk.' For numbers 203, 207, his proposed borrowing must be 'economically sound;' for 220 there must be 'a workable program.' Somewhere in the interstices lies a grey area. . . .[2]

The time exigencies of rehabilitation financing are not infrequently much more urgent than that of financing new housing

> An owner seeking rehabilitation financing on an existing structure is confronted with urgencies in time far different than the developer of vacant suburban land. He's confronted with a structure in being, with current and accruing charges for operation, for heating, for light and taxes. . . . delays in FHA processing, acceptable to an owner of vacant land, are catastrophic to an owner of improved property. Complaints over the country indicate inability on the part of FHA district offices to

process loan applications without months of delay. . . . Banks and savings and loans associations are able to decide loan applications in no more than a week to ten days. The FHA district office takes four months or longer.[3]

Certainly the past record of efforts to secure appropriate rehabilitation financing through FHA sources has been far from satisfactory. In Detroit, for example, in the Mack-Concord Pilot Conservation Area, the use of Section 220 was attempted. After much effort only eleven final commitments were made out of thirty-seven applications. The Detroit City Planning Group claimed that the FHA was too strict in refusing to approve applications.

FHA appraisal standards were maintained at the regular high level, rather than being modified in terms of the success of the conservation project. . . . Appraisers find it difficult to apply standards in conservation areas which are radically different from those that they habitually use in better neighborhoods.[4]

The Urban Renewal Administration has been cognizant of the weaknesses in rehabilitation financing, and certainly it can be expected that some of the newer legislation, particularly Section 221 with all of its various codicils, and the additional programs under consideration at this writing, may well change the situation. There are obvious problems, however, in the very nature of rehabilitation itself.[5] The rewards to the lending administrator upon making a rehabilitation loan are uncertain; the penalties if that loan turns out to be unsuccessful—and rehabilitation loans are high-risk difficult ones—are comparatively clear-cut.[6]

A number of state programs have been initiated to fill the gap. Most of these, however, though providing very low interest rates and long-term amortization, do so at the cost, from the landlords' point of view, of imposing rent ceilings. While they may bear some fruit, as of the moment they are still in the pilot stage of operation.

It is interesting, in the light of the enormous amount of government enabling legislation in the financing of rehabilitation, to analyze the response of landlords to the question, "Do you know of any financial programs sponsored by the Government for older properties?" As shown in Exhibit 10–1, the bulk of the respondents did not know of any government program of this nature. Of the three hundred eighty-seven responses, two hundred seventeen were negative. Eleven out of the one hundred seventy who an-

EXHIBIT 10-1
DO YOU KNOW OF ANY FINANCIAL PROGRAM SPONSORED BY THE GOVERNMENT FOR OLDER PROPERTIES?

	AREA 1		AREA 2A		AREA 2B		AREA 3A		AREA 3B		TOTAL	
	Num-ber	Per-cent	Num-ber	Per-cent	Num-ber	Per-cent	Num-ber	Per-cent	Num-ber	Per-cent	Num-ber	Per-cent
F.H.A. General	31	24.2	19	21.1	11	29.7	23	28.4	12	23.5	96	24.8
F.H.A. Title I	6	4.7	1	1.1	—	—	1	1.2	—	—	8	2.1
F.H.A. 203,220, 221	8	6.3	4	4.4	—	—	3	3.7	2	3.9	17	4.4
V.A.	—	—	4	4.4	1	2.7	2	2.5	3	5.9	10	2.6
Yes—nothing specific	10	7.8	8	8.9	2	5.4	5	6.2	3	5.9	28	7.3
No	7	5.5	4	4.4	1	2.7	—	—	—	—	12	3.1
Not for this area	9	7.0	2	2.2	—	—	—	—	—	—	11	2.8
Don't know	57	44.5	48	53.5	22	59.5	47	58.0	31	60.8	205	52.9
Total	128	100.0	90	100.0	37	100.0	81	100.0	51	100.0	387	100.0
No answer	—		1		—		4		—		5	

swered positively, said that there were government programs, but "not for this area." The majority of the positive answers simply indicated knowledge of the FHA in general. Only seventeen out of three hundred eighty-seven parcels were in the possession of owners who referred specifically to any of the 200 Series FHA legislation. As Exhibit 10–2 indicates, the degree of knowledge was directly proportional to the size of the holdings. *Small owners, frequently those with the least access to private financing, are least aware of potential government aid.* This ignorance is all the more remarkable when one considers the present cost of capital and sources of repair money which are used for improving slum tenements.

Sources and Costs of Capital for Rehabilitation

In earlier sections of this work, actual landlord experience in securing mortgage funds for the purchase of slum tenements has been discussed. The cost of this debt is obviously higher than that of the equivalent for other forms of residential realty.

In appraising the financing of rehabilitation, the landlord's *belief* in what repair money will cost and the length of time for which he can secure it, is perhaps even more important than the reality of cost and the repayment schedule. The former acts as an immobilizer, conceivably of landlord intent to improve; the latter presumes a degree of knowledge which can be built into the landlord's profit equation.

In Exhibit 10–3 are presented landlords' responses by area to the question, "What would you have to pay for improvement money?" Note that this does not necessarily mean that the landlords could secure money at these rates; this is rather a projection of the world as they see it. The sample is representative of the parcel ownership of three hundred ninety-two slum tenements. Of these, one hundred ten are in the possession of people who don't know what improvement money would cost. While this may be "playing it safe," it undoubtedly reflects a basic ignorance in this area, an ignorance that is perhaps a blend of a lack of interest, and *a lack of a hard selling effort by governmental authorities interested in rehabilitation financing.*

In general, the "live" answers reflect an unrealistically low cost of improvement money. In every area more than two-thirds of the parcels are in the hands of people who believe, or at least verbalize a belief, that they will be able to secure improvement money for 7 percent or less. Area 1, as

EXHIBIT 10-2

Do You Know of any Financial Program Sponsored by the Government for Older Properties Such as [Address]?

	Size of Holdings															
	NA/DK		Other		Over 12		7–12		4–6		2–3		1		Total	
	Number	Per-cent	Number	Per-cent	Number	Per-cent	Number	Per-cent	Number	Per-cent	Number	Per-cent	Number	Per-cent	Number	Per-cent
Don't know	1	25.0	—	—	11	18.7	14	45.1	14	32.6	52	62.7	113	67.6	205	52.9
No	—	—	—	—	1	1.7	2	6.5	3	6.9	2	2.4	4	2.4	12	3.1
Not for this area or parcel	—	—	—	—	6	10.2	2	6.5	—	—	2	2.4	1	0.6	11	2.8
Yes, nothing specific	—	—	—	—	8	13.5	2	6.5	—	—	7	8.4	11	6.6	28	7.3
F.H.A. General	3	75.0	—	—	15	25.4	7	22.5	23	53.5	17	20.5	31	18.6	96	24.8
F.H.A. Title I	—	—	—	—	2	3.4	4	12.9	2	4.7	—	—	—	—	8	2.1
F.H.A. 203, 220, 221	—	—	—	—	16	27.1	—	—	1	2.3	—	—	—	—	17	4.4
V.A.	—	—	—	—	—	—	—	—	—	—	3	3.6	7	4.2	10	2.6
NA	—	—	—	—	2	—	—	—	—	—	1	—	2	—	5	—
Sub-N	4		—		61		31		43		84		169		392	
Live sample	4		0		59		31		43		83		167		387	

EXHIBIT 10-3

WHAT WOULD YOU HAVE TO PAY FOR IMPROVEMENT MONEY?

	AREA 1		AREA 2A		AREA 2B		AREA 3A		AREA 3B		TOTAL	
	Number	Per-cent	Number	Per-cent	Number	Per-cent	Number	Per-cent	Number	Per-cent	Number	Per-cent
5% or under	—	—	3	5.9	—	—	1	2.1	—	—	4	1.6
5% up to 6%	13	14.6	12	23.5	4	15.4	6	12.5	4	13.8	39	16.0
6% up to 7%	56	62.9	29	56.9	18	69.2	30	62.5	20	69.0	153	63.0
7% up to 10%	5	5.6	2	3.9	1	3.8	9	18.8	3	10.3	20	8.2
Over 10%	15	16.9	5	9.8	3	11.6	2	4.1	2	6.9	27	11.2
Total (live sample)	89	100.0	51	100.0	26	100.0	48	100.0	29	100.0	243	100.0
Won't borrow	6		6		3		6		4		25	
NA	1		7		—		5		1		14	
Don't know	32		27		8		26		17		110	

would be anticipated, has the highest proportion of "costing over 10 per-cent" response.

In Exhibit 10–4, the same basic data is reviewed by size of landlord's holdings. Note that it is the large landlords, rather than the small ones, who have the highest and most realistic impression of what improvement money would cost. The "won't borrow" response will be returned to later in this chapter, but note that it is concentrated in the single-parcel owners. The basic ignorance of what improvement money would cost is also centered in small holder. Out of the one hundred sixty-nine single-parcel owner responses, seventy indicated that they did not know what improvement money would cost; this is a far higher proportion than that for any other landlord group.

Length of Financing

Perhaps even more significant than the cost of debt financing is the length of time over which repayment must be made. In Exhibit 10–5 is presented the landlords' impressions of how long a period of time for which they could secure improvement money. The analysis by area is most provocative. As would be guessed, in Area 1 there is the least sanguine of responses; more than two-thirds of the responses indicate that loans would be made for under five years. The differences between Areas 2A and 2B, and 3A and 3B, respectively, in this regard are most interesting. They, perhaps, reflect the difference in lending attitude between largely Negro areas and substantially white areas. Less than 10 percent of the parcel owners in Area 1 responded with the belief that they could secure improvement money for ten or more years. In 2A, the equivalent proportion, based on a small sample, was 5.2 percent; in 3A, 21 percent. The equivalent figures for 2B and 3B are 29.5 percent and 34.7 percent respectively. In Exhibit 10–6 the responses to the question of·longevity of loan are analyzed by the size of landlord's holdings. Once again, it is the large landlords who are least optimistic about the length of improvement loans that they can secure.

It is reasonably safe to assume that this lack of optimism is a reflection of the facts of borrowing, rather than a defensive maneuver on the part of major landlords to excuse lack of rehabilitation. Both in interviews at the local FHA office, as well as with the major lending institutions in the area, the impression secured by the author was that the only significant source of rehabilitation money was that of Title I, with its effective interest

EXHIBIT 10-4

WHAT WOULD YOU HAVE TO PAY FOR IMPROVEMENT MONEY?

Size of Holdings

	NA/DK		Other		Over 12		7–12		4–6		2–3		1		Total	
	Number	Per-cent	Number	Per-cent	Number	Per-cent	Number	Per-cent	Number	Per-cent	Number	Per-cent	Number	Per-cent	Number	Per-cent
5% or under	—	—	—	—	—	—	—	—	—	—	3	5.5	1	1.1	4	1.6
5% up to 6%	2	50.0	—	—	3	5.3	3	10.4	6	17.6	10	18.2	15	16.9	39	16.0
6% up to 7%	1	25.0	—	—	38	66.7	17	58.6	17	50.0	30	54.4	50	56.2	153	63.0
7% up to 10%	—	—	—	—	4	7.0	3	10.4	4	11.8	4	7.3	5	5.6	20	8.2
Over 10%	1	25.0	—	—	9	15.7	5	17.2	5	14.7	5	9.1	2	2.2	27	11.2
Won't borrow	—	—	—	—	3	—	1	—	2	—	3	—	16	—	25	—
NA	—	—	—	—	1	—	—	—	—	—	3	—	10	—	14	—
Don't know	—	—	—	—	3	—	2	—	9	—	26	—	70	—	110	—
Sub-N	4		—		61		31		43		84		169		392	
Live sample	4		0		57		29		34		55		89		243	

EXHIBIT 10-5

WHAT WOULD YOU HAVE TO PAY FOR IMPROVEMENT MONEY? (LENGTH OF LOAN)

	AREA 1		AREA 2A		AREA 2B		AREA 3A		AREA 3B		TOTAL	
	Number	Per cent	Number	Per cent	Number	Per cent	Number	Per cent	Number	Per cent	Number	Per cent
Under 3 years	7	9.7	2	5.1	2	11.8	1	2.6	3	13.0	15	7.9
3 up to 5	41	56.9	20	51.3	6	35.3	20	52.6	6	26.1	93	49.2
5 up to 10	11	15.3	8	20.5	1	5.9	3	7.9	2	8.7	25	13.2
10 years	3	4.2	1	2.6	2	11.8	3	7.9	2	8.7	11	5.8
10 up to 15	2	2.8	—	—	2	11.8	4	10.5	1	4.3	9	4.8
More	1	1.4	1	2.6	1	5.9	1	2.6	5	21.7	9	4.8
Total (live sample)	65	100.0	32	100.0	14	100.0	32	100.0	19	100.0	162	100.0
NA	12		16		7		18		10		63	
Don't know	44		36		13		29		18		140	
Won't borrow	7	—	7	—	3	—	6	—	4	—	27	—

EXHIBIT 10-6

WHAT WOULD YOU HAVE TO PAY FOR IMPROVEMENT MONEY? (LENGTH OF LOAN)

Size of Holdings

	NA/DK		Other		Over 12		7–12		4–6		2–3		1		Total	
	Number	Percent	Number	Percent	Number	Percent	Number	Percent	Number	Percent	Number	Percent	Number	Percent	Number	Percent
Under 3 years	—	—	—	—	5	10.6	1	5.0	1	3.3	1	2.8	7	13.2	15	7.9
3 up to 5	1	33.3	—	—	34	72.4	6	30.0	19	63.3	19	52.8	14	26.4	93	49.2
5 up to 10	1	33.3	—	—	1	2.1	5	25.0	5	16.7	6	16.7	7	13.2	25	13.2
10 years	—	—	—	—	1	2.1	4	20.0	—	—	3	8.3	3	5.7	11	5.8
10 up to 15	1	33.3	—	—	1	2.1	—	—	2	6.7	3	8.3	2	3.8	9	4.8
More	—	—	—	—	2	4.3	2	10.0	1	3.3	—	—	4	7.5	9	4.8
Won't borrow	—	—	—	—	3	6.4	2	10.0	2	6.7	4	11.1	16	30.2	27	14.3
NA	—	—	—	—	11	—	7	—	2	—	14	—	29	—	63	—
Don't know	1	—	—	—	3	—	4	—	11	—	34	—	87	—	140	—
Sub-N	4		—		61		31		43		84		169		392	
Live sample	3		0		47		20		30		36		53		189	

rates of 10 percent and effective maximum terms of five years. The only reasonably long-term, low-cost form of rehabilitation financing presently in use is that provided by rolling over mortgages for higher values, and thus securing the wherewithal to make improvements. As will be indicated in Chapter 12, however, this attitude is a reflection of the past with a host of legislation enabling considerable change.

The response to the question of "What source would you turn to if you needed money to make improvements on your property?" is shown in Exhibit 10-7. (The same data by size of holdings is shown in Exhibit 10-8.) As can be seen in this Exhibit, the finance company appears significant only in Area 1. The biggest single response centers around the use of banks, with personal resources representing 13.6 percent of the response. Note that the number of specific answers to this question was much higher than that of its two predecessors. A landlord may not have researched the question of borrowing terms, but his first port-of-call typically is his bank. Given the negative attitude of banks reflected in their lack of involvement in first mortgages in the hard-core areas, as indicated in Chapter 5, it is difficult to see them being particularly positive in approving of rehabilitation plans in those same areas. *To the degree that the bank is a consulting agency for the small landlord as well as the first port-of-call for borrowing, the dependence shown in these Exhibits may well be a serious inhibitor of thinking on rehabilitation by the landlord, as well as the actual securing of financing.*

The Landlord's Will to Improve if Given Mortgage Help

Is a weak mortgage market for purposes of rehabilitation the keystone of the problem of slum maintenance? Would landlords improve their tenement parcels if given adequate mortgaging? In order to research this area the following question was asked: "Would you improve this property if given a long-term mortgage?" The answers received are presented by area in Exhibit 10-9. [Note that questions of "would you, if?" variety tend to evoke more substantial positive responses than is actually the case, if by doing so they present the person being interviewed in a positive posture; it costs the respondent nothing to give the socially acceptable answer. Despite this built-in skew, the responses are substantially *negative*.] Only 19.5 percent of the total respondents indicated that they would improve, given long-term mortgaging with no restrictions; 3.8 percent indicated that they wanted tax

EXHIBIT 10-7

WHAT SOURCE WOULD YOU TURN TO IF YOU NEEDED MONEY TO MAKE IMPROVEMENTS ON YOUR PROPERTY?

	AREA 1		AREA 2A		AREA 2B		AREA 3A		AREA 3B		TOTAL	
	Number	Percent	Number	Percent	Number	Percent	Number	Percent	Number	Percent	Number	Percent
Savings bank	3	2.6	—	—	—	—	—	—	1	2.1	4	1.1
Mortgage broker	—	—	—	—	2	5.9	—	—	—	—	2	0.6
Finance company	20	17.1	3	3.6	1	2.9	6	8.6	3	6.3	33	9.3
Personal loan, commercial bank	—	—	2	2.4	—	—	1	1.4	—	—	3	0.8
Personal resources	16	13.7	9	10.7	7	20.6	10	14.3	6	12.5	48	13.6
Second mortgage, no source	1	0.9	3	3.6	—	—	5	7.1	—	—	9	2.5
Bank w/o detail	77	65.8	67	79.8	24	70.6	48	68.6	38	79.2	254	72.0
Total	117	100.0	84	100.0	34	100.0	70	100.0	48	100.0	353	100.0
NA	5		7		3		12		2		29	
DK	6		—		—		3		1		10	

EXHIBIT 10-8

WHAT SOURCE WOULD YOU TURN TO IF YOU NEEDED MONEY TO MAKE IMPROVEMENTS ON YOUR PROPERTY?

| | Size of Holdings | | | | | | | | | | | | | | | |
| | NA/DK | | Other | | Over 12 | | 7–12 | | 4–6 | | 2–3 | | 1 | | Total | |
	Num-ber	Per-cent	Num-ber	Per-cent	Num-ber	Per-cent	Num-ber	Per-cent	Num-ber	Per-cent	Num-ber	Per-cent	Num-ber	Per-cent	Num-ber	Per-cent
Savings bank	—	—	—	—	1	1.7	1	3.2	—	—	—	—	2	1.3	4	1.1
Mortgage broker	—	—	—	—	2	3.4	—	—	—	—	—	—	—	—	2	0.6
Finance company	1	25.0	—	—	7	12.1	5	16.1	3	7.7	8	10.7	9	6.0	33	9.3
Personal loan, commercial bank	—	—	—	—	—	—	—	—	1	2.6	1	1.3	1	0.7	3	0.8
Personal resources	—	—	—	—	10	17.2	5	16.1	3	7.7	10	13.3	20	13.4	48	13.6
Second mortgage, no resources	—	—	—	—	1	1.7	—	—	3	7.7	1	1.3	4	2.7	9	2.5
Bank w/o detail	3	75.0	—	—	37	63.9	20	64.6	29	74.3	54	73.4	111	75.9	254	72.0
NA	—	—	—	—	3	—	—	—	4	—	8	—	14	—	29	—
DK	—	—	—	—	—	—	—	—	—	—	2	—	8	—	10	—
Sub-N	4		—		61		31		43		84		169		392	
Live sample	4		0		58		31		39		74		147		353	

EXHIBIT 10-9

WOULD YOU IMPROVE THIS PROPERTY IF GIVEN A LONG-TERM MORTGAGE?

	AREA 1		AREA 2A		AREA 2B		AREA 3A		AREA 3B		TOTAL	
	Number	Per-cent	Number	Per-cent	Number	Per-cent	Number	Per-cent	Number	Per-cent	Number	Per-cent
Yes—No restrictions	25	19.5	20	24.2	6	17.6	11	14.7	10	20.4	72	19.5
Yes—If mortgage payts, equal increased revenue cost	2	1.6	—	—	—	—	—	—	—	—	2	0.5
Yes with taxes plus something else	3	2.3	2	2.4	—	—	8	10.7	1	2.0	14	3.8
Property doesn't need it	14	10.9	19	23.0	7	20.6	14	18.7	11	22.4	65	17.6
Neighborhood doesn't warrant it	17	13.3	8	9.6	3	8.8	6	8.0	6	12.2	40	10.8
Parcel not worth it	8	6.3	3	3.6	2	5.9	3	4.0	2	4.1	18	4.9
Parcel & neighborhood no good	18	14.1	5	6.0	2	5.9	4	5.3	2	4.1	31	8.4
No return	10	7.8	9	10.8	3	8.8	16	21.3	4	8.2	42	11.4
Don't want debt	12	9.4	8	9.6	8	23.5	5	6.7	9	18.4	42	11.4
No money	—	—	1	1.2	1	2.9	3	4.0	2	4.1	7	1.9
Taxes	4	3.1	—	—	1	2.9	—	—	—	—	5	1.4
U.R. taking property	14	10.9	7	8.4	—	—	5	6.7	—	—	26	7.0
Too old	1	0.8	1	1.2	1	2.9	—	—	2	4.1	5	1.4
Total	128	100.0	83	100.0	34	100.0	75	100.0	49	100.0	369	100.0
NA/DK	—		8		3		10		2		23	

EXHIBIT 10-10

WOULD YOU IMPROVE THIS PROPERTY IF GIVEN A LONG-TERM MORTGAGE?

| | Size of Holdings | | | | | | | | | | | | |
| | NA/DK | | Over 12 | | 7-12 | | 4-6 | | 2-3 | | 1 | | Total | |
	Num-ber	Per-cent	Num-ber	Per-cent	Num-ber	Per-cent	Num-ber	Per-cent	Num-ber	Per-cent	Num-ber	Per-cent	Num-ber	Per-cent
Yes—No restriction	1	33.3	12	20.7	6	22.2	7	17.1	23	28.0	23	14.6	72	19.5
Yes—If mortgage payts. equal increased revenue cost	—	—	1	1.7	—	—	1	2.4	—	—	—	—	2	0.5
Yes—With taxes plus something else	—	—	—	—	—	—	4	9.8	3	3.7	7	4.4	14	3.8
Property doesn't need it	—	—	17	29.4	3	11.1	6	14.6	10	12.2	29	18.4	65	17.6
Neighborhood doesn't warrant it	1	33.3	6	10.3	2	7.4	4	9.8	12	14.6	15	9.5	40	10.8
Parcel isn't worth it	—	—	—	—	7	26.0	—	—	5	6.1	6	3.8	18	4.9
Parcel & neigh-borhood no good	1	33.3	8	13.8	4	14.8	6	14.6	4	4.9	8	5.1	31	8.4
No return	—	—	7	12.1	4	14.8	11	26.8	10	12.2	10	6.3	42	11.4
Don't want to go into debt	—	—	2	3.4	—	—	—	—	5	6.1	35	22.2	42	11.4
No money	—	—	—	—	—	—	—	—	—	—	7	4.4	7	1.9
Taxes	—	—	4	6.9	—	—	—	—	—	—	1	0.6	5	1.4
U.R. taking property	—	—	1	1.7	1	3.7	2	4.9	9	11.0	13	8.2	26	7.0
Too old	—	—	—	—	—	—	—	—	1	1.2	4	2.5	5	1.4
NA/DK	2	—	3	—	3	—	2	—	2	—	11	—	23	—
Sub-N	5		61		30		43		84		169		392	
Live sample	3		58		27		41		82		158		369	

aid in addition. A small fraction of a percent indicated that they would improve only if increased revenue equaled costs.

In essence, more than three-quarters of the respondents indicated that they would not improve given long-term mortgages. The reasons for this are numerous. In general, however, the bulk of the negatives revolved around the fact of the parcel and/or the area not being worthy of investment. It is most particularly true in Area 1, where some 33.7 percent of the total response fell into the several subsets of this category. In Areas 2B and 3B, the "don't want to go into debt response" was dominant, representing twice the fraction that the same response received in other areas.

In Exhibit 10–10 responses are analyzed by size of landlord's holdings. It is the single-parcel owners who are most loathe to get involved in mortgage debt, while multiple-parcel owners are much more positive in their response to the question; it is the former who have the least faith in the value of their holdings, and/or the neighborhoods in which these holdings are located, as a worthwhile investment for additional funds.

The fear of going into debt is very strongly held by smaller landlords. "I am an old man and can't get money easy, and I don't want to leave my family with a lot of debts," was one typical response. The attitude of a middle-aged Negro roofer exemplified the feeling, which was voiced with numerous variations among small owners, both Negro and white—"There ain't nothing we want to do big enough to borrow money for, but if there was, we'd think hard before we went into debt."

In response to an earlier question regarding the ranking of landlord problems (these will be analyzed in the next chapter), owners of single tenements frequently would indicate that mortgaging costs and mortgaging length (two of the areas which were to be rated) were not significant because "they had paid off their house." Implicit in this statement is that the goal of repayment was so hard fought that the single-parcel owner refuses to go back into debt under any circumstances. There is considerable question whether even those owners who said "yes, without restriction" to the possibilities of improving parcels if given long-term mortgages, would actually do so. For example, Number 85, an owner of eight tenements in Area 1, gave a positive answer to the question, but on the other hand, indicated that Area 1 was so bad that "I improve just to keep the parcel rentable, and to keep it from being vandalized when vacant." Given this statement, it is difficult to believe very substantial rehabilitation investment, even with long-term cheap funds, would be made.

The material presented above should not be thought of as minimizing the importance of providing adequate financing for tenement rehabilitation. It does indicate, however, that the entrepreneurial will to improve is far from vigorous. Obviously, it will require more than mortgage help alone to overcome the inertia indicated by the responses. Could a change in tax policy make a major contribution toward this end? In the next chapter, the potential of this policy will be analyzed.

REFERENCES

1 Nash, Residential . . . , p. 156.
2 Charles Haar, Federal Credit and Private Housing (McGraw-Hill, 1960), pp. 251–2.
3 Levy, "Problems . . . ," p. 315.
4 Detroit City Planning Commission, Renewal and Revenue (Detroit, 1962), pp. 63–4.
5 For additional data on the administrative problems, see particularly Greer and Miner, "The Political Side of Urban Development and Redevelopment" in the Annals of the American Academy of Political and Social Science, March 1964. See also, "The Hiatus Between the Administration of Federal Housing Administration Mortgage Insurance and the Planners of Urban Renewal," p. 67, same source.
6 The Federal Housing Administration has been the chief funnel through which Federal funds have flowed to aid rehabilitation in older areas. As noted in Chapter 1, the balance between the desire for rehabilitation and conservative banking practices have often been weighted towards the latter at the cost of providing adequate flows of capital into rehabilitation. Here, too, the attitude seems to be changing. (For example, see Philip N. Brownstein, Commissioner, Federal Housing Administration Letter #38, dated Nov. 8, 1965.)

Chapter 11

TAXES AND SLUMS

THE connection of municipal tax policy with the growth and perpetuation of slums has been a favorite thesis of many observers. For example, an editorial in a Newark newspaper stated:

> The property that requires the least service, the well-maintained residential property with modern facilities, is assessed the highest tax bill. The worst property of the slums that are a drain on the police, fire, and health resources of the city, is encouraged with the lowest tax bills. The slums, in effect, are subsidized by the tax system, and the decent housing properties penalized. As long as the tax system helps to make slums big money earners for their owners and, by contrast, severely limits the profits to be made on good housing, the government does much more to spread slums than any housing court can do to combat them. . . . The present tax system . . . tends to make more slums.[1]

The basic idea voiced here, that poorly-maintained parcels are relatively underassessed at the cost of overburdening well-maintained parcels, has been much elaborated on by observers. Not infrequently the thesis is advanced that the landlord in fear of taxation tends to under-maintain at least the outward appearances of his parcel. The inverse of this, that the landlord would maintain his parcel in a more appropriate fashion if there were no fear of taxes, is at least implicit in these comments. With the very high tax rates that prevail in Newark (see Chapter 2), the city provides an excellent laboratory within which to study the phenomenon of tax impact.

There are several questions which must be answered on this subject: How significant are taxes on the slums? What is the actual tax impact? Is there a significant difference in the taxation levied upon well-maintained versus poorly-maintained parcels? On slums versus nonslum property? And most important of all—What is the landlord's response to tax impact? The chapter will close with an evaluation of the potential of tax abatements and reductions.

Actual Tax Assessments and Their Implications

Exhibit 11–1 contains data on assessments per square foot for combined land and improvements for the tenements within the study areas. As is evident, there is little variation of assessment per square foot by area. For the sample total of five hundred sixty-two parcels for which adequate data was available (several parcels were dropped because of the difficulties of estimating the total footage of their irregular lots), the median figure is $4.43 per square foot. There is little variation in the interquartile range, running as it does between roughly $3.50 and $5.50. In a separate calculation, not reproduced here, the same analysis was made eliminating parcels housing commercial facilities. The data gave nearly the same results.

From the municipality's point of view it should be remembered that a substantial proportion of each developed acre of land must be given over to nontaxable productive uses such as roads, sidewalks, and so on. Out of a typical acre, no more than thirty thousand to thirty-five thousand square feet represent improved parcels. It is clear, therefore, that the yield of a hypothetical gross acre of multi-family tenements to the city is little more than $150,000 in real estate assessment.

While assessment/sales ratios will be observed in more detail later in this chapter, it should be noted that the market value of the parcels in the

EXHIBIT 11–1
TOTAL ASSESSMENT PER SQUARE FOOT
LAND PLUS TENEMENT IMPROVEMENTS

TOPIC	AREA 1	AREA 2A	AREA 2B	AREA 3A	AREA 3B	TOTAL SAMPLE
Live sample	185	128	53	113	83	562
Median	$4.71	$4.33	$4.31	$4.42	$4.38	$4.43
Interquartile Range	$3.38–5.87	$3.26–5.49	$3.32–5.32	$3.56–5.15	$3.69–4.98	$3.41–5.52

hypothetical acre would probably be a little more than 110 percent of their assessments. Prime industrial land in the suburbs outside of Newark currently sells for roughly $50,000 an acre. The gap, therefore, between the current market for acreage in the slum areas of Newark and competitive industrial tracts outside the city averages approximately $115,000 per acre. While this figure is relatively modest for small tracts of land to be written down under Urban Renewal for improvement, if it is considered that the five groups of census tracts that make up the area under consideration amount to somewhere on the order of three thousand to four thousand acres, the cost of land acquisition and write-down becomes all too evident.

In sum, market prices for spot clearance are not inordinate. For total clearance, however, the property cost alone, regardless of all the other costs, both financial and human, that would be involved, *is* more than a little overwhelming.

From the municipal cost/revenue point of view, the problem of the city becomes clear. A six-family tenement will usually, depending on its amenities, be assessed at from $12,000–$18,000. Given the age distributions and size of slum families, the building may easily house more than thirty people, including a dozen school children. The needs of these people must be met by the city on approximately $500 per capita of ratables.

Given the limited commercial/industrial growth which characterizes the typical older United States city, the strain on tax rates, and municipal service quality, is all too clear.

In this connection it is interesting to note the data presented in Exhibit 11–2. In this Exhibit is summarized land assessments per square foot

EXHIBIT 11–2

TENEMENT IMPROVED LAND ASSESSMENT PER SQUARE FOOT

TOPIC	AREA 1	AREA 2	AREA 3
Live sample	186	179	197
Median	$.72	$.72	$.67
Interquartile Range	$.60–1.03	$.64–.99	$.60–.86

within the three major subsets of the study area. (There is very little difference between A and B in Areas 2 and 3.) As can be seen from the Exhibit, there is a broad range of land assessment. The interquartile ranges, however, are relatively tight, and they indicate that these areas, most of which are within a mile of the city's central business district, are assessed at approximately $30,000 per acre in terms of privately-owned multiple-tenancy land sites. *In sum, land values, as represented by assessments within the slum belt surrounding the city's core, are on a par with areas zoned for industry in the suburbs and not very much higher than equivalent suburban acreage zoned for garden apartments.*

That this is not a function of underassessment of land at the cost of overassessment of improvements is indicated by the ratio between median land assessment to total assessment. The relationship of roughly 15 percent does not seem to this writer at all out of line with usual experience.

EXHIBIT 11–3

1964 ASSESSMENT AS A PERCENTAGE OF SALES PRICE*

CITY	RANGE	MEDIAN	INTERQUARTILE RANGE
Newark	39.3–387.2	87.7	74.9–110.6

* $\dfrac{\text{Assessment}}{\text{Sales price}} = \text{percent}$

Source: New Jersey Bureau of Local Taxation, unpublished material.

In Exhibit 11–3, data from the New Jersey Bureau of Local Taxation, based upon its study of two hundred fifty-one parcels with four or more dwelling units which were sold in 1964, is presented. There is obviously a very broad range of assessment to sales ratios. The median figure of 87.7 percent, however, is in line with that of equivalent ratios for slum tenements.[2]

To the degree that assessment policy should be based upon market values, and this is an injunction which is most specific in the New Jersey State Constitution as well as that in the laws of most other taxing authorities, the assessment to sales experience relationship is in reasonable order.

Tax Assessments of Well-Kept Parcels vs. Poorly-Kept Parcels

Within the same type of housing, i.e. essentially slum tenements, is there a difference in assessment/sales ratios between those parcels which are well-kept and those parcels which are poorly-kept?

Exhibits 11–4, 11–5, and 11–6 attempt to come to grips with this provocative question. Exhibit 11–4 indicates assessment-as-of-1964 to sales-as-of-the-year-consummated ratios for all the five hundred sixty-six parcels in the sample.

EXHIBIT 11–4
ASSESSMENT TO SALES RATIO

Year	1 A/S Median Entire Sample)	2 A/S Median (Well- kept)	3 A/S (Well-kept) ——————— A/S (Entire Sample)	4 A/S Median (Poorly- kept)	5 A/S (Poorly-kept) ——————— A/S (Entire Sample)
1939	—	3.480	—	—	—
1940	2.320	—	—	—	—
1941	1.493	2.197	1.471	—	—
1942	2.166	2.228	1.029	1.994	.921
1943	2.072	—	—	2.050	.989
1944	2.019	1.872	.927	1.383	.685
1945	2.929	2.250	.768	—	—
1946	1.942	1.506	.775	1.733	.892
1947	1.580	1.573	.996	1.455	.921
1948	1.333	1.115	.836	1.413	1.060
1949	1.925	1.171	.608	—	—
1950	1.119	1.053	.941	.541	.483
1951	1.149	1.107	.963	1.065	.927
1952	1.239	.943	.761	1.540	1.243
1953	.880	.848	.964	.914	1.039
1954	1.091	.993	.910	.681	.624
1955	1.200	.851	.709	1.040	.867
1956	1.285	1.625	1.265	—	—
1957	1.026	.830	.809	1.275	1.243
1958	1.068	—	—	1.185	1.110
1959	1.028	.986	.959	.978	.951
1960	.789	1.344	1.703	.997	1.263
1961	.845	.771	.912	.716	.847
1962	.800	.738	.923	.744	.930
1963	.954	.651	.682	1.019	1.068
1964	.929	.684	.736	.463	.498
AVERAGE			.966		.975

The median ratio was chosen for each of the several years presented in order to avoid the skew factor which might be generated by occasional extreme ratios.

By focusing on column 1 in Exhibit 11–4 which presents the data for the entire sample year, it can be seen that the prices of slum tenements as measured by current assessments have risen sharply since 1940. As indicated in an earlier chapter, however, there seems to be some evidence that this price rise has come to an end, and in the last two years has been reversed. Columns 2 and 4 present the equivalent data for the well-kept parcels and

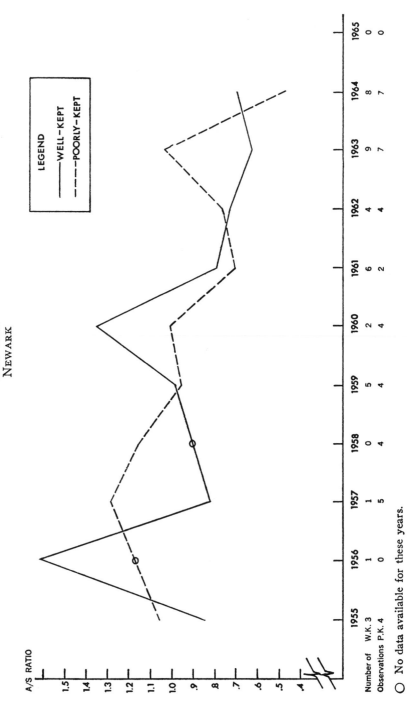

EXHIBIT 11-5

A/S Ratio by Year—Poorly-kept vs. Well-kept Parcels
1955–1965
Newark

EXHIBIT 11–6

A/S Ratio of Well-kept Parcels as a Percentage
of the A/S Ratio of Poorly-kept Parcels

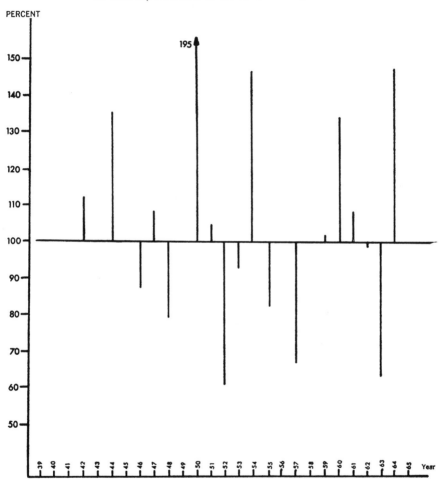

the poorly-kept parcels, respectively, in the sample. (For the definition of these terms and the approach used to segregate these categories, see Appendix I on Methodology.)

In order to remove the price inflation factor from the data, the median figure for the entire sample for each of the several years has been used as a deflator of columns 2 and 4. Columns 3 and 5, therefore, are corrected for price changes as a function of time. In theory, if there were no difference between the assessment/sales ratio of a well-kept parcel as against the assessment/sales ratio of the general run of parcels and, in addition, there was no noise factor due to smallness of sample and atypical sales or assessments, column 3, for example, should be close to 1.0 for each of the several years, and the equivalent would be the case for column 5. Unfortunately, the disparate facts of the world being as they are, there obviously is a significant year-to-year variation. When summarized, however, as it is at the bottom of columns 3 and 5, it can be seen that the average figure, that is the average of the relationships indicated in the columns respectively, is practically identical. *To the degree that the assessment/sales ratios have been effectively measured, by this means well-kept parcels and poorly-kept parcels show very little difference in assessment/sales ratios.*

It should be noted that this type of analysis is presented with a considerable measure of diffidence. Its basic presumption, that there is little in the way of major capital improvements in the parcels under consideration over the years which might effect their assessments as against those improvements of maintenance which at least in theory should not increase assessment, is an extremely hazardous one. The noise factor attendant to the analysis of any one year, as a function of the relatively small sample in that one year, certainly is evident. As can be seen, however, if the data with its admitted limitations is accepted, there seems to be little variation in assessment/sales ratios.

Taxes as a Percentage of Gross Income

Care must be taken, however, not to equate the equivalence of assessment/ sales ratios with that of operating costs. The mere fact that well-maintained and poorly-maintained parcels typically are assessed at ratios which are in line with their sale prices does not mean that taxes will be equally as large in the landlord's operating statement for disparately-maintained parcels. It can be shown that *the policy of assessing upon sales value practically guarantees that this will not be the case.*

The variation is a function in the multiplier which is extended to well-maintained versus poorly-maintained parcels. The landlord who buys the latter knows that he is in danger of punitive action by city authorities; which is accompanied by a considerable potential for additional capital investment. The multiple of gross income which he will extend for going into this comparatively risky situation is low. A well-maintained parcel, on the other hand, tends to command a broader market. It presents fewer "problems" and for that reason tends to sell for a somewhat higher multiple. (This generalization has been checked out and agreed upon by all of the real estate investors with whom we have spoken in the course of this study.) Taxes, therefore, as a percentage of gross income will always be higher for the well-maintained parcel than for its poorly maintained equivalent.[3]

Simplified Case Study

	Well-maintained Parcel	*Poorly-maintained Parcel*
Annual Gross Rent	$10,000	$10,000
Multiplier	×4	×3
Sale Price	$40,000	$30,000
Tax @6%	×.06	×.06
Annual Tax Bill	$ 2,400	$ 1,800

Full market value taxation, therefore, tends to impose a higher tax rate as a percentage of gross income on well-maintained parcels versus poorly-maintained ones. This should not, however, be equated with the statement that poorly-maintained parcels produce a greater net profit than their well-maintained equivalent. Taxes are merely one among a variety of factors which influence net profit and investment policy. Such elements, noted in earlier chapters, as vacancy rates, type of financing, landlord characteristics, and a whole host of other factors, are most influential here. Nevertheless, the disproportion of taxes is clear.

Perhaps even more important than the actualities of taxes, however, are the landlords' vision of their impact. The data indicates that taxes are being levied on well-maintained and poorly-maintained parcels in accordance with the State Constitution's injunction on sales value. But what is the landlords' view?

The Landlords' View of Taxes

There is little evidence to indicate that tax assessments in terms of sale value of parcel are unfair in terms of resale value, but most landlords are not selling their parcels, at least not immediately. Even if they were aware, which as will be shown is not the case, that ultimately upon resale they would get their investment in improvements back, this still might not relieve the potential inhibition of fear of immediate income loss because of tax reassessment based upon improvement. Is this a significant factor?

In order to answer this question, a number of approaches were tried. The first of these involved asking the landlord the following question: "There are many problems in maintaining and improving properties. In the case of [address] how would you rate the following categories in order of importance to you?" At the same time, the landlord who was being interviewed was shown a card on which the following factors were listed:

1. Tenants
2. Mortgaging cost
3. Mortgaging length
4. Tax level
5. Tax reassessment
6. Builder requirements

In addition, the interviewer was instructed to record any other factors which the landlord might mention.

Exhibit 11–7 presents the results of this question tabulated by the size of landlord holding. For the purposes of this Exhibit, in order to secure comparability, an inverse rank weighting was used; the factor cited as most important was given a weight of six, the second most important was given a weight of five, and so on down to the sixth factor which was given a weight of one. The sum of the weights was then divided by the total number of respondents.

As can be seen, there is a substantial difference between the several elements and also between the responses as a function of size of landlord holding. *The larger the size of holding the more the landlord views the tenantry as his number one problem in maintenance and improvement. On the other hand, the small holder gives the least weight to tenantry problems.* In the last chapter focus will be placed on the importance of this fact.

An inverse relationship exists as far as tax levels are concerned. While of great importance to all groups, their greatest impact is upon small holders and, conversely, are least important to large holders. Once again, as has been stressed in earlier chapters, the large landlord is least impressed by tax requirements. As a commercial dealer, and a relatively sophisticated one, he buys a parcel with a knowledge of present and future tax problems in mind. It is the small holder, a holder who not uncommonly depends upon his holding as a prime source of income, who finds himself most squeezed

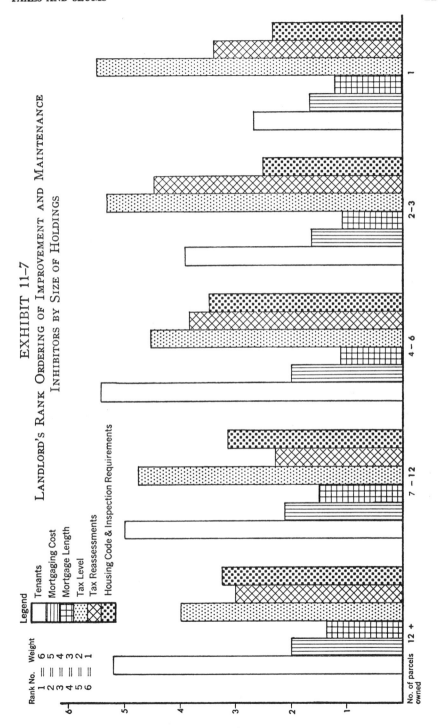

EXHIBIT 11-7

LANDLORD'S RANK ORDERING OF IMPROVEMENT AND MAINTENANCE
INHIBITORS BY SIZE OF HOLDINGS

Legend

Tenants
Mortgaging Cost
Mortgage Length
Tax Level
Tax Reassessments
Housing Code & Inspection Requirements

Rank No.	Weight
1 =	6
2 =	5
3 =	4
4 =	3
5 =	2
6 =	1

No. of parcels owned

1   2-3   4-6   7-12   12+

by tax levels. Neither mortgaging cost nor mortgaging length compare with either of the two factors mentioned earlier in importance.

The attitudes toward tax reassessment varied in a fashion somewhat similar to that of tax levels. It is the major holder who fears it least. As the material on landlord behavior has indicated, the large-scale holder either makes improvements because of their profit potential, despite awareness of the tax implications, or makes no improvement. It is the relatively unsophisticated small holder, particularly those with two or three parcels, who are most intimidated by the possibility of tax reassessment.

In sum, there is no question of the significance of taxes in landlords' *verbalizations* of what are the prime inhibitors of additional investments in their parcels.

The second question in the interview sequence on this point was: "You did (or you did not) mention taxes." The answers which were received covered a very broad span of response. In general, they reflected a strong feeling that the tax levels essentially had crippled the resale market and made the advisability of additional investment most uncertain. *In the face of rent level plateaus, the increasing level of the tax rate, which Newark and many other municipalities have found necessary, has reduced the profitability of slum investment. The typical landlord response has been to reduce maintenance and avoid additional investment.*

In the face of tax uncertainty, combined with the other negative factors which have been detailed, the slum market mechanism has been immobilized and with it a substantial part of the private potential for better slum maintenance and improvement.

Landlord Knowledge of Non-Reassessable Improvements

In Exhibit 11–8 is presented the landlords' responses to a series of questions about the tax impact of a variety of different improvements. Note the variation in response both on the absolute level for any one improvement and also between the several sizes of landlords.

More than a third of the parcels were in the hands of owners who indicated that repairing and replacing porches and steps would result in reassessment. More than a third thought that central heat could be installed without reassessment.

According to city tax authorities, *the former can be done without reassessment while the latter involves an increase of the assessment figure.*

EXHIBIT 11-8
What Improvements Can You Make without Reassessment?

	NA/DK		Other		Over 12		7–12		4–6		2–3		1		Total	
	Number	Per cent	Number	Per cent	Number	Per cent	Number	Per cent	Number	Per cent	Number	Per cent	Number	Per cent	Number	Per cent
A. REPAIRING PORCHES, etc.																
Yes, will be reassessed	—	—	—	—	17	30.9	5	17.9	9	21.4	28	41.2	59	50.0	118	37.5
No reassessment	4	100.0	—	—	38	69.1	23	82.1	33	78.6	40	58.8	59	50.0	197	62.5
NA/DK	—	—	—	—	6	—	3	—	1	—	16	—	51	—	77	—
Live sample	4		0		55		28		42		68		118		315	
B. ELECTRICAL WIRING																
Yes, will be reassessed	—	—	—	—	22	40.0	4	14.3	5	11.9	14	20.0	41	33.9	86	26.9
No reassessment	4	100.0	—	—	33	60.0	24	85.7	37	88.1	56	80.0	80	66.1	243	73.1
NA/DK	—	—	—	—	6	—	3	—	1	—	14	—	48	—	72	—
Live sample	4		0		55		28		42		70		121		320	
C. WATER HEATER																
Yes, will be reassessed	1	25.0	—	—	13	24.1	8	28.6	13	31.0	19	27.9	47	39.8	101	32.2
No reassessment	3	75.0	—	—	41	75.9	20	71.4	29	69.0	49	72.1	71	60.2	213	67.8
NA/DK	—	—	—	—	7	—	3	—	1	—	16	—	51	—	78	—
Live sample	4		0		54		28		42		68		118		314	
D. CENTRAL HEAT																
Yes, will be reassessed	2	50.0	—	—	50	90.9	21	75.0	30	71.4	31	41.3	68	57.6	202	63.7
No reassessment	2	50.0	—	—	5	9.1	7	25.0	12	28.6	39	55.7	50	42.4	115	36.3
NA/DK	—	—	—	—	6	—	3	—	1	—	14	—	51	—	75	—
Live sample	4		0		55		28		42		70		118		317	
E. OUTSIDE REFACING																
Yes, will be reassessed	1	25.0	—	—	34	61.8	6	22.2	21	50.0	38	56.7	87	74.4	187	59.9
No reassessment	3	75.0	—	—	21	38.2	21	77.8	21	50.0	29	43.3	30	25.6	125	40.1
NA/DK	—	—	—	—	6	—	4	—	1	—	17	—	52	—	80	—
Live sample	4		0		55		27		42		67		117		312	
Sub-N	4															
For entire set (A–E)	4		—		61		31		43		84		169		392	

A substantial number of the respondents think that automatic hot water heater installation or the installation of new electrical wiring will result in reassessment. The responses to outside refacing, another improvement which, again according to city authorities, can be done without reassessment, were substantially fearful. About 60 percent felt that they would be reassessed if they made this type of improvement.

A number of the landlords pointed to the fact that though they might not get reassessed for a specific improvement at the time of the improvement, there was a substantial probability of their getting reassessed in the course of the periodic reassessment that the city goes through.

The fear of external improvement was confirmed by the thirty-three respondents who summarized their answers by volunteering comments which in essence said that any kind of outside improvement would lead to reassessment. One said, "If you make the improvement inside without a permit you're okay." Another, who owns a considerable number of parcels and is a member of a neighborhood rehabilitation committee which has put out a pamphlet reassuring landlords on the non-reassessibility of good maintenance and outside improvement, said that, "Anything which enhances a parcel will cause reassessment." And still another owner, who has more than seven hundred fifty dwelling units in Newark, responded to the question of repairing or replacing steps by saying: "If you're smart and get a carpenter without a permit it's no problem. You've got to keep away from getting a building permit as far as getting taxed for repairs is concerned."

The question of illegal improvement came up a number of times. In this context the point was made by several landlords that at one time, back "in the days when the contractors and the unions were too busy to keep a good look out" it was possible to make substantial repairs without securing a building permit. Now that the contracting business "wasn't so good," the unions, it was claimed, keep a very close watch on all deliveries from major building supply houses, and will tip-off the building inspectors on non union, nonpermit jobs.[4]

The fear of small owners toward tax increases was most evident. For example, Parcel Number 420: Negro owner and wife; both over sixty-five; husband is blind; they live on social security and the rentals from two parcels which they own.

"We have repaired the steps and porches, but you have to be careful about too much improving on the outside because they can ride by and see it!" The same owner when asked—"What improvements would you make on this property if you were sure of not getting a boost in taxes?"—replied, "The painting of the porch on the outside."

As has been noted before, a number of the individual parcel owners and the two to three parcel owners are poor people. As such, they frequently have little means and perhaps even less initiative with which to repair their homes. It is for this reason perhaps that taxes rank so very large in their thinking. Given a very limited income from parcel ownership, the pinch of taxes is most acute. As one of them said, "I'm too old to pay more taxes, I'm retired."

Tax Relief Potential

What would be the results of a municipal policy of guarantees of no tax increases as a result of improvements? In Exhibits 11–9, 11–10, 11–11, and 11–12 are examined the responses to this question, first by area and then by size of holdings. The response, to say the least, is not particularly heartening. In all of the areas, with the exception of 2B, the bulk of the response was negative. There would be no repairs, even minor ones, despite guarantees against tax boost. (See Exhibit 11–9.) The only exception is Area 2B with a relatively small sample under consideration. Note that there is, with this exception, no significant variation between the several areas. In essence, there is no variation as a function of area in response towards tax guarantees. If the sample had included an area which was even less run down than the Group 3 tracts, conceivably there might be a significant change. This is not the case, however, for a reasonably representative sample of 40 percent of Newark.

This lack of variation is perhaps, in part, explained by Exhibit 11–10 which attempts to indicate what reasons were given for disinclination to make improvements even with tax guarantees. Note that while only 38.2 percent of the responses in Area 1 indicated that in the opinion of the landlord, at least as verbalized, the parcel "doesn't need it," the percentage rises in Area 2B, for example, to 75 percent and in Area 3B to 60.5 percent. There is a significant variation between the A and B groups in both Areas 2 and 3.

The other reasons for lack of initiative at this offer are varied in character. If the "rentals too limited" response is lumped together with the "not worth it" response and the "neighborhood no good" response, the field is pretty well bracketed. As in the case of mortgage aid, a small proportion of our responses revolve around the fear of urban renewal.

EXHIBIT 11-9

WHAT IMPROVEMENTS WOULD YOU MAKE IF YOU WERE SURE OF NOT GETTING A BOOST IN TAXES?

	AREA 1		AREA 2A		AREA 2B		AREA 3A		AREA 3B		TOTAL	
	Number	Per cent	Number	Per cent	Number	Per cent	Number	Per cent	Number	Per cent	Number	Per cent
Major internal and external	16	12.7	6	7.1	2	5.9	8	10.7	4	7.8	36	9.7
External major	8	6.3	6	7.1	8	23.5	3	4.0	4	7.8	29	7.8
Internal major	4	3.2	3	3.6	4	11.8	10	13.3	3	5.9	24	6.5
External minor	5	4.0	2	2.4	2	5.9	2	2.7	3	5.9	14	3.8
Internal minor	1	0.8	2	2.4	1	2.9	2	2.7	—	—	6	1.6
Doing it w/o regard for taxes	6	4.8	9	10.7	2	5.9	5	6.7	4	7.8	26	7.0
Few or none	76	60.3	53	63.1	15	44.1	43	57.3	33	64.7	220	59.5
Won't because of urban renewal	10	7.9	3	3.6	—	—	2	2.7	—	—	15	4.1
Total	126	100.0	84	100.0	34	100.0	75	100.0	51	100.0	370	100.0
NA/DK	2		6		3		6		2		19	
No response indicated	3		—		—		—		—		3	—

EXHIBIT 11–10

WHAT IMPROVEMENTS WOULD YOU MAKE IF YOU WERE SURE OF NOT GETTING A BOOST IN TAXES?

	AREA 1		AREA 2A		AREA 2B		AREA 3A		AREA 3B		TOTAL	
	Num-ber	Per-cent	Num-ber	Per-cent	Num-ber	Per-cent	Num-ber	Per-cent	Num-ber	Per-cent	Num-ber	Per-cent
Can't afford it	2	2.6	5	8.2	1	6.3	2	4.7	3	7.9	13	5.6
Doesn't need it	29	38.2	26	42.6	12	75.0	20	46.5	23	60.5	110	47.0
Neighborhood no good	11	14.5	7	11.5	—	—	8	18.6	—	—	26	11.1
Would need financing	—	—	—	—	—	—	—	—	—	—	—	—
Other requirement	1	1.3	—	—	—	—	—	—	—	—	1	0.4
Rentals too limited	8	10.5	6	9.8	2	12.5	2	4.7	1	2.6	19	8.1
Tenants no good	7	9.2	3	4.9	—	—	2	4.7	—	—	12	5.1
Not worth it	18	23.7	14	22.9	1	6.3	9	20.9	11	28.9	53	22.6
Total*	76	100.0	61	100.0	16	100.0	43	100.0	38	100.0	234	100.0
NA/DK	52		29		21		38		15		155	
No response indicated	3		—		—		—		—		3	

* Some multiple answers.

Exhibits 11–11 and 11–12 analyze the responses in terms of size of holding. There is little variation in the respondents who would make few or no improvements. A similar result is indicated for those who plan major repairs. There is, however, a substantial variation, as indicated in Exhibit 11–12, in the reasons given for this lack of interest. While the proportion of "twelve-plus" holders who feel that their parcels "don't need improvements" is even larger than those for smaller holders, this is not true for those holders who have been indicated as perhaps the poorest maintainers of parcels, i.e. the intermediate-sized holder. Similarly, multiple-parcel owners seem to be more affected by the neighborhood "being no good" than are single-parcel owners. Only 5.3 percent of the latter indicated the neighborhood as their reason for being disinclined to improve, while the figures for the "twelve-plus" parcel holders are 14.3 percent, the six to twelve holders are 22.2 percent, and the three to six parcel holders are 24 percent, respectively.

A similar relationship exists among those who give the response that the rentals are too limited. The answer that "the parcel is not worth it" received remarkably homogeneous response, with the exception of the "twelve-plus" category. It is these professional large-scale holders who, as has been indicated in an earlier chapter, are most likely to take advantage of any subsidization.

Conclusions

There is no question that the fear of tax increases plays a major role in inhibiting improvements. This is perhaps more a function of tax rates than of assessment increases. Attitudes toward the latter indicate an enormous degree of ignorance (or perhaps it is sophistication?) on the part of landholders toward the city's attitude on what constitutes an assessable improvement. When responses are received to the question, "What improvements would you make in this property if you were sure of not getting a tax boost?" are on the order of "I would just do a painting job," the effects of this uncertainty are all too clear. *Though the results of this question in the cases cited may be disappointing to those who would hope for more extensive improvements, implicit in the remark is the fact that fear of tax boost is inhibiting even the painting of the exterior of the parcel.* The Puerto Rican owner who indicated that "any improvement will increase taxes" speaks from a basic fear of government and the mysteries and uncertainties that surround its conduct.

EXHIBIT 11-11

WHAT IMPROVEMENTS WOULD YOU MAKE IF YOU WERE SURE OF NOT GETTING A BOOST IN TAXES?

	NA/DK		Other		Over 12		7–12		4–6		2–3		1		Total	
	Number	Per cent	Number	Per cent	Number	Per cent	Number	Per cent	Number	Per cent	Number	Per cent	Number	Per cent	Number	Per cent
Major internal and external	—	—	—	—	6	10.3	4	13.8	3	7.1	9	11.3	14	8.9	36	9.7
External major	—	—	—	—	4	6.9	2	6.9	3	7.1	2	2.5	18	11.5	29	7.5
Internal major	—	—	—	—	3	5.2	1	3.4	5	11.9	4	5.0	11	7.0	24	6.5
External minor	—	—	—	—	1	1.7	—	—	1	2.4	4	5.0	7	4.5	13	3.5
Internal minor	—	—	—	—	1	1.7	3	10.3	1	2.4	—	—	1	0.6	6	1.6
Doing it w/o regard for taxes	1	33.3	—	—	3	5.2	5	17.2	3	7.1	5	6.3	9	5.7	26	7.1
Few or none	2	66.7	—	—	36	62.1	14	48.4	25	59.6	54	67.4	93	56.7	224	60.0
Won't because of urban renewal	—	—	—	—	4	6.9	—	—	1	2.4	2	2.5	8	5.1	15	4.1
NA/DK	1	—	—	—	3	—	2	—	1	—	4	—	8	—	19	—
Sub-N	4		—		61		31		43		84		169		392	
Live sample	3		0		58		29		42		80		161		373	

EXHIBIT 11-12

WHAT IMPROVEMENTS WOULD YOU MAKE IF YOU WERE SURE OF NOT GETTING A BOOST IN TAXES?

	NA/DK		Other		Over 12		7–12		4–6		2–3		1		Total	
	Number	Per-cent	Number	Per-cent	Number	Per-cent	Number	Per-cent	Number	Per-cent	Number	Per-cent	Number	Per-cent	Number	Per-cent
Can't afford it	—	—	—	—	—	—	—	—	—	—	4	7.1	10	10.6	14	5.9
Doesn't need it	2	66.7	—	—	23	54.7	7	38.8	7	28.0	24	42.9	49	52.2	112	47.1
Neighborhood no good—	—	—	—	—	6	14.3	4	22.2	6	24.0	6	10.7	5	5.3	27	11.3
Would need financing	—	—	—	—	—	—	—	—	—	—	—	—	—	—	—	—
Other requirement	—	—	—	—	—	—	1	5.6	—	—	—	—	—	—	1	0.4
Rentals too limited	1	33.3	—	—	5	11.9	—	—	4	16.0	4	7.1	5	5.3	19	8.0
Tenants no good—doesn't warrant	—	—	—	—	2	4.8	1	5.6	2	8.0	5	8.9	2	2.1	12	5.0
Not worth it	—	—	—	—	6	14.3	5	27.8	6	24.0	13	23.3	23	24.5	53	22.3
NA/DK	1	—	—	—	19	—	13	—	18	—	28	—	75	—	154	—
Sub-N	4		—		61		31		43		84		169		392	
Live sample	3		0		42		18		25		56		94		238	

While the removal of these fears and uncertainties certainly would result in some improvement, there is substantial question as to whether this would be very extensive. How "truthful" (reflective of a mental attitude making for action) are the attitudes which we have presented here. Let us take one case study.

> Case 73—a major professional owner of realty with over a dozen parcels in Newark. He indicated that outside refacing could be done without incurring new assessment and that the case was similar for automatic hot water heating. The owner has two parcels in our survey area on —————— Street, one of which has been substantially improved while the other is a run-down cold-water operation. The latter has apartments renting for $45 per month, the former has units that rent for nearly double that figure. When asked why the second parcel was not improved the landlord said, "If I improved I would still be scared to raise the rents and the people would move out and the area just doesn't warrant more investment." He said further, "I'd like other landlords on —————— Street to get together and make more improvements, but unless we do it together it just doesn't make any sense for one of us to do it alone."

It is this fear of neighborhood impact and even more its corollary, failure to secure tenants willing to pay for the improvements, which inhibits improvements. Guarantees against tax increases, even if they were forthcoming and *believed*, do not necessarily generate a larger rent roll in themselves. The market situation in the areas of the older city which are under consideration has degenerated to the point of reaching a dynamic spiral: lack of maintenance leads to poorer rent rolls, poorer rent rolls lead to lack of maintenance. While certainly the tax level has in part accounted for the situation, it is far from being a lonely villain. A more enlightened tax policy would probably secure its greatest results from the two ends of the ownership spectrum—the very large owners and the individual parcel holders. Indeed, it is perhaps the latter group who have the most overall potential as bootstrappers of the slums. They are the group least inhibited by fear of neighborhood.

In our concluding chapter we shall attempt to pull together the many strands which we have in part explored, and conclude with policies for governmental action.

REFERENCES

1 *Newark Star Ledger*, August 30, 1954, p. 14.
2 On the question of low tax valuations on slums, note that in a study of sales assessment ratios in Pittsburgh the mean ratios of assessed values to sale prices of houses
  in the wards occupied by the lowest income groups are uniformly higher than those in
  the newer wards. Raymond L. Richmond, *The Theory and Practice of Site—Value
  Taxation in Pittsburgh* (Pittsburgh: September 17, 1964, mimeographed).
3 Note that Rapkin, in his study of good versus poor structures on West Side
  New York, found that expenditures were in general agreement by landlords of both
  types of parcels, with the major exception of real estate taxes. For good properties,
  taxes absorb $.20 out of every rent dollar while $.15 went for taxes on the poor
  properties. Rapkin, *The Real Estate Market* . . ., pp. 71–2.
4 The discrepancy which has been noted by a number of authorities, between the
  housing statistics of 1950 and 1960, even if allowance is made for demolitions and
  building-permit-accompanied-improvements, undoubtedly is a function of the enormous number of nonlicensed improvements that were made in the decade. Based on
  the observations above, it may be questioned whether the same can be anticipated in
  the 1960–1970 decade.

Chapter 12

GOVERNMENT POLICIES
FOR ACTION

The entangled mesh of ownership patterns, of changes in the form and function of the older city and the folkways of its inhabitants, the great migration patterns which have dominated the demographic considerations in and about the United States metropolitan areas, the rising standards of expectation, all provide the matrix within which the data presented in our earlier chapters have taken form. Any efforts at improving attitudes toward slum maintenance and rehabilitation must in turn take this matrix into account, or prove unsuccessful.

The present market situation is one of virtual stagnation in the hard-core slum areas. The combination of risk, decreasing profitability, and loss of potential for capital gains has substantially restricted the kinds of professional owners who are willing to invest in slum properties. It takes a highly insensitive individual to become a professional nonresident owner of slum property, in the light of present societal attitudes. This is not an individual who is easily influenced to invest his money unless an appropriate return can be secured. Given the relative weakness of the slum apartment market, a weakness which has been aided in Newark's case by substantial amounts of public housing, as well as the shifts out of the central city which have been indicated in Chapter 3, the professional landlord has been faced with the choice of basically two alternatives: to stand pat and not increase his investment, or to attempt to improve his parcel in order to secure higher rentals.

The pattern that was observed in the course of this study indicates that the choice substantially has been the former. The observer cannot fail to be struck by the "heads you win, tails we lose" nature of this phenomenon. When the apartment market is very strong the landlord need not improve; when the apartment market is very weak the landlord fears for his investment and does not improve. What can municipal authorities use to break this impasse? Code enforcement is the usual reply. Code enforcement, however, must be, as will be noted later in more detail, accompanied by financing help and tax reassurance. Without this accompaniment it will merely lead to wholesale evasion and corruption. Before pursuing these matters in more detail, it is essential that the basic question be resolved—what the city, as a reflection of society, is or should be doing with slums and their occupants.

What Is, or Should Be, The Cities' Attitude Toward Slums and Slum Dwellers?

If this writer may be permitted a gross oversimplification, the problem of the slums is one both of plumbing and morale. It has largely been viewed in the past as consisting solely of plumbing. This is not to denigrate the former; but the provision of appropriate housing amenities is certainly an essential step toward improving the outlook and aspiration level of slum dwellers. However, the morale problem cannot be cured merely by providing physical amenities. The relatively limited success of public housing bears testimony on this point.

Government policy towards the slums must have as its primary aim the improvement of the aspiration level and capacity for goal realization of the slums' inhabitants. Tax policy, code enforcement, financing aid, and municipal services; all of these must be viewed within the context of the overall objective.

The community must face the realities of the slum situation fairly, without self-deception or romanticism, and at the same time move for change. A review of slum conditions as they exist is in order.

1. In Newark, as in many of other Northern industrial cities, the overwhelming majority of hard-core slum area residents are Negroes. The whites, who continue to decrease in number, are typically an elderly remnant of earlier immigration.

2. There is little evidence of a substantial return of the white middle class to the slum areas of the city.

3. A substantial proportion of slum tenements are owned by absentee

white owners. These owners are not merely absentees from the slums per se, they are also absentees, at least as residents, from the city in which they own property.

4. The factor of ownership is the single most basic variable which accounts for variations in the maintenance of slum properties. Good parcel maintenance typically is a function of resident ownership.

5. Dependent upon major programs of land clearance for purposes of urban renewal and/or highway construction, a population vacuum will develop in the slums. The tidal wave of Southern Negro migration has slowed down and is substantially bypassing some of the Northern cities which were its traditional goals.[1] With virtual stability in the Puerto Rican population size, there is no new depressed group on the horizon to fill the older slums.

6. While this population decrease makes the problem of relocation much simpler, it also tends to limit the landlords' capacity and will to improve parcels.

7. Given a substantial dependence upon land taxes in the face of increased demands upon the municipality for services, taxes have become a major inhibitor of entrepreneural activity in the central city. Both in terms of their impact, and in terms of the uncertainty which surround their administration, current municipal tax policies are leading to further degeneration of the slums.

8. The relationship of client and patron, which plays a dominant role in the dealings between government, both municipal and federal, and the poor population of the slums, is deleterious to the morale of the individuals concerned.

Within these parameters are there policies which would improve present slum conditions, both in terms of buildings and of people? Over the past year a whole armory of enabling legislation has been passed by Congress. Local authorities have been given the essential weapons for the fight against blight and for better housing conditions. The Housing and Urban Development Act of 1965 is indicative of the growing sophistication of government policies in rehabilitation. From a direct loan program, which provides long-term 3 percent loans, to the rehabilitation grant procedure under section 115 of Title I of the 1964 act, and to the demolition grant and aid to code enforcement divisions, a vast armory has been supplied to local authority.[2]

It should be stressed that the enabling legislation mentioned above is strictly that—enabling legislation. It remains for local authority to take the initiative in implementing programs which will take advantage of this legislation. There are certain to be many difficulties on the road to implementing this legislation. There is no new legislation that does not require some degree of experience in its utilization. Certainly, however, the community is better armed for rehabilitation than has ever before been the case.

The discussion which follows will focus first on the development of resident landlords, and the ancillary elements which this will require, such as guidance and financing arrangements, as well as tax policy. From this the discussion turns to the question of municipal services and the problem of the hard-core slum and code enforcement.

Boosting the Proportion of Resident Landlords in Slum Tenements

As Exhibit 9–2 in Chapter 9 indicated most forcefully, *there is no question of the significance of landlord residence, particularly of single-parcel landlords, as insurance of proper maintenance of slum tenements.* Given the priority accorded by multiple-parcel owners to tenant problems as an inhibitor, as shown in Exhibit 11–7 in Chapter 11, the lack of feeling on this score by resident landlords, coupled with their good record in maintenance, is most significant. *It is the resident landlord, and only the resident landlord, who is in a position to properly screen and supervise his tenantry. No one-shot wave of maintenance and paint up-sweep up campaign can provide the day-to-day maintenance which is required in slum areas.* Given the relatively small size of Newark tenement units, and others like them, this can only be accomplished by a resident landlord. The record of these landlords, as we have indicated, is such as to inspire confidence in their future behavior on this score.

By making it feasible for more residents to become' owners, we further encourage the development of local leadership which is so sorely lacking in most slums. The role of resident owners as guides and creators of life patterns for the youth of the slums to follow is clearly evident.[3]

How could this type of development be stimulated? There are several prime requirements. The first of these, obviously, is financing help. In Exhibit 12–1 is presented a table which indicates cash flow requirements as a function of mortgage term and interest rates. As can be noted in the Ex-

EXHIBIT 12–1

MONTHLY LEVEL PAYMENTS REQUIRED TO AMORTIZE $1,000 OVER
VARIOUS TERMS AND AT VARIOUS INTEREST RATES

Interest Rate (Percent)	Term (in years)						
	10	15	20	25	30	35	40
6.0	$11.10	$8.44	$7.16	$6.44	$6.00	$5.70	$5.50
5.5	10.85	8.17	6.88	6.14	5.68	5.37	5.16
5.0	10.61	7.91	6.60	5.85	5.37	5.05	4.82
4.5	10.36	7.65	6.33	5.56	5.07	4.73	4.50
4.0	10.12	7.40	6.06	5.28	4.77	4.43	4.18
3.5	9.89	7.15	5.80	5.01	4.49	4.13	3.87

Source: Ernest M. Fisher, *Urban Real Estate Markets: Characteristics and Financing* (N. Y. C.: National Bureau of Economic Research, 1951) p. 71.

hibit, the term of mortgages is much more significant from a cash flow point of view than are interest rates. For example, a mortgage at 6 percent which is written for a fifteen-year period imposes a smaller cash flow burden than an equivalent size mortgage for ten-year period at 3.5 percent. Given the dearth of available financing, which is currently the case in the slums, there is obviously no alternative but to provide something in the way of long-term FHA guaranteed mortgages for slum tenement purchases *by residents*. The analogy with the early Homestead Act springs readily to mind. In that case, government lands were provided at relatively reasonable rates and with liberal financing to those who would live on them. The same thing must be done in the slums. The 1965 Housing Act is a beginning on the road.

With this must be coupled inexpensive fire and liability insurance for resident owners in slum areas. The expense and difficulty of securing these necessities is rising rapidly and it strikes hardest upon the poor landlord who has limited leverage with an underwriter.

Financing, however, is merely one of the several steps which is required. Earlier in this work reference was made to the *storm window syndrome*. This is merely one symptom of the frequent victimization of relatively innocent new resident buyers of slum tenements by a variety of home improvement services. The pride of these people in ownership makes them easy marks for "pay later" operators. The point raised by a money lender interviewed in the course of this study should be kept in sight here. He pointed to the fact that commonly when he has to repossess a parcel, the typical cause is that the owner has burdened the parcel with two or more home improvement loans. Just as the Agriculture Department provides a variety of advisory services for the farmer, so the city and/or the Federal Government must provide equivalent advisory services for the new home owner in the slum areas. These advisors must be competent not merely in home improvements, but also in financing and appraising parcels. It would seem entirely possible that among the ranks of senior savings and loan people, as well as within the ranks of the present FHA personnel, such individuals could be found. Technical competence, however, must be linked with a basic sympathy with the aspiration level of the new owner and with none of the *deus ex machina* attitude that so often exists in government relations with the poor.

The question of tax policy is a most significant one on this score, as it is in terms of the general problem of slums. It may well behoove the city to continue its policy of full assessment based upon market values. Obviously, where broad-based taxation is available on a basis other than land, it may reduce some of the strain. Reassessment policy, however, must be more clearly defined than is presently the case. The landlord should have no reason to fear city reassessment merely because of painting the outside of his house.

It is essential that the city not merely adopt a more reasonable attitude toward taxation, but also *sell* the facts of this attitude to those who may be influenced by misconceptions as to its reality. In addition, in the long run it may very well pay the city to provide the equivalent of homestead rebates for resident landlords. This is a format (which will be recognized by those readers who are familiar for example, with tax policy in a city such as Miami Beach) in which the homesteader, i.e. the resident landlord, receives either a reduction or a rebate in his real estate taxes. This might well be coupled with a stipulation that the rebate be employed in the improvement of the parcel in question. The area of uncertainty and suspicion which surrounds current taxing procedures must be clarified. Its existence clearly inhibits improvements. Once again the reader may wish to review the data presented in Chapter 11 which indicates the fears of landlords on municipal tax policy. *This fear has been justified frequently in fact because of the financial bind of a municipality dependent on realty taxes in the face of expanding needs and a static base. In these circumstances, pressure on the landlord's pocket is a constant. While, as has been indicated, tax relief in itself will not generate improvement—it is an essential step toward fostering it. Alternative means of financing municipal needs, therefore, must be found.*

Municipal Services

There seems to be ample evidence that the level of municipal services required by the slum areas is higher than that required by nonslum equivalent areas. At the same time there is reason to believe that the actual delivery level of these services is reversed with poorer areas being slighted. The comments of a Negro owner on this subject are most apropos.

> Parcel #330 was purchased in 1935. "You know the neighborhood has really changed terribly since we moved in here. At first it was mostly German and Jewish, and the police in the city took care of things. No trucks parked overnight in the streets and no noise or anything like that. Now there is mostly Negro and they don't seem to come any more. If you complain they want to put you in jail.—Many of the owners here would like to stay, but the neighborhood is run down so that most of them sell just to get away. Since Negroes have become predominant, the city has allowed things that they would not allow when I just first moved here."

One should notice that the parcel was very well maintained. The owner commented that he was sure that continued municipal surveillance would have saved the neighborhood regardless of who moved in. The backyard of this parcel which has a very handsome garden, looks out upon a sea of debris. The owners complain that they have had to screen their back porches to keep the rats out. Another Negro landlord made the following comment:

> "When I went to complain to the police department about overnight truck parking and teenage hoodlums on the block, the cops made me feel like a criminal. I was glad to go home and kind of hide myself behind the door."

These comments mirror attitudes which are most common among current resident landlords.

Every effort must be made by the city to provide an optimum level of services within the slums. Such functions as police protection, street lighting, parking restrictions, garbage collection, and a host of others could be named here. Not least among these is the question of educational facilities. While this is a subject whose depth is beyond the scope of this study, it cannot be omitted. Without substantial efforts on all of these fronts, the efforts at rehabilitating the slums must falter.

The Future of the Hard-core Slum

As has been noted in the section on "Who Owns the Slums," there are clear-cut indications that new resident buyers are unwilling to move into an area which is as far gone as is Area 1. The dominance of large-scale absentee landlordism in that area is a tribute to the fact that they are the only landlords who are willing to invest in such problem situations. One can seriously question the potential of such an area for rehabilitation. Given the relatively loose housing market, which presently exists in center-city Newark, the bulldozer approach to such hard-core areas would seem to be the only answer. This should not wait upon redevelopers. The existence of such hard-core blight (it should be recalled that the area in question has less than 25 percent sound housing on the basis of the 1960 Census) can only serve to drag down the neighborhoods peripheral to it.

The loss of tax revenue to the municipality through this process of demolition must be accepted as surgery essential to preserve the surrounding areas from the spread of deep-seated blight. Obviously, the scale of this blight will require considerable discretion on the part of municipal authorities on the phasing and speed of demolition. Given the present functioning of the market, as has been indicated earlier, private enterprise cannot be depended on to remove buildings which are no longer usable. Again, new urban renewal legislation to ease this process was adopted in 1965, it must be vigorously utilized.

There is some question whether a change in tax policy to encourage demolition might not be in order. The needs of the city for more open space, the potential of already assembled and cleared substantial size tracts in encouraging further development, must be depended upon to generate future use for the areas in question. The maintenance of the hard-core blight areas, given the facts of alternative housing availability, cannot be justified upon tax income reasons alone.

Code Enforcement

Parallel with all of the suggestions above is the requirement that code enforcement be made much more rigorous. But prior to this, there is required a much more adequate definition of just what the code should be. For example, the requirement of central heat is observed least in some of the better housing areas in Area 3. It is not uncommon, particularly among members of earlier immigrant groups, that cold-water flats with suitable decentralized heating facilities are preferred to those whose heat supply is subject to the administration of the landlord and of the vagaries of the heating system. *Adequate insect and rodent control, plumbing that works, paint, and general cleanliness may be much more significant to the inhabitants of a tenement both physically and spiritually than the existence of central heat or plaster walls.* Whether the studs used in a repair are 16 inches on center or are 20 inches on center may be completely irrevelant to a tenant. A building which is completely satisfactory on the basis of existing codes, may be completely unsatisfactory in terms of its effect upon its occupants.

Code enforcement, therefore, must require a much more subjective approach than has previously been the case. This is particularly the case with those buildings in the hands of landlords who cannot afford repairs. In these cases, it may be necessary to work out a long-term plan of rehabilitating the parcel in question, with major emphasis being given to the paint and cleanliness functions, those most easily encompassed by "sweat equity." Good maintenance and resident landlordism are much more significant than mechanical adherence to a mechanical code. With the legality of multiple housing codes clarified, the city has a new avenue of creative action.

The responsibility of social workers to appreciate the fact that the loose housing market does enable them to move their clients "up" into better quarters is clear, though far from universally acted on. At least one of the major owners interviewed for this study is upgrading his parcels for welfare tenants whose housing allowances have been "opened up" slightly and who have alert social workers as guides.

No False Romanticism!

The self-help capacity of the poor is limited. Some resident landlords are elderly, others are uneducated, and some lack an appropriate aspiration level. The fact remains, however, that as a group, they are presently the best landlords in the slums, and provide probably the major hope for better maintenance in the future. It will require a talented and understanding guidance operation to help generate landlord enthusiasm while restraining over-expenditure. The problems here should not be underestimated. It is essential if this operation is to be truly successful, particularly from a morale standpoint, and also from the standpoint of securing *long-run* improvement, that the advisory service be a guide and an inspiration, not a directorate.

The present and future strains on the municipalities' budget, coupled with limited increases in revenue, will make it most difficult to pay for the services which are required. The alternative, however, of increasing degeneration is all too clear-cut. From a fiscal point of view, the program outlined above is a most burdensome one; this point should not be evaded. There is no other answer, however, from the city's point of view.

Tax policy must be directed toward aiding the good landlord, and penalizing those owners who do not properly maintain their properties. A tax policy based on sales value, as shown in Chapter 11, can easily have the reverse effect. The potential of homestead exemption, of rigorous code enforcement, and of self-help stimulating devices, must be rigorously exploited.

Rehabilitation and Rent Increases

There is a well-founded fear on the part of the tenantry that rehabilitation leads to rent increases. This must be accepted as a fact of the market. Although tax policy can somewhat relieve this factor, particularly when coupled with more adequate financing, this fact should be faced. *The potential of rent subsidies for the underincomed with which to pay better rents is quite clear here. There is no substitute for this approach. This is not to underestimate the value of code enforcement—but rather to add a carrot to the stick. There is more positive achievement by making rehabilitation profitable than in attempting to secure it through punitive measures.* The reward in terms of the aspiration level and general morale of the slum dweller will, I think, outweigh the cost. This is particularly true when the cost/benefits are contrasted with those of institutionalized public housing.

The key to improving the slums from a "people" point of view, is the creation of a resident responsible middle class within those areas—not a middle class which while physically in the area does not belong to it, as is the case with the efforts to create new middle class housing within slum areas cleared by urban renewal. This has no organic unity with the tenements per se, and can only provide frustration rather than leadership and emulation. These goals can best be accomplished and living conditions within the slum areas most enhanced by increasing the number of owner residents of slum tenements. This will require a highly coordinated effort in terms of tax policy, financing help, code enforcement, and advisory services. The rewards of a successful program are very great. The cost of present policies are equally evident.

REFERENCES

1 The nonwhite population of the United States is continuing to leave the South, but the outflow has been slowed considerably. Out-migration of Negroes from the South has averaged little more than seventy thousand per year in the period from 1960 to 1963, or only half that of the 1950 to 1960 period. This is based on a study done by the Metropolitan Life Insurance Company, See MLIC, *Statistical Bulletin,* April 1965, p. 3.

2 See H.H.F.A., *Local Public Agency Letters* 340, 341, 342, 343, 345, & 349 [Washington, 1965].

3 Given the lack of a masculine image which has been commented on as a not unfamiliar shortcoming of family upbringing among the poor, the significance of a resident owner *peer unter pares* to slum youth as a potential goal setter is clear-cut.

AREA TRACT
RACIAL CHANGES

DETERIORATING
OR DILAPIDATED
DWELLING UNITS

APPENDIX II

EXHIBIT A II-1

AREA TRACT RACIAL CHANGES 1940-50-60

Tract	1940						1950						1960†					
	White		Nonwhite		Total		White		Nonwhite		Total		White		Nonwhite		Total	
	Number	Per-cent	Number	Per-cent	Number	Per-cent	Number	Per-cent	Number	Per-cent	Number	Per-cent	Number	Per-cent	Number	Per-cent	Number	Per-cent
Area 1																		
12	2,783	71.1	1,131	28.9	3,914	100	1,977	46.1	2,312	53.9	4,289	100	545	13.8	3,401	86.2	3,946	100
15	3,950	95.3	195	4.7	4,145	100	3,477	84.6	633	15.4	4,110	100	1,508	37.4	2,525	62.6	4,033	100
30	3,270	63.8	1,854	36.2	5,124	100	2,065	39.3	3,192	60.7	5,257	100	502	12.9	3,379	87.1	3,881	100
33	4,229	98.9	46	1.1	4,275	100	3,932	93.9	254	6.1	4,186	100	1,838	43.5	2,389	56.5	4,227	100
63	1,249	37.5	2,080	62.5	3,329	100	641	17.1	3,116	82.9	3,757	100	135	5.3	2,408	94.7	2,543	100
82	2,386	51.6	2,241	48.4	4,627	100	1,512	32.0	3,211	68.0	4,723	100	423	11.6	3,232	88.4	3,655	100
83	3,049	70.4	1,280	29.6	4,329	100	2,356	56.5	1,812	43.5	4,168	100	1,254	41.8	1,744	58.2	2,998	100
Total Area 1	20,916	70.3	8,827	29.7	29,743	100	15,960	52.3	14,530	47.7	30,490	100	6,205	24.5	19,078	75.5	25,283	100
Area 2A																		
11	3,165	72.5	1,198	27.5	4,363	100	2,394	61.2	1,515	38.8	3,909	100	1,162	35.7	2,097	64.3	3,259	100
17	4,329	87.8	602	12.2	4,931	110	3,271	64.0	1,843	36.0	5,114	100	1,361	27.8	3,536	72.2	4,897	100
38	4,998	87.7	704	12.3	5,702	100	4,139	75.8	1,324	24.2	5,463	100	1,334	23.7	4,285	76.3	5,619	100
55	4,025	98.3	68	1.7	4,093	100	3,525	91.1	346	8.9	3,871	100	835	20.0	3,345	80.0	4,180	100
59	4,959	90.9	496	9.1	5,455	100	4,678	83.0	960	17.0	5,638	100	1,815	31.6	3,927	68.4	5,742	100
64	3,567	59.0	2,474	41.0	6,041	100	2,125	33.8	4,168	66.2	6,293	100	603	12.4	4,272	87.6	4,875	100
65	2,260	65.0	1,217	35.0	3,477	100	1,675	35.3	3,074	64.7	4,749	100	487	16.3	2,494	83.7	2,981	100
81	3,735	66.9	1,847	33.1	5,582	100	3,104	54.9	2,553	45.1	5,657	100	1,463	34.9	2,727	65.1	4,190	100
Total Area 2A	31,038	78.3	8,606	21.7	39,644	100	24,911	61.2	15,783	38.8	40,694	100	9,060	25.3	26,683	74.7	35,743	100
Area 2B																		
14	5,542	99.3	41	0.7	5,583	100	5,461	99.2	46	0.8	5,507	100	3,893	72.9	1,446	27.1	5,339	100
68	4,088	80.1	1,014	19.9	5,102	100	3,871	76.5	1,186	23.5	5,057	100	2,667	67.8	1,264	32.2	3,931	100
80	2,903	76.0	915	24.0	3,818	100	3,059	64.4	1,694	35.6	4,753	100	1,516	47.0	1,710	53.0	3,226	100

APPENDIX II—Continued

EXHIBIT A II-1

AREA TRACT RACIAL CHANGES 1940–50–60

	1940						1950						1960†					
	White		Nonwhite		Total		White		Nonwhite		Total		White		Nonwhite		Total	
Tract	Number	Per cent	Number	Per cent	Number	Per cent	Number	Per cent	Number	Per cent	Number	Per cent	Number	Per cent	Number	Per cent	Number	Per cent
Total Area 2B																		
	12,533	86.4	1,970	13.6	14,503	100	12,391	80.9	2,926	19.1	15,317	100	8,076	64.6	4,420	35.4	12,496	100
Total Area 2(A + B)																		
	43,571	80.5	10,576	19.5	54,147	100	37,302	66.6	18,709	33.4	56,011	100	17,136	35.5	31,103	64.5	48,239	100
Area 3A																		
29	4,897	98.0	100	2.0	4,997	100	4,115	91.4	389	8.6	4,504	100	2,234	53.8	1,915	46.2	4,149	100
31	3,306	82.3	712	17.7	4,018	100	2,520	64.0	1,418	36.0	3,938	100	751	13.8	4,677	86.2	5,428	100
32	4,969	98.8	58	1.2	5,027	100	4,298	95.5	202	4.5	4,500	100	2,074	45.4	2,493	54.6	4,567	100
39	2,044	61.6	1,272	38.4	3,316	100	1,828	42.6	2,466	57.4	4,294	100	553	15.5	3,011	84.5	3,564	100
40	4,347	89.5	509	10.5	4,856	100	3,301	71.3	1,329	28.7	4,630	100	529	11.2	4,176	88.8	4,705	100
57	5,315	79.9	1,336	20.1	6,651	100	4,104	65.7	2,141	34.3	6,245	100	1,890	33.8	3,701	66.2	5,591	100
58	4,672	99.6	20	0.4	4,692	100	4,333	89.3	518	10.7	4,851	100	1,761	32.8	3,610	67.2	5,371	100
60	1,774	41.1	2,538	58.9	4,312	100	893	17.7	4,138	82.3	5,031	100	265	6.8	3,626	93.2	3,891	100
62	1,129	21.5	4,131	78.5	5,260	100	634	11.1	5,089	88.9	5,723	100	280	7.5	3,469	92.5	3,749	100
66	1,417	22.8	4,803	77.2	6,220	100	1,074	16.1	5,601	83.9	6,675	100	578	12.3	4,135	87.7	4,713	100
84	2,311	66.6	1,158	33.4	3,469	100	2,340	69.6	1,020	30.4	3,360	100	1,252	49.0	1,304	51.0	2,556	100
Total Area 3A	36,181	68.5	16,637	31.5	52,818	100	29,440	54.8	24,311	45.2	53,751	100	12,167	25.2	36,117	74.8	48,284	100
Area 3B																		
2	2,327	84.1	440	15.9	2,767	100	1,963	79.7	500	20.3	2,463	100	1,476	74.3	511	25.7	1,987	100
10	3,528	95.0	184	5.0	3,712	100	3,243	93.2	237	6.8	3,480	100	2,511	73.9	885	26.1	3,396	100
16	4,986	91.6	459	8.4	5,445	100	5,397	88.2	724	11.8	6,121	100	3,845	68.0	1,806	32.0	5,651	100
36	3,834	99.8	8	0.2	3,842	100	3,535	99.7	10	0.3	3,545	100	3,064	92.3	256	7.7	3,320	100
67	4,005	91.6	368	8.4	4,373	100	4,803	89.2	579	10.8	5,382	100	3,174	65.8	1,650	34.2	4,824	100

APPENDIX II—Continued

EXHIBIT A II-1

AREA TRACT RACIAL CHANGES 1940–50–60

	1940						1950						1960†					
	White		Nonwhite		Total		White		Nonwhite		Total		White		Nonwhite		Total	
Tract	Number	Per-cent	Number	Per-cent	Number	Per-cent	Number	Per-cent	Number	Per-cent	Number	Per-cent	Number	Per-cent	Number	Per-cent	Number	Per-cent
Area 3B—*Continued*																		
75A	7,881	98.1	150	1.9	8,031	100	9,638	92.5	787	7.5	10,425	100	3,697	78.4	1,019	21.6	4,716	100
*75B	—	—	—	—	—	—	—	—	—	—	—	—	3,417	82.3	733	17.7	4,150	100
76	3,355	94.5	196	5.5	3,551	100	2,836	91.5	264	8.5	3,100	100	1,971	90.7	203	9.3	2,174	100
78	3,569	94.1	222	5.9	3,791	100	3,168	90.4	336	9.6	3,504	100	2,798	89.5	329	10.5	3,127	100
85	6,389	93.1	474	6.9	6,863	100	5,874	84.4	1,083	15.6	6,957	100	3,587	65.2	1,911	34.8	5,498	100
88	4,777	91.5	442	8.5	5,219	100	3,946	88.1	534	11.9	4,480	100	4,443	77.3	1,303	22.7	5,746	100
Total Area 3B	44,651	93.8	2,943	6.2	47,594	100	44,403	89.8	5,054	10.2	49,457	100	33,983	76.2	10,606	23.8	44,589	100
Total Area 3(A + B)	80,832	80.5	19,580	19.5	100,412	100	73,843	71.5	29,365	28.5	103,208	100	46,150	49.7	46,723	50.3	92,873	100
Total All Tracts	145,319	78.8	38,983	21.2	184,302	100	127,105	67.0	62,604	33.0	189,709	100	69,491	41.8	96,904	58.2	166,395	100
Balance of City	238,215	97.0	7,243	3.0	245,458	100	236,044	94.8	13,023	5.2	249,067	100	196,398	82.2	42,427	17.8	238,825	100
Total City	383,534	89.2	46,226	10.8	429,760	100	363,149	82.8	75,627	17.2	438,776	100	265,889	65.6	139,331	34.4	405,220	100

* Tract 75A and 75B were all one tract in the 1940 and 1950 Censuses,

† Data from 1960 contained in the 1960 Census listed "White," "Negro," and "Other Races." For the sake of comparability of data, "White" was maintained as a separate category, while "Negro" and "Other Races," were combined to form the "Nonwhite" category used here.

Sources: A, B, C, D, E (See Appendix III, "Source References")

EXHIBIT A II–2
DETERIORATING OR DILAPIDATED DWELLING UNITS—1960*

Tracts	Total Housing Units	Deteriorated or Dilapidated	Percent Deteriorated or Dilapidated
GROUP 1			
12	1,073	932	86.9
15	1,011	910	90.0
30	1,289	1,205	93.5
33	1,358	1,235	90.9
63	870	850	97.7
82	1,175	1,127	95.9
83	1,053	867	82.3
TOTAL	7,829	7,126	91.0
GROUP 2A			
11	864	613	70.9
17	1,368	958	70.0
38	1,604	867	54.1
55	1,144	755	66.0
59	2,091	1,234	59.0
64	1,552	1,070	68.9
65	1,190	835	70.2
81	1,991	1,059	53.2
TOTAL	11,804	7,391	62.6
GROUP 2B			
14	1,627	1,009	62.0
68	1,226	840	68.5
80	1,151	844	73.3
TOTAL	4,004	2,693	67.3
GROUP 2(A + B)	15,808	10,084	63.8
GROUP 3A			
29	1,276	523	41.0
31	1,466	526	35.9
32	1,228	568	46.3
39	1,045	517	49.5
40	1,374	457	33.3
57	2,156	952	44.2
58	1,934	933	48.2
60	1,472	733	49.8
62	1,984	889	44.8
66	2,044	745	36.4
84	806	390	48.4
TOTAL	16,785	7,233	43.1

EXHIBIT A II–2—Continued
DETERIORATING OR DILAPIDATED DWELLING UNITS—1960*

Tracts	Total Housing Units	Deteriorated or Dilapidated	Percent Deteriorated or Dilapidated
GROUP 3B			
2	647	282	43.6
10	1,016	366	36.0
16	1,585	583	36.8
36	1,123	467	41.6
67	2,294	1,120	48.8
75B	1,161	463	39.9
76	766	310	40.5
78	966	321	33.2
85	1,963	895	45.6
88	1,740	658	37.8
TOTAL	13,261	5,465	41.2
GROUP 3(A + B)	30,046	12,698	—
Percent of Number Reporting	100.0	42.3	—
ALL TRACTS	53,683	29,908	55.7
CITY TOTAL	134,872	39,114	—
Percent of Number Reporting	100.0	29.0	—

* Sources: See Appendix III.

CENSUS TERMINOLOGY AND SOURCES

1. *Deteriorated or dilapidated dwelling units*—The census field worker determined the condition of the housing unit by observation, on the basis of specified criteria. Nevertheless, the application of these criteria involved some judgment on the part of the individual enumerator. The training program for enumerators was designed to minimize differences in judgment. Deteriorating housing needs more care than would be provided in the course of regular maintenance. It has one or more defects of an intermediate nature that must be corrected if the unit is to continue to provide safe and adequate shelter. Dilapidated housing does not. It has one or more critical defects, or has a combination of intermediate defects in sufficient number to require extensive repair or rebuilding, or is of inadequate original construction. Critical defects result from continued neglect, or lack of repair, or indicate serious damage to the structure.

2. In contrast to 1960, the 1940 and 1950 Censuses listed a category of "Needing Major Repairs" in place of what was listed as "Deteriorated or Dilapidated" dwelling units in the 1960 Census. This "Needing Major Repairs" category was used "when repairs were needed on such parts of the structure as floors, roof, plaster, walls, or foundations, the continued neglect of which would impair the soundness of the structure and create a hazard to its safety as a place of residence."

3. *Definition of census tract*—Census tracts are small areas into which large cities and adjacent areas are divided for statistical purposes. Tract boundaries were established cooperatively by a local committee and the Bureau of the Census, and were generally designed to be relatively uniform with respect to population characteristics, economic status, and

living conditions. The average tract has about four thousand residents. Tract boundaries are established with the intention of being maintained over a long time so that comparisons may be made from census to census.

In the decennial censuses, the Bureau of the Census tabulates population and housing information for each census tract. The practice of local agencies to tabulate locally collected data by tracts has increased the value of census tract data in many areas.

Population Characteristics

Race and color—The three major race categories distinguished in this report are white, Negro, and other races. Among persons of "other races" are American Indians, Japanese, Chinese, Filipinos, Koreans, Asian Indians, and Malayans. Negroes and persons of "other races" taken together constitute "nonwhite" persons. Persons of Mexican birth or descent, who are not definitely of Indian or other nonwhite race, are classified as white. In addition to persons of Negro and of mixed Negro and white descent, the category "Negro" includes persons of mixed Indian and Negro descent unless the Indian ancestry very definitely predominates or unless the person is regarded as an Indian in the community.

Housing Characteristics

1. *Living quarters*—Living quarters were enumerated as housing units or group quarters. Occupied living quarters were classified as housing units or group quarters on the basis of information supplied by household members on the Advance Census Report and questions asked by the enumerator where necessary. Identification of vacant housing units was based partly on observation by the enumerator and partly on information obtained from owners, landlords, or neighbors.

A house, an apartment or other group of rooms, or a single room is regarded as a *housing unit* when it is occupied or intended for occupancy as separate living quarters, that is, when the occupants do not live and eat with any other persons in the structure and there is either (1) direct access from the outside or through a common hall or (2) a kitchen or cooking equipment for the exclusive use of the occupants of the unit.

Occupied quarters which do not qualify as housing units are classified as group quarters. They are located most frequently in institutions, hospitals, nurses' homes, rooming and boarding houses, military and other types of barracks, college dormitories, fraternity and sorority houses, convents, and monasteries. Group quarters are also located in a house or apartment in which the living quarters are shared by the person in charge and five or more persons unrelated to him. Group quarters are not included in the housing inventory, although the count of persons living in them is included in the population figures.

The inventory of housing units includes both vacant and occupied units. Newly constructed vacant units were included in the inventory if construction had reached the point that all the exterior windows and doors were installed and the final usable floors were in place. Dilapidated vacant units were included provided they were still usable as living quarters; they were excluded if they were being demolished or if there was positive evidence that they were to be demolished.

Trailers, tents, boats, and railroad cars were included in the housing inventory if they were occupied as housing units. They were excluded if they were vacant, used only for extra sleeping space or used only for vacations or business.

In 1950, the unit of enumeration was the dwelling unit. Although the definition of the housing unit in 1960 is essentially similar to that of the dwelling unit in 1950, the housing unit definition was designed to encompass all private living quarters, whereas the dwelling unit definition did not completely cover all private living accommodations. The main difference between housing units and dwelling units is as follows: In 1960, *separate* living quarters consisting of one room with direct access, but without separate cooking equipment, qualified as a housing unit whether in an apartment house, rooming house, or house converted to apartment use; in hotels, a single room qualifies as a housing unit if occupied by a person whose usual residence is the hotel or a person who has no usual residence elsewhere. In 1950, a one-room unit without cooking equipment qualified as a dwelling unit only when located in a regular apartment house or when the room constituted the only living quarters in the structure.

The evidence thus far suggests that using the housing unit concept in 1960, instead of the dwelling unit concept as in 1950, had relatively little effect on the counts for large areas and for the Nation. Any effect which the change in concept may have on comparability can be expected to be greatest in statistics for certain census tracts and blocks. Living quarters classified as housing units in 1960 but which would not have been classified as dwelling units in 1950, tend to be clustered in tracts where many persons live separately in single rooms in hotels, rooming houses, and other light house-keeping quarters. In such areas, the 1960 housing unit count for an individual tract may be higher than the 1950 dwelling unit count, even though no units were added by new construction or conversion.

2. *Occupied housing unit*—A housing unit was "occupied" if it was the usual place of residence for the person or group of persons living in it at the time of enumeration. Included are units occupied by persons who were only temporarily absent (for example, on vacation) and units occupied by persons with no usual place of residence elsewhere.

3. *Vacant housing unit*—A housing unit was "vacant" if no persons were living in it at the time of enumeration. However, if its occupants were only temporarily absent, the unit was considered occupied. Units temporarily occupied by persons having a usual place of residence elsewhere were considered vacant (classified as "nonresident" units in 1950).

Year-round vacant units are those intended for occupancy at any time of the year. Seasonal vacant units are those intended for occupancy during only a season of the year.

4. *Available* vacant units are those which are on the market for year-round occupancy, are in either sound or deteriorating condition, and are offered for rent or for sale. The group "for sale only" is limited to available units for sale only and excludes units "for rent or sale." The group "for rent" consists of units offered "for rent" and those offered "for rent or sale." The 1960 category "available vacant" is comparable with the 1950 category "vacant nonseasonal not dilapidated, for rent or sale."

5. *Other* vacant units comprise the remaining vacant housing units. They include dilapidated units, seasonal units, units rented or sold and awaiting occupancy, units held for occasional use, and units held off the market for other reasons. This category is comparable with the 1950 category "other vacant and nonresident."

6. *Tenure*—A housing unit is "owner occupied" if the owner or co-owner lives in the unit, even if it is mortgaged or not fully paid for. All other occupied units are classified as "renter occupied," whether or not cash rent is paid. Examples of units for which no cash rent is paid include units occupied in exchange for services rendered, units owned by relatives and occupied without payment of rent, and units occupied by sharecroppers.

7. *Persons*—All persons enumerated in the 1960 Census of Population as members of the household were counted in determining the number of persons who occupied the housing unit. These persons include any lodgers,

foster children, wards, and resident employees who shared the living quarters of the household head.

In the computation of the median number of persons, a continuous distribution was assumed, with the whole number of persons as the midpoint of the class interval. For example, when the median was in the three-person group, the lower and upper limits were assumed to be two and a half and three and a half persons, respectively. The median may be based on a sample or on the complete count of units.

8. *Persons per room*—The number of persons per room was computed for each occupied housing unit by dividing the number of persons by the number of rooms in the unit.

9. *Year moved into unit*—Data on year moved into unit are based on the information reported for the head of the household. The question relates to the year of latest move.

10. *Units in structure*—A structure is defined as a separate building that either has open space on all four sides, or is separated from other structures by dividing walls that extend from ground to roof.

Statistics are presented in terms of the number of housing units rather than the number of residential structures. However, the number of structures for the first two categories may be derived. For one-unit structures (which include trailers), the number of housing units and the number of structures are the same. For two-unit structures, the number of housing units is twice the number of structures. For the remaining categories, the number of structures cannot be derived from the data as tabulated.

The categories for number of housing units in the structure in 1960 are not directly comparable with those in 1950, particularly for one- and two-unit structures. In the 1950 tract report, units in detached or attached structures were shown separately, but those in semidetached structures containing one or two units were combined into one category. Comparability between 1950 and 1960 data may also be affected by the change in concept from dwelling unit to housing unit.

11. *Year structure built*—"Year built" refers to the date the original construction of the structure was completed, not to any later remodeling, addition, or conversion.

The figures on the number of units built during a given period do not necessarily represent the number of housing units added to the inventory during that period. The figures represent the number of units constructed during a given period plus the number created by conversions in structures originally built during that period, minus the number lost in structures built during the period. Losses occur through demolition, fire, flood, disaster, and conversion to nonresidential use or to fewer housing units.

12. *Rooms*—The number of rooms is the count of whole rooms used for living purposes, such as living rooms, dining rooms, bedrooms, kitchens, finished attic or basement rooms, recreation rooms, lodgers' rooms, and rooms used for offices by a person living in the unit. Not counted as rooms are bathrooms; halls, foyers, or vestibules; closets; alcoves; pantries; strip or pullman kitchens; laundry or furnace rooms; unfinished attics, basements, and other space used for storage.

In the computation of the median number of rooms, a continuous distribution was assumed, with the whole number of rooms as the midpoint of the class interval. For example, when the median was in the three-room group, the lower and upper limits were assumed to be two and a half and three and a half rooms, respectively. The median was computed on the basis of the tabulation groups shown in the table. If the median falls in the category "eight rooms or more," it is shown in the table as "seven and a half plus" rooms.

Condition and Plumbing

Data are presented on condition and plumbing facilities in combination. The categories represent various levels of housing quality.

The enumerator determined the condition of the housing unit by observation, on the basis of specified criteria. Nevertheless, the application of these criteria involved some judgment on the part of the individual enumerator. The training program for enumerators was designed to minimize differences in judgment.

1. *Sound housing* is defined as that which has no defects, or slight ones which are normally corrected during the course of regular maintenance.

2. *Deteriorating housing* needs more repair than would be provided in the course of regular maintenance. It has one or more defects of an intermediate nature that must be corrected if the unit is to continue to provide safe and adequate shelter.

3. *Dilapidated housing* does not provide safe and adequate shelter. It has one or more critical defects, or has a combination of intermediate defects in sufficient number to require extensive repair or rebuilding, or is of inadequate original construction. Critical defects result from continued neglect or lack of repair or indicate serious damage to the structure.

In 1950, the enumerator classified each unit in one of two categories, not dilapidated or dilapidated, as compared with the three categories of sound, deteriorating, and dilapidated in 1960. Although the definition of "dilapidated" was the same in 1960 as in 1950, it is possible that the change in the categories introduced an element of difference between the 1960 and 1950 statistics.

4. *The category "with all plumbing facilities"* consists of units which have hot and cold water inside the structure, and flush toilet and bathtub (or shower) inside the structure for the exclusive use of the occupants of the unit. Equipment is for exclusive use when it is used only by the persons in one housing unit, including any lodgers living in the unit.

5. *Units "lacking only hot water"* have all the facilities except hot water. Units "lacking other plumbing facilities" may or may not have hot water but lack one or more of the other specified facilities. Also included in this category are units whose occupants share toilet or bathing facilities with the occupants of another housing unit. The combination of "lacking only hot water" and "lacking other plumbing facilities" is presented as "lacking some or all facilities" in some census reports.

The categories of plumbing facilities presented in the 1960 report are not entirely comparable with those in the 1950 report. However, the 1950 category "no private bath or dilapidated" is equivalent to the following 1960 categories: "Dilapidated," "sound, lacking other plumbing facilities," and "deteriorating, lacking other plumbing facilities."

6. *Bathroom*—A housing unit is classified as having a bathroom if it has a flush toilet and bathtub (or shower) for the exclusive use of the occupants of the unit and also has hot water. The facilities must be located inside the structure, but need not be in the same room. Units which have an additional toilet or bathtub (or shower) for exclusive use are classified as having "more than one bathroom."

7. *Heating equipment*—The main type of heating equipment was to be reported even if it was temporarily out of order at the time of enumeration. For vacant units from which the heating equipment had been removed, the equipment used by the last occupant was to be reported.

"Steam or hot water" refers to a central heating system in which heat from steam or hot water is delivered through radiators or heating coils. "Warm air furnace" refers to a central system which provides warm air through ducts leading to the various rooms. "Built-in room units" are permanently installed heating units in floors, walls, or ceilings. They include floor, wall, or pipeless furnaces as well as built-in electrical units. Floor, wall, and pipeless furnaces deliver warm air to immediately adjacent rooms but do not have ducts leading to other rooms. "Other means—with flue" describes stoves, radiant gas heaters, fireplaces, and the like, connected to a chimney or flue which carries off the smoke or fumes. "Other means— without flue" describes portable or plug-in devices not connected to a chimney or flue, such as electric heaters, electric steam radiators, kerosene heaters, and radiant gas heaters.

Rent

1. *Contract rent*—Contract rent is that agreed upon regardless of furnishings, utilities, or services that may be included. Renter-occupied units for which no cash rent was paid were excluded from the computation of the median.

In the 1950 tract report, contract rent was not published separately for renter-occupied units (except for nonwhite renter-occupied units) but was shown in combination with vacant units available for rent.

2. *Gross rent*—The computed rent termed "gross rent" is the contract rent plus the average monthly cost of utilities (water, electricity, gas) and fuels such as wood, coal, and oil, if these items are paid for by the renter in addition to contract rent. Thus, gross rent eliminates rent differentials which result from varying practices with respect to the inclusion of heat and utilities as part of the rental payment.

Renter-occupied units for which no cash rent was paid are shown separately in the tabulation, but were excluded from the computation of the median. The median was computed on the basis of more detailed tabulation groups than are shown in the tables.

SOURCE REFERENCES

A. Population and Housing, Statistics for Census Tracts, Newark, N. J., 16th Census of the United States 1940. U. S. Government Printing Office, Washington: 1942.
B. Housing, Supplement to the First Series of Housing Bulletin for New Jersey, Newark Block Statistics, 16th Census of the United States 1940. U. S. Government Printing Office, Washington: 1942.
C. Block Statistics, Newark, New Jersey, United States Census of Housing, 1950; Volume V, Part 119. U. S. Government Printing Office, Washington: 1952.
D. 1950 United States Census, Population Data of Newark, New Jersey by Census Tracts; prepared by Newark Central Planning Board, Newark, N. J.
E. U. S. Censuses of Population and Housing: 1960. Census Tracts. Final Report PHC (1)–105, Newark, New Jersey. U. S. Bureau of the Census. U. S. Government Printing Office, Washington, D. C., 1962.

PARCEL CHOICE METHODOLOGY

Field Survey—The Parcel:

1. Draw a simple map of the block indicating the names of the bordering streets.

2. Choose parcel as indicated in procedure.

3. Indicate how many buildings your chosen parcel is from specific street corner, i.e. how many *address* numbers. This is essential for tax records which are based on *block* and *lot* numbers.

Procedure:

1. Start at SE corner of block.

2. Going clockwise, count the number of parcels on the block—going completely around it to starting point. *All* parcels that incorporate three or more apartments are to be included.

3. From Random Number Table take in sequence two digit numbers until one small enough to be in the block is found. (i.e., if thirty-two parcels, disregard all numbers over thirty-two until one of thirty-two or less comes up). This is the first parcel chosen.

See attached list for content and description material desired.

4. For each additional parcel use the same sequence counting from the *original starting point. Do not* repeat the random number sequences already used as you proceed through your sample choice. Cross off used numbers. Read the table as you would a book.

Field Survey Parcel Check List

ADDRESS:

Column Key

1–2	Census Tract Number
3–4	Census Block Number
5–8	Tax Block Number
9–11	Tax Lot Number

12   *Tract Category*
- (1) Less than 25 percent Sound designated as Area 1
- (2) 25–50 percent designated as Area 2B
- (3) 50–68 percent designated as Area 3A

13   *Occupancy*
- (1) Occupied
- (2) Partially occupied
- (3) Vacant

14   *Size of Parcel—No. of Apartments* (Each family represents a unit)
- (1) 3–6 Units
- (2) 7–12 Units
- (3) 13–24 Units
- (4) 25 or more Units

15   *Type of Construction*
- (1) Frame
- (2) Frame with reasonable to good condition siding
- (3) Frame with bad condition siding
- (4) Masonry

16   *Quality of External Appearance* (Compare to neighboring parcel)
- (1) Poorer than neighbors
- (2) Same as neighbors
- (3) Better than neighbors

17   *Absolute Quality* (Landlord's maintenance)
- (1) Reasonably kept
- (2) Poorly kept
- (3) Well kept
  (Criteria)

a. Garbage facilities

b. Health hazards (dirty halls, broken stairs)

c. Safety measures, i.e. fire escapes, sturdy porches, and stairs

18–19   *Quality of Street vs. Block* (Compare parcel to both sides of the street)

(1)   Same as

(2)   Better than

(3)   Poorer than

20–21   *Alterations and Improvements*

22   *Degree of Commercial Occupancy* (Specify type of business, if any)

(1)   None

(2)   Minor—less than 30 percent rent of parcel

(3)   Significant—30 percent or more

23   *Proximity of Nuisances*

(1)   Bars—in proximity to parcel

(2)   Loitering by undesirables

(3)   Junk yards

(4)   Factories

(5)   Heavy traffic

24–26   *General Comments* (Surveyors comments and evaluation of the parcel in general)

Parcel Ownership Check List

(Note the Tax Block Number in Columns 5–8 and Tax Parcel Number in Columns 9–11 before starting this page. *Give full answers. Do not mark keys.*

Column Key

Name of Owner

27   (1)   Individual (including joint ownership by husband and wife)

(2)   Two or more individuals

(3)   Realty corporations

(4)   Financial institutions

(5)   Nonfinancial institutions

(6)   Estates

Address of Owner

28 (1) Same address
    (2) Same general area of Newark (i.e. within _____ miles)
    (3) Newark other
    (4) New Jersey other than Newark
    (5) Outside New Jersey

Date of Title: _____

29 (1) 0–1 year old
    (2) 2–4 years old
    (3) 5–6 years old
    (4) 7–10 years old
    (5) 11–15 years old
    (6) 16–20 years old
    (7) Over 20 years old
    (8) Not recorded

Property Class

30 (1) 2
    (2) 4A
    (3) 4B
    (4) 4C
    (5) Other

Lot Size—(as stated, i.e. frontage × depth) include symbols

31–35 (1) Approximate square feet

Land Assessment

36–41 (1)

Building Assessment

42–47

Land Assessment Per Square Foot—

48–51 (1)

Land Assessment Classification Per Square Foot—

52 (1)   (6)
    (2)   (7)
    (3)   (8)
    (4)   (9)
    (5)   (10)

Mortgage Source—By Name

53   (1)   Savings bank
     (2)   Commercial bank
     (3)   Savings and loan
     (4)   Individual grantee
     (5)   Prior owner
     (6)   Mortgage company
     (7)   No mortgage shown
     (8)   Realty and construction company
     (9)   Not given
   (10)   Government agency

First Mortgage Amount—$_____

54–59   (1)

First Mortgage Terms

60	(1)	Not listed	(6)	6% plus to 7%
	(2)	4% plus to 4.5%	(7)	7% plus to 8%
	(3)	4.5% plus to 5%	(8)	8% plus
	(4)	5% plus to 5.5%	(9)	Bond
	(5)	5.5% plus to 6%	(10)	Other

Mortgage Types

61   (1)   B (Blanket Mortgage of Consideration)—Blanket—more than one parcel in transaction
     (2)   Clear-Cut First Mortgage
     (3)   S (Subject Mortgage)
     (4)   Subj (Encumbrances on Record)
     (5)   Other-Note

Amount Paid for Property—$_____

62–67 $ (Be careful to note method for determining this item)

Value Category of Property—

68   (1)   Up to $8,000
     (2) $8,000 up to but not including $10,000
     (3) $10,000 up to but not including $12,000
     (4) $12,000 up to but not including $15,000
     (5) $15,000 up to but not including $20,000
     (6) $20,000 up to but not including $30,000
     (7) $30,000 up to but not including $50,000
     (8) $50,000 up to but not including $100,000

(9) $100,000 up to but not including $250,000
(10) Not available

69   (1)   In renewal area
    (2)   Not in renewal area

Bona-Fide Sale

70   (1)   Previous nominal transfer
    (2)   No previous nominal transfer
    (3)   Nominal transfer

71   (1)   Sale price can't be determined
    (2)   Blanket mtgs.
    (3)   Foreclosure—price unclear
    (4)   Sale price can't be determined—last sale before record
    (5)   Sales price n.g.—Subject mtg.

Second Mortgage

72   (1)   Yes
    (2)   No
    (3)   3rd Mtg.

Second Mortgage Source by Name

73   (1)   Savings bank
    (2)   Commercial bank
    (3)   Savings and loan
    (4)   Individual grantee
    (5)   Mortgage company
    (6)   Construction or home improvements

74–78   *Second Mortgage Amount*

Second Mortgage Type

79   (1)   B (Blanket Mortgage of Consideration)
    (2)   Clear-cut second mortgage
    (3)   S (Subject Mortgage)
    (4)   Subj (Encumbrances on Record)
    (5)   Purchase Money
    (6)   At time of transfer (within 6 months)
    (7)   At time of transfer (more than 6 months)
    (8)   Other

80   (1)   −1

INTERVIEW QUESTIONNAIRE

Case No._____

1. When did you first become an owner of rental real estate?
2. Why did you buy the property at _____?
3. Is (are) this still your reason(s) for keeping it? (If sale is hoped for, find out if parcel is listed w/broker.)
4. Do you use a manager or a rent collector for your properties?
5. Do you collect your rents by the week or monthly?
6. Furnished or unfurnished at _____ St.
7. I assume you own other rental properties than the one at _____ _____. Is it similar to this property? (Probe for extent and location and type), i.e. number of families, etc.
8. Lead in—"Then you make (or don't make) your living from real estate holdings?"
9. Our sheet indicates that _____ has _____ to _____ apartments, is that correct?
10. Do you have Negro or white tenants at _____?
11. In your opinion has the vacancy rate changed in the past several years in the general area of _____?
12. Has the vacancy rate changed in your property _____ in the last couple of years?
13. Do you hire someone to do your repair work or do you do it yourself?
14. How much of your time does operating your rental properties take?

15. Would you say that *most owners* of properties similar to _____ are looking for return through rental or profit through sales?
    (Referring to Number 15)

16. Would you differ with this opinion?
    (Hand Card #1 to owner—follow directions in manual.)

17. There are many problems in maintaining and improving properties. In the case of _____, how would you rate the following categories in order of importance to you?
    (Important)

18. You did or did not mention taxes.
    (Hand Card #2 to owner and ask him or her to tell you which ones he knows about by number, i.e. 1, 2, 3, 4, which ones can be made without reassessments.)

19. As a property owner, we know there are improvements we can make to our property without an increase in our tax assessment.

20. What improvements would you make in this property at _____ if you were sure of not getting a boost in taxes?

21. I know that real estate taxes in Newark have gone up. Would you say that as a percentage of the rent at _____ the taxes have changed much since you have owned the property? (If applicable.) Why hasn't income from parcels matched the tax increase? [Probe whether tax boosts are passed on.]

22. Is the resale market such that you can get the money invested on improvement back?

23. If you improved the property at _____, could you get an adequate return through improved rents?
    (Interviewer check flexibility of rent of parcel and a change in the vacancy rate.)

24. Would you improve this property if given a long-term mortgage?

25. Do you know of any financial program sponsored by the government for older properties such as _____ St?

26. What would you have to pay for improvement money? (Terms and repayment.)

27. What source would you turn to if you needed money to make improvements on your property?

28. We all know that building and health inspectors visit our properties from time to time. How have these visits affected your property?

29. Are you in an area which is scheduled for urban renewal?

30. If your property is taken for urban renewal, will you be able to get back the investment you made by making improvements?

(If answer to #30 is No, ask)

31. Why not?

32. Mr. (Mrs.) _____, you have been most cooperative in answering the above questions, and there are just a few points of additional information that we would appreciate.

(Hand Card #3 to owner—Income)

33. Mr. (Mrs.) _____, we would appreciate it very much if you would circle the number that applies to you.

                                                        Case No._____

Interviewer's Summary Sheet

A. Name of owner
B. Sex
C. Address of owner
D. Resident or nonresident

Place of Interview
Date of Interview
Time
Travel

Interview from _____ to _____

Cooperation of Owner:
    a. None
    b. Poor
    c. Average
    d. Good
    e. Excellent

Name of Interviewer _____

Date submitted to Office _____

Interview received by _____

Interviewer's comments and remarks:

Appendix VI

THE INTERVIEWER'S MANUAL

Introduction

This manual is intended to help the interviewer to understand the objectives of the interview itself, and also to provide some alternative approaches to the questions. The interview pattern which follows is a compound of objective and depth questions. There are certain finite parameters which we want clearly defined and for that purpose, as you will note, we have certain answers which are to be checked off if possible. In addition, however, for a number of questions we are depending upon the perceptiveness of the interviewers to provide information in depth. In this type of interviewing, it is essential that some degree of rapport with the person being interviewed be established. Our point of view is that this is the first study to examine the low-end rental real estate market from a *landlord's* point of view. Our aim, and it is a very difficult aim, is to communicate effectively enough so that some of the ritualistic answers which are very common place in this field can be avoided. It will be up to you, as the interviewer, to determine how genuine are the responses being made by the landlord being interviewed and how adequately the results of the interview reflect, in your judgment, the realities of the situation. Do not feel under any obligation to rush the interview, on the other hand, you may find that you will be listening to a monologue on a particular point which soon loses its value. In this case, do feel free to subtly reshape the interview pattern.

Some comments follow which elaborate the nature of the several questions of the interview:

_260

Question 1.

We are interested here in finding out when this individual became associated with the real estate market. This is not necessarily when he bought the particular parcel which directed him to us. Any background data such as, "my father was in the real estate business and I inherited it," would be most welcome. (You will note by the way that there is space after each of the questions to amplify any of the structured responses which we have indicated.)

Question 2.

The areas that we are interested in here are such questions as: was the parcel bought as an investment with the hope of future capital gains, was it bought as a rental property, or was it inherited and the present owner has continued its holding without any clear objective. In some cases, I am sure we are going to find that these parcels were purchased as homes. In these cases please find out why they bought this particular parcel, as against perhaps moving from Newark.

Question 3.

Here we are interested in what changes in attitude have taken place since the parcel was purchased. Hopefully, this will give us insight as to the operational characteristics and problems involved with the parcel. If the response is "now I am planning to sell the parcel," find out whether the parcel is actively for sale, i.e. listed with a broker or other steps taken.

Question 4.

This should be relatively easily answered. If there is some pattern other than the ones which we have already structured for your response, please indicate it.

Question 5.

Here we are interested in the type of financial service which the landlord renders his tenants. Find out whether this is much of a problem. If there is a mixed pattern in the parcel in question, please indicate such.

Question 6.

This again should be easily answered. In some cases the parcel may be mixed. If it's furnished—ask why.

Questions 7 and 8.

These questions are going to require considerable care and skill on the part of the interviewer. We want to find out whether the owner of the parcel in question is a professional owner, i.e. making a living or substantial hunk of his living from the parcel, or just a part-time investor. If he is the former, we would like to find out what kinds of real estate he owns. Does he own other slum properties, or is this the only one of its kind that he does own? And further, where are these properties located; are they all in and around Newark? Does he own parcels in several other areas? Based upon this, we have suggested the leading question that you "make or do not make your living from real estate holding."

Question 9.

This is a simple question which the landlord should have no difficulty in answering. If he is not sure, we would like to know that he has this degree of unfamiliarity with his parcel. If the definition of apartment is unclear, we typically mean the number of housing units as defined by the possession of distinct cooking facilities.

Question 10.

Again this should be a very simple concomitant of Question 9.

Questions 11 and 12.

These questions are incorporated, even though there is a considerable degree of redundancy, in the hopes of generating some internal checks on what the trends and absolute figures of vacancies are in parcels similar to the one being questioned.

Questions 13 and 14.

These questions are somewhat linked. In 13—"do you hire someone to do your repair work or do you do it yourself?"—we are asking basically does the owner actually do his own repairs either in part, in total, or not at all, and by this we mean physically do his own repairs as against securing outside services. Question 14 reverts back basically to Questions 6 and 7. The categories that are indicated full time or nearly full time, half time, quarter time—one day a week with or without evenings besides some other full time job, or less, are very rough approximations based upon our test interviews. If the answer which you secure does not fit into those categories, please indicate the response in full.

Questions 15 and 16.

These questions are essentially linked. Question 15 asks the owner to talk about other owners of properties similar to the one that he is being questioned about. We want to find out whether, in his opinion, they are being held for return on rents or profit through sales. Obviously, very few of the responses are going to be clear-cut one way or the other. We would like to have some feeling for the weighting. This holds true, obviously, of Question 16 also.

Question 17.

This question is a very crucial one. We want the landlord to indicate the respective weights of the problems indicated, with specific reference to the particular parcel that we are interviewing him on. If there is some factor, other than the ones indicated which he feels is very significant, please indicate this. Try to get him to put them in a rank ordering, i.e. number 1 is the tenants, number 2 is the tax level, etc.

Questions 18 through 21.

Questions 18 through 21 are concerned with taxes. Our basic objective is to find out whether the tax levels themselves, or the possibility of reassessment, or the possibility of increases in taxes and tax rates in general, inhibit landlords from improving their parcels. This is a very delicate area. The potential for securing a ritual answer that the tax rates excuse all misbehaviors on the part of the landlord is very evident. So WATCH OUT!

Question 18.

"You did (or did not) mention taxes?" It is to be slipped in to the landlord, hopefully, before he has really thought the thing out. Try to jot down his responses here such as "they are very significant, they are not significant, sure they are significant, but other things are more significant," etc.

Question 19.

This question should be self-evident. We want the landlord to indicate what, to the best of his knowledge or guessing as of the moment, are improvements which he can make that will involve him in tax boosts or that can be made without involvement in taxes. If he has some anecdotal material about an improvement which he did make which involved him in a substantial reassessment, please indicate this.

Question 20.

This question attempts to drive the landlord to the sticking point. It's a tough one because it's the basic question of would you "if"—but we are interested here in whatever reactions you can detail.

Question 21.

We are interested here in finding out whether tax boosts in Newark have essentially been passed on to the tenant in the form of boosted rents. Obviously, this is only possible in a relatively tight rental situation. So we should be able to decide, based upon the response to this question, whether the rental housing market in Newark is still tight, and also whether tax increases are paid for by tenants.

Questions 22 and 23

These concern the economical advisability of the landlords investing additional funds in their parcels.

Question 22.

Here we are concerned with resales of parcels. If you improve a parcel, will the improved parcel sell at such an increment over the price of the unimproved parcel as to make it economically worthwhile?

Question 23.

This supplements Question 22 and concerns the question of whether there is a flexible market in terms of improved parcels and tenantry. Are there tenants for improved parcels at increased prices? Alternatively, is it possible that the vacancy rate on unimproved parcels is high, and that the economic feasibility of improving a parcel may be warranted in terms of lowering vacancy rates? These two questions obviously complement each other.

Questions 24 through 27

These questions are concerned with financing improvements.

Question 24.

This is addressed to the question of whether given a long-term mortgage, the landlord would improve his parcel or would not.

Question 25.

This question is clear-cut. We want to know if the landlord does know of any financial programs sponsored by government and if he mentions any specific programs, please indicate what they are—even if the description is quite rough.

Question 26.

What would you have to pay for improvement money? Here we are interested *both* in the terms, i.e. what *interest* payments he would have to make and/or discounts on principal, i.e. bonuses of one kind or another and, in addition, what repayment schedule he would have to make—would it be a five-year loan—a ten-year loan—a twenty-year loan, i.e. what sort of *amortization* would he have to meet.

Question 27.

This question is concerned with the sources which the specific landlord would turn to if he wanted to make improvements. This could be anything from his brother-in-law, his mother, or his wife, to refinancing his present mortgage, to getting a home-improvement loan from a bank or any of a variety of other things.

Question 28.

Question 28 is an open end question. In all probability you will get lots of anecdotal material here. Try to separate the wheat from the chaff, if at all possible. "Building and health inspection is reasonable because of blank, blank, or is not reasonable because of blank, blank" are the kinds of responses that we would like you to secure.

Questions 29 and 30.

Question 29.

We ask whether the landlord is or thinks he is in an urban renewal area. It is the landlord's opinion of his parcel that we are looking for here. His opinion of the imminence of land-taking may be quite unrealistic or quite well informed. In either case we want his vision of his parcel vis-a-vis urban renewal in terms of its being taken for the purpose.

Question 30.

If the parcel is taken for urban renewal, does the landlord envision getting a reasonable return for improvements on the parcel or is he inhibited about making improvements because he feels that in the process of land-taking, he simply will not secure an adequate return for capital invested over and above original acquisition costs?

Question 31.

This obviously just amplifies question 30.

I think you are going to find the interviews themselves most interesting, and I hope that we are going to find a surprising degree of cooperation. Let me warn you once again about any editorializing in your interviews. You're not carrying the torch for any particular approach to housing problems. This is a fact-finding mission. The success of this research depends upon your perceptiveness and sensitivity. Any hostility or overt steering of the person being interviewed will only distort the results of the interviews themselves. Note once again that we have assured the landlords that all interviews will be completely confidential.

LIST OF PUBLICATIONS CITED

F. Allnutt and G. Mossinghoff, "Housing and Health Inspection," *George Washington Law Review*, (January, 1960).

Action Report, Municipal Housing Codes in the Courts, (N.Y.C.: Action, 1956).

Martin Anderson, *The Federal Bulldozer*, (Cambridge, Mass.: M.I.T. Press, 1964).

Annual Report of the Division of Local Government, State of New Jersey, Statement of Financial Condition of Counties and Municipalities, (Trenton: N. J. Department of the Treasury, Division of Local Government, 1939–1963).

Association of the Bar of the City of New York, Special Committee on Housing and Urban Development, *Memorandum 305/63/9*.

Kirk W. Back, *Slums, Projects and People*, (Durham, N. C.: Duke University Press, 1962).

Raymond Bauer, *et al.*, "The Marketing Dilemma of Negroes," *Journal of Marketing*, (July, 1965).

Morris Beck, *Property Taxation and Urban Land Use in Northeastern New Jersey*, (Washington, D. C.: Urban Land Institute, 1963).

Walter J. Blum & A. Dunham, "Income Tax Law and Slums," *Columbia Law Review*, (April, 1960).

Hans Blumenfeld, "The Tidal Wave of Metropolitan Expansion," *Journal of the American Institute of Planners*, (Winter, 1954).

Harvey Brazer, *Some Fiscal Implications of Metropolitanism*, (Washington, D. C.: Brookings Institution, 1962).

David B. Carlson, "Rehabilitation: Stepchild of Urban Renewal," *Architectural Forum*, (1962).

Chicago Housing Authority, *The Slum . . . Is Rehabilitation Possible?*, (Chicago: 1960).

Commerce Clearing House, Inc., *Explanation 1964 Revenue Act*.

Committee on Housing and Urban Development, *Code Enforcement for Multiple Dwellings in New York City*, (N.Y.C.: Community Service Society of New York, n.d.).

Detroit City Planning Commission, *Renewal and Revenue*, (Detroit: 1962).

John W. Dyckman and R. R. Isaacs, *Capital Requirement for Urban Development and Renewal*, (New York: McGraw-Hill, 1961).

Walter Firey, *Land Use in Central Boston*, (Cambridge: Harvard University Press, 1943).

Ernest M. Fisher, *Urban Real Estate Markets: Characteristics and Financing*, (New York: National Bureau of Economic Research, 1951).

Robert M. Fisher, *Twenty Years of Public Housing*, (New York: Harper & Bro., 1959).

Bernard J. Frieden, *The Future of Old Neighborhoods*, (Cambridge, Mass.: M.I.T. Press, 1964).

Mason Gaffney, *Property Taxes and the Frequency of Urban Renewal*, (Paper presented at National Tax Association, Pittsburgh, September 17, 1964, mimeo).

Leo Grebler, *et al.*, *Capital Formation in Residential Real Estate*, (Princeton: Princeton University Press, 1956).

——, *Experience in Urban Real Estate Investment*, (New York: Columbia University, 1955).

——, *Housing Market Behavior In a Declining Area*, (New York: Columbia University Press, 1952).

Scott Greer and David W. Minar, "The Political Side of Urban Development and Redevelopment," *Annals of the American Academy of Political and Social Science*, (March, 1964), Volume 352.

William G. Grigsby, *Housing Markets and Public Policy*, (Philadelphia, Pa.: University of Pennsylvania Press, 1963).

——, *The Residential Real Estate Market in an Area Undergoing Racial Transition*, (Unpublished doctoral dissertation, Columbia University, 1958).

Charles Haar, *Federal Credit and Private Housing*, (New York: McGraw-Hill, 1960).

Jane Jacob, "How Money Can Make or Break Our Cities," *The Reporter*, (October 12, 1961).

Journal of Property Management, *Exchange of Rental Income and Operating Expense Data*, (Chicago: Institute of Real Estate Management of the National Association of Real Estate Boards, 1964).

Harold Kaplan, *Urban Renewal Politics*, (N. Y.: Columbia University Press, 1963).

Julian H. Levi, "Problems in the Rehabilitation of Blighted Areas," *Federal Bar Journal*, (Summer, 1961).

Ira S. Lowry, "Filtering and Housing Standards—A Conceptual Analysis," *Land Economics*, (August, 1960).

Ruth L. Mace, *Municipal Cost-Revenue Research in the United States*, (Chapel Hill, N. C.: University of North Carolina, 1964).

Market Planning Corporation, *Newark—A City In Transition*, (N.P., 1959).

Metropolitan Housing and Planning Council of Chicago, *Interim Report on Housing the Economically and Socially Disadvantaged Groups in the Population*, (Chicago: 1960).

Martin Meyerson and Edward C. Banfield, *Politics, Planning and the Public Interest*, (Glencoe, Ill.: Free Press, 1955).

Martin Millspaugh, *The Human Side of Urban Renewal*, (New York: Washburn, 1960).

——, "Problems and Opportunities of Relocation," *Law and Contemporary Problems*, (Durham, N. C.: Duke University, Winter, 1961).

Walter A. Morton, *Housing Taxation*, (Madison, Wisconsin: University of Wisconsin Press, 1955).

William W. Nash, *Residential Rehabilitation* . . . , (N. Y.: McGraw-Hill, 1959).

National Housing Agency, *Who Owns the Slums?; Where Does Money Spent for Slum Property Go?*, (National Housing Bulletin 6, March, 1946).

Richard L. Nelson, *The Changing Composition of Capitalization Rates*, Monograph prepared from a speech by Mr. Nelson before the Southeastern Regional Conference of the Society of Real Estate Appraisers, May 1, 1964, Georgia State College.

Newark Central Planning Board, *New Newark*, (Newark, N. J.: 1961).

Newark, New Jersey, *Project Conference Committee, Capital Program 1964 to 1969*, (Newark, N. J.: Dec. 1963).

Newark Star Ledger, (August 30, 1954).

New York State Division of Housing Conservation, *Housing Codes, The Key to Housing Conservation*, (New York: 1960).

New York State Temporary State Housing Commission, *Prospects for Rehabilitation*, (Albany, N. Y.: 1960).

Northeastern New Jersey Regional Urban Renewal Survey, *A Guide to Urban Renewal*, (Trenton, New Jersey: 1963).

City of Philadelphia, *Partnership for Renewal—A Working Program*, (Philadelphia: 1960).

Chester Rapkin, *et al.*, *Group Relations in Newark, 1957, A Report to the Mayor's Commission On Group Relations*, (New York: Urban Research, 1957).

——, *The Real Estate Market in an Urban Renewal Area*, (N.Y.C., Planning Commission, 1969).

Raymond L. Richmond, *The Theory and Practice of Site—Value Taxation in Pittsburgh*, (Pittsburgh: September 17, 1964, mimeographed).

A. H. Schaaf, *Economic Aspects of Urban Renewal*, (Berkeley: University of California, 1960).

Alvin L. Schorr, *Slums and Social Insecurity*, (U. S. Department of Health, Education and Welfare, Social Security Administration, Division of Research and Statistics, 1963).

William L. Slayton, "Bottlenecks of Urban Renewal," *Federal Bar Journal*, (Summer, 1961), Volume 281.

Arthur D. Sporn, "Empirical Studies in the Economics of Slum Ownership," *Land Economics*, (Nov., 1960).

——, "Some Contributions of the Income Tax Law to the Growth and Prevalence of Slums," *Columbia Law Review*, (November, 1959).

George Sternlieb, *The Future of the Downtown Department Store*, (Cambridge: Harvard University Press, 1962).

——, "Is Business Abandoning the Big City?," *Harvard Business Review*, (January, 1961).

United States Savings and Loan League, *Proceedings—Conference on Savings and Residential Financing*, (Chicago, Illinois: May 10–11, 1962).

Lewis G. Watts, et al., *The Middle Income Negro Family Faces Urban Renewal*, (Waltham: Brandeis University, 1965).

Louis Winnick, *Rental Housing: Opportunities for Private Investment*, (New York: McGraw-Hill, 1958).